Lecture Notes of the Institute
for Computer Sciences, Social Informatics
and Telecommunications Engineering 117

T0212671

Vinu V. Das   Passent Elkafrawy (Eds.)

Signal Processing and Information Technology

Second International Joint Conference, SPIT 2012
Dubai, UAE, September 20-21, 2012
Revised Selected Papers

 Springer

Volume Editors

Vinu V. Das
Institute of Doctors Engineering and Scientists (The IDES)
Network Security Group, Kerala, India
E-mail: vinuvdas@gmail.com

Passent Elkafrawy
Menoufia University
Mathematics and Computer Science, Cairo, Egypt
E-mail: passentmk@gmail.com

ISSN 1867-8211   e-ISSN 1867-822X
ISBN 978-3-319-11628-0   e-ISBN 978-3-319-11629-7
DOI 10.1007/978-3-319-11629-7
Springer Heidelberg New York Dordrecht London

Library of Congress Control Number: 2014949918

Typesetting: Camera-ready by author, data conversion by Scientific Publishing Services, Chennai, India

Printed on acid-free paper

Springer is part of Springer Science+Business Media (www.springer.com)

Preface

It is our honor to bestow the proceedings upon you of the Second International Joint Conference on Advances in Signal Processing and Information Technology – SPIT 2012, organized by the Association of Computer Electronics and Electrical Engineers (ACEEE) during September 20–21, 2012, in DUBAI. The conference promotes recent research and advances in computer science, computer technology, information processing and signal processing.

Proceedings will be published by Springer LNICST Series and it will be available in the Springer Digital Library. The conference committee received 330 papers where 88 papers were accepted and 32 papers were registered as long papers, and short papers. All the papers are held for presentation and discussion.

On behalf of the conference organizing committee I thank all those who contributed to the organization of this year technical program, in particular the program committee members, the executive committee and members of the conference for their great effort and support to conduct the conference. Our deep gratitude to Prof. PM Thankachan, and Dr. Janahallal Stephen (ILAHIA, INDIA) for his continues guidance and support. Special gratitude to the Springer LINCST editors to produce this high quality proceeding

September 2012

Passent Elkafrawy
Vinu V. Das

Preface

Organization

Organizing Committee

Honorary Chair

Mohiy Hadhoud	Menoufia University, Egypt
Waiel Fathi Abd EL-Wahed	Menoufia University, Shiben EL-Kom, EGYPT

Technical Chair

Ali Fahmy	Cairo University, Cairo, Egypt
Mohamed Fahmy Tolba	Ain Shams University, Cairo, Egypt
ElMeligy	Menoufia University, Egypt

Technical Co-chair

Fatma Omara	Cairo University, Cairo, Egypt
Abd elBadeeh M Salem	Ain Shams University, Cairo, Egypt
Hatem Mohamed Sayed Ahmed	Menoufia University, Egypt
Mohamed Amin	Menoufia University, Egypt
Mostafa abd elhaleem	Menoufia University, Egypt
Osama Abd EL-Raoof	Menoufia University, Egypt
Hamdy Mossa	Menoufia University, Egypt
Fathi ElSaid	Menoufia University, Egypt
Walid Fakhry	Cairo University, Cairo, Egypt
Hadj Hamma Tadjine	für Volkswagen AG, Wolfsburg, Germany
Mingli Song	Hong Kong Polytechnical University, Hong Kong
Tianhao Zhang	UPENN, US
Huiqiong Wang	City University, Hong Kong
Harjanto Prabowo	Bina Nusantara University, Indonesia
Gerardus Polla	Bina Nusantara University, Indonesia

Organizing Chair

Passent M. El-Kafrawy	Menoufia University, Shiben EL-Kom, EGYPT
Janahanlal Stephen (Dean)	Ilahina College of Engg. College, India

General Chair

Vinu V. Das	The IDES
Yogesh Chaba	Guru Jambheshwar University of Science and Technology, Hisar

Finance Chair

PM Thankachan   Mar Ivnios College, Trivandrum

Publication Chair

Vijayakumar   MG University, India
Gylson Thomas   MES College of Engineering, India

Publicity Chair

O.P. Rishi   BITS Ranchi, India
A. Louise Perkins   University of Sounth Mississippi, USA
R.D. Sudhakar Samueli   S.J. College of Engg., India

Poster Chair

Ashadi Salim   Bina Nusantara University, Indonesia

National Advisory Committees

Togar Alam Napitupulu   Bina Nusantara University, Indonesi

Program Committee Chair

Raymond Kosala   Bina Nusantara University, Indonesia
Richard Kumaradjaja   Bina Nusantara University, Indonesia

International Advisory Committee

Marc van Dongen   University College Cork, Ireland
Hooman Mohseni   Northwestern University, USA
Suresh Subramoniam   Prince Sultan University, Saudi Arabia
A. Louise Perkins   University of Sothern Mississippi, USA
Sumanth Yenduri   The University of Southern Mississippi, USA
Hamid Bagheri   Sharif University of Technology, Iran
Mehran Garmehi   Bojnord University, IRAN
Kabekode V. Bhat   The Pennsylvania State University, USA
Gordon Reynolds   Dublin Institute of Technology, Ireland
Shashi Phoha   The Pennsylvania State University, USA
Chilukuri K. Mohan   Syracuse University, USA
Debopam Acharya   Georgia Southern University, USA
David Hall   Louisiana Tech University, USA
Cecilia Chan   University of Hong Kong, Hong Kong
Kristian J. Hammond   Northwestern University, USA
Long Que   Louisiana Tech University, USA
Peter Vadasz   Northern Arizona University, USA

Review Committee

Haryono Soeparno	Bina Nusantara University, Indonesia
Suryadi Liawatimena	Bina Nusantara University, Indonesia
Diaz Santika (M.Sc.)	LIPI, Indonesia
Eng. Anto Satriyo Nugroho	BPPT, Indonesia
Dwi Handoko	BPPT, Indonesia
M. Mustafa Sarinanto	BPPT, Indonesia
Ir. Tatang Akhmad Taufik (M.Sc.)	BPPT, Indonesia
Eng Bernadetta Kwintiana	Universität Stuttgart, Germany
Eng. Rahmat Widyanto	UI, Indonesia
Eng. Son Kuswadi	ITS, Indonesia
Eng. Rila Mandala	ITB, Indonesia
Ir. Pekik Argo Dahono	ITS, Indonesia
Ir. Eko Tjipto Rahardjo (MSc., PhD.)	UI, Indonesia
Arnold Ph Djiwatampu	IEEE Indonesia
Ir Dadang Gunawan (M.Eng)	UI, Indonesia
Ir.Wahidin Wahab, Ph.D	UI, Indonesia
Henri Uranus	UPH, Indonesia
Gunawan Wibisono	UI, Indonesia

Program Committee Members

Shu-Ching Chen	Florida International University, USA
Stefan Wagner	Fakultät für Informatik Technische Universität München, Boltzmannstr
Juha Puustjärvi	Helsinki University of Technology
Selwyn Piramuthu	University of Florida
Werner Retschitzegger	University of Linz, Austria
Habibollah Haro	Universiti Teknologi Malaysia
Derek Molloy	Dublin City University, Ireland
Anirban Mukhopadhyay	University of Kalyani, India
Malabika Basu	Dublin Institute of Technology, Ireland
Tahseen Al-Doori	American University in Dubai
V.K. Bhat	SMVD University, India
Ranjit Abraham	Armia Systems, India
Naomie Salim	Universiti Teknologi Malaysia
Abdullah Ibrahim	Universiti Malaysia Pahang
Charles McCorkell	Dublin City University, Ireland
Neeraj Nehra	SMVD University, India
Muhammad Nubli	Universiti Malaysia Pahang
Zhenyu Y Angz	Florida International University, USA

Table of Contents

Effort Estimation in Software Cost Using Team Characteristics Based on Fuzzy Analogy Method – A Diverse Approach

S. Malathi[1] and S. Sridhar[2]

[1] Dept of CSE, Sathyabama University,
Chennai, Tamilnadu, India
malathi_raghu@hotmail.com
[2] Dept of CSE & IT, Sathyabama University,
Chennai, Tamilnadu, India
drssridhar@yahoo.com

Abstract. The dramatic increase in the scope of software cost estimation has paved way for the enhanced research to develop different methods for estimating the software effort. Estimation of effort in software cost based on Fuzzy Analogy is one of the most popular existing methods. Usually, only the project characteristics are considered for the effort estimation whereas the team characteristics also play a significant role. This paper presents a diverse approach where the features of team characteristics like joy and skill are considered in addition to the project features. The empirical results are validated with the historical datasets having both categorical and numerical data by considering hypothetical data of team characteristics. The outcome of this paper signifies that the usage of team characteristics improves the performance and accuracy of software effort estimation.

Keywords: cost estimation, fuzzy analogy, team characteristics, effort estimation, hypothetical data.

1   Introduction

A critical factor during the software development process [1] is the ability of estimating the effort accurately at the early stages of development. Moreover, it is noted that none of the existing methods have dealt with the team characteristics effectively. A project team is a social system where personal and co-operative characters play an important role to the success of the organization. The team members in a project have emotions such as joy and skill, which can be either positive or negative, [2] during the duration of the project. The positive feature is related to joy and negative feature is related to fear. However, the degree of joy is one of the salient features affecting the project features.

All estimation methods consider only project features for effort estimation. In this paper, a different approach based on Fuzzy Analogy method has been proposed

V.V. Das and P.M. El-Kafrawy (Eds.): SPIT 2012, LNICST 117, pp. 1–8, 2014.

incorporating the team member characters like joy and skill. The hypothetical data of team member characteristics is considered for this study to estimate the effort.

Section 2 deals with the milieu of study including analogy, fuzzy logic, personality and emotion while Section 3 depicts the proposed method. Section 4 evaluates the performance and Section 5 concludes the paper.

2   Related Work

2.1   Analogy

Analogy based estimation is the process of finding the similar projects among existing ones and assess the estimate for the target project in the incipient stage [3]. Many researchers accept the solution of analogy method since it is derived on the basis of human way of reasoning rather than arcane chains of layers. The drawback of analogy is the degree of similarity between the historic and the target project [4]. Genetic algorithm [5] is used in analogy as one of the search technique for the similarity measure and also overcome the complex optimization issues.

2.2   Fuzzy Method

The term fuzzy came into existence with the fuzzy sets [6] for dealing the linguistic variables. However, fuzzy method cannot overcome the imprecision and uncertainty problem in an effective manner while handling the categorical datasets [7]. Fuzzy integrated with analogy, fuzzy analogy, [8] was developed to overcome this problem. The performance of the effort is improved by using the feature subset algorithm based on fuzzy logic in analogy concept [9].

2.3   Personality and Emotion

Personality [10] and mood plays an important role in the human behaviour. This forms a key characteristic feature for the team members during the project period. The personality behaviour is evaluated based on personnel opinion, attitude and other features related to team operation [11]. Every member in a team will have a topology which dominates the formation of a group based on five personality factors [12] relating the team personality and performance effort. Out of the five, two features, joy and skill are considered. Joy is one of the pairs of emotions used to produce the initial mood whereas skill is the capability of doing things in an innovative way and also being intellectual [13]. These features are also closely linked to an agile software method [14].

3   Propose Work

The proposed method is done in two steps.

3.1   Fuzzy Analogy

Fuzzy analogy [15] is the fuzzification of classical analogy procedure. It is comprised of three steps. 1) Identification of cases, 2) Retrieval of similar cases and 3) Case adaptation.

3.1.1   Identification of Cases

In this case, the objective is to estimate the software project effort. In the case of numerical value x_0, its fuzzification will be done by the membership function which takes the value of 1 when x is equal to x_0 and 0 otherwise. For categorical value, let us have M attributes and for each attribute M_j, a measure with linguistic values is defined (A_k^j). Each linguistic value, A_k^j, is represented by a fuzzy set with a membership function ($\mu_{A_k^j}$).Rules formulated, based on the fuzzy sets of modes, sizes and efforts .

3.1.2   Retrieval of Similar Cases

This step is based on the choice of a software project similarity measure.These measures evaluate the overall similarity of two projects P_1 and P_2, $d(P_1,P_2)$ by combining all the individual similarities if P_1 and P_2 associated with the various linguistic variables V_j describing P_1 and P_2, $d_{V_j}(P_1,P_2)$. Here, the distance can be measured by employing Euclidean distance method.

$$d_{V_j}(P_1,P_2)=\begin{cases} \max_{k} \ \min(\mu_{A_k^j}(P_1),\mu_{A_k^j}(P_2)) \\ \max-\min \quad aggregation \\ \sum_k \mu_{A_k^j}(P_1)\times\mu_{A_k^j}(P_2) \\ sum-product \quad aggregation \end{cases} \tag{1}$$

Where V_j are the linguistic variable describing the project P_1 and P_2. A_k^j are the fuzzy sets associated with V_j and $\mu_{A_k^j}$ are the membership functions representing fuzzy sets A_k^j.

3.1.3 Case Adaptation

The objective of this step is to derive an estimate for the new project by using the known effort values of similar projects. The objective of this step is to take only the k first projects which are similar to the new project. In the proposed method, all the projects in the data set are used to derive an estimate of the new project. Each historical project will contribute, in the calculation of the effort of the new project, according to its degree of similarity with this project.

3.2 Team Characteristics Evaluation

A personality trait is an enduring pattern of inner behaviour that is extremely inflexible, deviates markedly from the expectation of a person's culture and mood that causes distress. Two of the factors of personality trait are the joy and skill that can increase or decrease the software effort based on their values accordingly. Let Jy and Sl are the joy and skill character value that represent the mood of the members in a software team. Consider them in a class where the value Z can be measured.

> If $Jy > thr$ then
>
> Set Sl less than Jy
>
> Else
>
> Set Sl greater than Jy
>
> Endif
>
> If $Jy < thr$ then
>
> $Z = value$
>
> Endif
>
> If $Sl > thr$ then
>
> $Z = value$
>
> Endif

Pseudo code for finding the team characteristics

Since the vagueness and uncertainty of software effort drivers cannot be avoided, a fuzzy model has the advantage of easily verifying the cost drivers by adopting fuzzy sets.

$$Effort = A*(SIZE)^{B+0.01*\sum_{i=1}^{N} d_i} * \prod_{i=1}^{n} EM_i \pm Z \qquad (2)$$

where A and B are constants, d is the distance and EM effort multipliers. By using the above formula the effort is estimated.

4   Results and Discussion

The proposed methodology is implemented in JAVA Net Beans. The datasets used in the study is NASA 60[16]. Consider the dataset based on hypothetical assumption having N projects and each project may have different number of workers m. The overall average percentage of the team characters of joy and skill of the employees in a dataset is identified by circulating an analysis form for every individual after the completion of a period or module. The report consists of various objective type questions in two sections related to the behaviour and the performance of the members involved in the project which will be filled by the individuals. Every answer has a credit point and from the report, total weightage is found based on the credit points answered by the individual member. The same procedure is followed for each member in one project and finally the average is taken in terms of percentage. This is repeated for other projects and an overall average percentage is found for the individual characters in a dataset. Therefore the formula for finding the team member characteristics are computed as

$$J_{avg} = \frac{1}{N}\left[\sum_{i=1}^{N}\left(\left(\sum_{i=1}^{m} J_i\right) * f\right)\right] \tag{3}$$

$$S_{avg} = \frac{1}{N}\left[\sum_{i=1}^{N}\left(\left(\sum_{i=1}^{m} S_i\right) * f\right)\right] \tag{4}$$

J_i – represents the credit got for each Joy question.
J_{avg} – represents the value of the average credit for Joy in a team.
m- represents the number of joy questions.

N- Number of persons in a team.
S_i – represents the credit got for each Skill question.
S_{avg} – represents the value of the average credit for Skill in a team.
f – threshold factor which varies for joy and skill.

The threshold factor is predicted based on the analysis of various reviews conducted during the process. Consider the overall average percentage for the characters like joy and skill hypothetically for Nasa60 dataset are 75% and 45.5%. Figure 1 shows the effort values obtained in using the team characters for Nasa60 dataset.

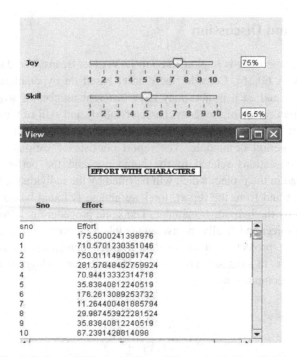

Fig. 1. Estimated Effort with Team Characters for Nasa60 dataset

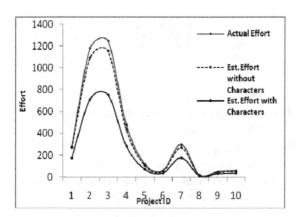

Fig. 2. Comparative Analysis of Effort for Nasa60 dataset

Figure 2 depicts the comparative analysis of the actual and estimated effort for the dataset with and without the team characteristic features. It is clearly seen that better results are obtained when the team characteristic features are included along with the project features. The overall average effort for the dataset in the proposed method is tabulated in table 1 and its comparison is given in figure 3.

Table 1. Avg. Effort comparison with and without team characters

Dataset	No. of Projects	Actual Avg.Effort	Estimated Avg.Effort without Characters	Estimated Avg.Effort with Characters
Nasa60	60	406.413	359.324	234.534

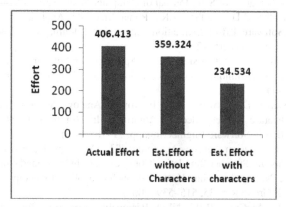

Fig. 3. Comparative Analysis of Average Effort for Nasa60 dataset

5   Conclusion

The complexity of new software has made the estimation of software effort very difficult for the project management. The existing techniques use only the project features for software effort estimation and not the team characteristics in an effective manner. This research paper proposes a different approach using Fuzzy Analogy for the team characteristic features like joy and skill of the employees during the project schedule for estimating the software effort resourcefully. This method is based on reasoning by analogy, fuzzy logic and linguistic quantifiers with team characteristics and can be used for the software projects. From the analysis of results, it is deduced that the proposed method effectively estimates the effort for historical datasets based on the hypothetical models. In addition, the studies have showed a good performance in overcoming the imprecision and uncertainty problem. The future research can be embarked on with real time data and considering other characteristics like neuroticism, agreeableness and culture to predict the effort efficiently.

References

1. Chiu, N.H., Huang, S.-J.: The adjusted analogy-based software effort estimation based on similarity distances. The Journal of Systems and Software 80, 628–640 (2007)
2. Kazemifard, M., Zaeri, A., Ghasem-Aghaee, N., Nematbakhsh, M.A., Mardukhi, F.: Fuzzy Emotional COCOMO II Software Cost Estimation (FECSCE) using Multi-Agent Systems. Applied Soft Computing 11, 2260–2270 (2011)

3. Li, J., Ruhe, G., Al-Emran, A., Richter, M.M.: A Flexible Method for Software Effort Estimation by Analogy. Empirical Software Engineering 12, 65–106 (2006)
4. Azzeh, M., Neagu, D., Cowling, P.I.: Analogy-based software effort estimation using Fuzzy numbers. The Journal of Systems and Software 84, 270–284 (2011)
5. Fedotova, O., Teixeira, L., Alvelos, H.: Software Effort Estimation with Multiple Linear Regression: review and practical application. Journal of Information Science and Engineering (2011)
6. Satyananda Reddy, C., Raju, K.: Improving the Accuracy of Effort Estimation through Fuzzy Set Representation of Size. Journal of Computer Science 5(6), 451–455 (2009)
7. Prasad Reddy, P.V.G.D., Sudha, K.R., Rama Sree, P.: Application of Fuzzy Logic Approach to Software Effort Estimation. International Journal of Advanced Computer Science and Applications 2(5) (2011)
8. Malathi, S., Sridhar, S.: A Classical Fuzzy Approach for Software Effort Estimation on Machine Learning Technique. International Journal of Computer Science Issues 8(6)(1) (November 2011)
9. Azzeh, M., Neagu, D., Cowling, P.I.: Improving Analogy Software Effort Estimation using Fuzzy Feature Subset Selection Algorithm. In: 4th International Conference on Predictive Models in Software Engineering, pp. 71–78 (2008)
10. Kazemifard, M., Ghasem-Aghaee, N., Oren, T.I.: An event based implementation of emotional agents. In: Summer Simulation Conference, Calgary, Canada, pp. 63–67 (2006)
11. Molleman, E., Nauta, A., Jehn, K.A.: Person-Job applied to teamwork: a multilevel approach. Small Group Res. 35, 515–539 (2004)
12. Costa Jr., P.T., McCrae, R.R.: NEO Personality Inventry, Revised. Psychological Assessment Resources, Odessa (1992); (Spanish version, TEA Ediciones, Madrid) (2002)
13. Ghasem-Aghaee, N., Oren, T.I.: Towards fuzzy agents with dynamic personality for human behavior simulation. In: Summer Computer Simulation Conference, Montreal, Canada, pp. 3–10 (2003)
14. Beck, K.: Extreme Programming Explained: Embrace Change. Addison-Wesley, Reading (1999)
15. Malathi, S., Sridhar, S.: Optimization of Fuzzy Analogy in Software cost estimation using linguistic Variables. In: International Conference on Modeling, Optimization and Computing, ICMOC (2012)
16. Sayyad Shirabad, J., Menzies, T.J.: The PROMISE Repository of Software Engineering Databases. School of Information Technology and Engineering, University of Ottawa, Canada (2005), http://promise.site.uottawa.ca/SERepository

A SVD-Chaos Digital Image Watermarking Scheme Based on Multiple Chaotic System

Niaz Khorrami[1,*], Peyman Ayubi[2,*], Sohrab Behnia[3], and Jila Ayubi[4]

[1] Department of Mathematics, Salams Branch, Islamic Azad University, Salmas, Iran
n.khorrami@iausalmas.ac.ir
[2] Department of Computer Engineering, Urmia Branch, Islamic Azad University, Urmia, Iran
p.ayubi@iaurmia.ac.ir
[3] Department of Physics, UrmiaUniversity of Technology, Urmia, Iran
[4] Department of Electrical Engineering, Sistan and Baluchestan University, Zahedan, Iran

Abstract. In this letter a new watermarking scheme for Gray scale image is proposed based on a family of the chaotic maps and Singular Value Decomposition. Jacobian elliptic map is used to encrypt the watermark logo to improve the security of watermarked image. Quantum map is also used to determine the location of image's block for the watermark embedding. To test the robustness and effectiveness of our proposed method, several attacks are applied to the watermarked image and the best results have been reported. The purpose of this algorithm is to improve the shortcoming of watermarking such as small key space and low security. The experimental results demonstrate that the key space is large enough to resist the attack and the distribution of grey values of the encrypted image has a random-like behavior, which makes it a potential candidate for encryption of multimedia data such as images, audios and even videos.

Keywords: Blind Digital Image Watermarking, Chaos, Singular Value Decomposition, Chaotic Map.

1 Introduction

Watermarking technique is one of the active research fields in recent years, which can be used for protection of multimedia information, content authentication, and so on [1]. A watermark typically contains information about origin, status, and/or destination of the host data [2], [3].

Image scrambling is one of the most prevailing encryption algorithms these years [4], [5], [6]. However, these methods are not so many. The majority of watermarking schemes proposed to date, use watermarks generated from pseudo random number sequences [7].

Chaotic systems have been studied for more than 50 years. In 1963, Edward Lorenz discovered the first chaotic system and has been established by many different

---

[*] Corresponding authors.

V.V. Das and P.M. El-Kafrawy (Eds.): SPIT 2012, LNICST 117, pp. 9–18, 2014.
© Institute for Computer Sciences, Social Informatics and Telecommunications Engineering 2014

research areas, such as physics, mathematics, and engineering. This paper chiefly focuses on the application of quantum chaos and jacobian elliptic in encryption techniques of watermark logo. Quantum chaos and jacobian elliptic chaos began as an attempt to find chaos in the sense of extreme sensitivity to changes in initial conditions. It was found however, that in quantum mechanics, it is the sensitivity of quantum trajectories with respect to changes in control parameters that is likely to define quantum chaos [8]. Chaotic functions such as Markov Maps, Bernoulli Maps, Skew Tent Map, and Logistic Map have been widely used to generate watermark sequences [9,10].

Singular Value Decomposition (SVD) is said to be a significant topic in linear algebra by many renowned mathematicians.SVD was introduced by Eckart and Young [11] and has become one of the most widely used techniques of computational algebra and multivariate statistical analysis applied for data approximation, reduction and visualization. The use of singular value decomposition (SVD) in digital image watermarking has been widely studied [12-15].

The chaotic maps are employed to improve the security of a watermarked image, and an improved SVD embedding and extraction procedure has been used to encrypt the watermark logo. The upgraded mapping method determines the location of image's block where the watermark is embedded. The proposed method increases the security of watermarking and also it enables to hide more information in the watermarked image. The robustness of the proposed method has been evaluated against various attacks including common signal processing methods and geometric transformations.

2   Chaotic Maps

2.1   Jacobian Elliptic Maps

One-parameter families of jacobian elliptic rational maps [16] of the interval [0,1] with an invariant measure can be defined as:

$$X_{N+1} = \frac{4\alpha^2 x(1-k^2 X_N)(1-X_N)}{(1-k^2 X^2{}_n)^2 + 4(\alpha^2 - 1)X_N(1-k^2 X_N)(1-X_N)} \qquad (1)$$

Where $X_0 \in [0,1]$, $\alpha \in [0,4]$ and $\in [0,1]$, k (modulus) represent the parameter of the elliptic functions. Jacobian elliptic map is used in this paper as follow:

$$CX_{N+1}^1 = \begin{cases} 0 & X_{N+1} \leq 0.5 \\ 1 & X_{N+1} > 0 \end{cases} \qquad (2)$$

2.2   Quantum Map

The quantum rotators model has been widely used to study the dynamics of classically chaotic quantum systems and is specified in a simple form by:

$$X_{N+1}^1 = r(X_N - X_N^2)Cos^k(-\lambda \frac{e^{-mb}}{b}) \qquad (3)$$

Where $X_0 \in [0,1]$, $r \in [3.6,4]$, $\lambda \in [0,1]$, $\in [1,4]$, $b \in [1,4]$ and $k \in [2,10]$.

The 2D quantum map can be defined as:

$$
\begin{cases}
X_{N+1}^1 = r_1(X_N - X_N^2)Cos_1^k(-\lambda_1 \dfrac{e^{-m_1 b_1}}{b_1}) \\
Y_{N+1}^1 = r_2(Y_N - Y_N^2)Cos_2^k(-\lambda_2 \dfrac{e^{-m_2 b_2}}{b_2})
\end{cases}
\tag{4}
$$

This map is used for embedding and extraction process as follow:

$$
\begin{cases}
X_{N+1}^1 = (X_{N+1} \times 10^{14})mod M \\
Y_{N+1}^1 = (Y_{N+1} \times 10^{14})mod N
\end{cases}
\tag{5}
$$

Where M, N denotes the row and column of blocked image, respectively.

2.3   Elliptic Map for Watermark Logo Encryption

The watermark logo encryption proposed in this paper consists of the following major steps:

- The plain logo $W_{m \times n}$ is transformed into a one-dimensional array $W_{(m \times n) \times 1}$.
- The secret keys, including initial conditions and control parameters are set, and chaotic map in Eq.(2) are iterated 500 times.
- Ciphered values are computed by:

$$
C_i = (cx_i^1 \oplus W_i)
\tag{6}
$$

Where C_i is one dimensional array considered for storing the ciphered value.
- When all the pixels were encrypted, the matrix $C_{(m \times n) \times 1}$ is transformed into C $_{m \times n}$ and cipher watermark logo is exported to next step of watermarking algorithm.

Process of decryption is very similar to the encryption process. Just steps mentioned in the encryption process are repeated.

2.4   Selecting Location Embedded by Quantum Map

Using the coordinate i, j position of watermark pixel as the initial condition and through setting a value for the control parameter in Eq.(5), chaotic map is iterated after which, the embedding position of the pixels from the watermark image to host image can be obtained. The watermark pixels will get different embedding positions, so, the embedded watermark pixels will spread on the host image randomly.

3   Singular Value Decomposition

An $m \times n$ matrix A can be factorized as:

$$
A = USV^T
\tag{7}
$$

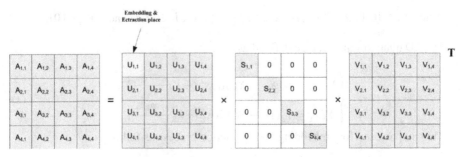

Fig. 1. Singular value decomposition of 4×4 block of digital image

Or

$$A = \sum u_i s_i v_i^T = u_1 s_1 v_1^T + u_2 s_2 v_2^T + \cdots + u_r s_r v_r^T \qquad (8)$$

Where U is an $m \times m$ orthogonal matrix, V is an $n \times n$ orthogonal matrix, S is an $m \times n$ diagonal matrix with non-negative entries as follows

$$S_{m \times n} = \begin{bmatrix} D & O_1 \\ O_2 & O_3 \end{bmatrix} \qquad (9)$$

Where O_1, O_2, O_3 are zero matrices and D is a diagonal matrix whose diagonal entries Σ have nonzero singular values of A :

$$D = \begin{bmatrix} S_1 & 0 & \cdots & 0 & 0 \\ 0 & & & & 0 \\ \vdots & & \ddots & & \vdots \\ 0 & & & & 0 \\ 0 & 0 & \cdots & 0 & S_r \end{bmatrix}, S_1 \geq S_2 \geq \cdots \geq S_r \geq 0 \qquad (10)$$

Where r is the rank of A .

The factorization in (1) is called the singular value decomposition of A .For a matrix with more rows than columns, in an alternate definition of the singular value decomposition, the matrix U is $m \times n$ with orthogonal columns, and S is a $m \times m$ diagonal matrix with nonnegative entries. Likewise, for a matrix with more columns than rows, the singular value decomposition can be defined above but with the matrix V being $n \times m$ with orthogonal columns, and S is a $m \times m$ diagonal with nonnegative entries.

Given an $m \times n$ matrix A , a rank-k approximation of A is a matrix A_k of the same size and of rank at most k that minimizes that difference with A .A rank-k approximation to A is obtained by taking the first k terms of the SVD:

$$A_k = \sum_{i=1}^{k} u_i \sigma_i v_i^T \qquad (11)$$

Fig.1 is shown singular value decomposition for 4×4 block in digital image.

4   Watermark Embedding and Extraction

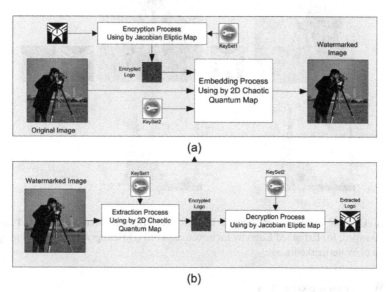

(a)

(b)

Fig. 2. Block Diagram of (a) embedding process (b) extraction process

4.1   Watermark Embedding

In this section the algorithm of embedding are discussed. The embedding process proposed in this paper consists of the following major parts:

- Step 1: Encryption process is applied to input watermark logo.
- Step 2: Position of block in original image is selected by quantum map and pixel values in block are stored in $Block_{4\times4}$.
- Step 3: The SVD coefficients are computed as follow:

$$[U,S,V] = SVD(Block_{4\times4})$$

Where U, S, V has values in 4×4 arrays (See Fig.1) and $SVD(.)$ denotes the singular value decomposition computational function.

- Step 4: U_{11} coefficient is updated as follow:

$$\begin{cases} U_{11} = Sign(U_{11}) \times (U_{21} + T) & if\ W_{ij} = 1 \\ U_{11} = Sign(U_{11}) \times (U_{21} - T) & if\ W_{ij} = 0 \end{cases}$$

Where W_{ij} denotes the binary pixel value of watermark logo in location (i,j) and T is threshold value (T=0.02).

- Step 5: Inverse of singular value decomposition is computed to obtain block pixels as follow:

$$Block_{4\times4} = U \times S \times V^T$$

Where (.)^T is transpose operation.

Step 6: step 2 to 5 is iterated, when all pixels in watermark logo are embedded to original image and final watermarked image is obtained

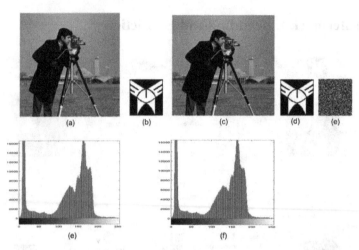

Fig. 3. (a) Original Image, (b) Watermark Logo (c) Watermarked Image(d)Extracted Logo by correct password, (e) Extracted Logo by incorrectpassword (f) Histogram of Original image (g) Histogram of Watermarkedimage

4.2   Watermark Extraction

Watermark extraction process is very similar to the embedding process. This process consists of the following major parts:

- Step 1: Position of block in watermarked image is selected by quantum map and pixel values in block are stored in $Block_{4\times4}$.
- Step 2: The SVD coefficients are computed as follow:

$$[U, S, V] = SVD(Block_{4\times4})$$

Where U, S, V has values in 4×4 arrays (See Fig.1) and $SVD(.)$ denotes the singular value decomposition computational function.

- Step 4:W_{ij} is extracted as follow:

$$\begin{cases} W_{ij} = 1 & if\ ABS(U_{11}) > ABS(U_{21}) \\ W_{ij} = 0 & if\ ABS(U_{11}) \leq ABS(U_{21}) \end{cases}$$

Where W_{ij} denotes the binary pixel value of watermark logo in location (i , j) and $ABS(.)$ denotes the absolute function in mathematics.

- Step 5: Step 1 to 4 is iterated, when all pixels in watermark logo are extracted from watermarked image and encrypted watermark logo is obtained
- Step 6: Decryption process is applied to obtained watermark logo in Step 5.

5   Experimental Result

This section will present and discuss the experimental results of our proposed scheme. Digital watermarking techniques must satisfy the following properties.

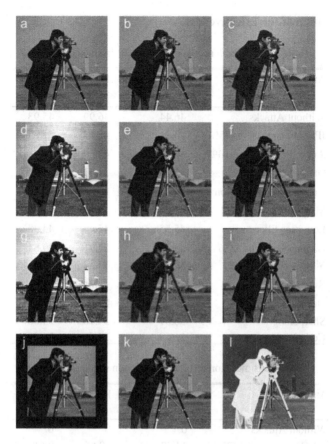

Fig. 4. Watermarked image under different attacks. (a) JPEG compression (70%),(b) Salt &pepper noise (10%), (c) Gaussian noise (0,0.01), (d)HistogramEqualization, (e) Median filter [3×3], (f) Low-pass filter [5×5], (g) Gammacorrection (0.6^o) (h) Motion blur (45°) (i) Rotation (1°), (j) Cropping (25%) (k) Sharpening (l) Complement.

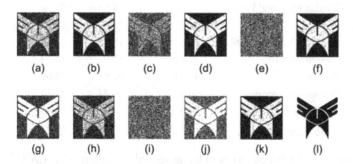

Fig. 5. Extracted Watermark logo under different attacks. (a) JPEG compression (70%),(b) Salt &pepper noise (10%), (c) Gaussian noise (0,0.01), (d)HistogramEqualization, (e) Median filter [3×3], (f) low-pass filter [5×5], (g) Gammacorrection (0.6^o) (h) motion blur (45°) (i) Rotation (1°), (j) Cropping (25%) (k) sharpening(l) complement.

5.1   Evaluation of the Effectiveness

Table 1. Simulation results of PSNR(dB) in standard images

Attack	Cameraman	Peppers	Boat
Without Attacks	46.44	46.99	45.93
JPEG compression (75%)	43.34	42.62	41.85
Salt & Pepper noise 10%	42.24	42.39	41.88
Gaussian noise (0,0.1)	31.68	31.47	31.44
Histogram Equalization	29.43	29.66	29.96
Median Filtering[3×3]	48.00	45.30	43.12
Low pass filter	45.55	45.44	44.38
Gamma Correction 0.6^0	29.32	27.21	29.64
Motion Blur 15°	35.48	35.52	33.64
Rotation 1°	32.76	32.26	31.01
One quarter cropped	27.62	27.66	27.63
Sharpening	36.09	34.10	33.08
Complement	26.59	27.50	26.01

Table 2. Simulation result of BER(%) in standard images

Attack	Cameraman	Peppers	Boat
Without Attacks	0	0	0
JPEG compression (75%)	14.22	10.66	9.61
Salt & Pepper noise 10%	4.22	3.69	3.80
Gaussian noise (0,0.1)	35.03	35.29	32.90
Histogram Equalization	2.88	2.16	1.86
Median Filtering[3×3]	47.28	48.66	49.54
Low pass filter	2.52	2.22	1.90
Gamma Correction 0.6^0	15.58	15.96	11.09
Motion Blur 15°	17.90	15.02	18.54
Rotation 1°	49.81	50.61	49.69
One quarter cropped	26.53	26.34	26.34
Sharpening	3.57	3.42	3.44
Complement	100	100	100

To demonstrate the effectiveness of the proposed algorithm, MATLAB simulations are performed by using 512× 512 pixel gray level "Cameraman" image and 128 ×128 pixel binary watermark logo "IAU". Fig. 3 demonstrates the invisibility of watermark. Figs.3(a) and Fig.3(b) show the original host image and watermark logo ,respectively. Figs.3(c-e) shows the watermarked image, the extracted watermark logo by correct keys and the extracted watermark logo by incorrect keys, respectively. The watermark embedding process is said to be imperceptible if the original data and watermarked data cannot be distinguished. To quantitatively evaluate the performance of the proposed scheme, the peak signal-to-noise ratio (PSNR) was adopted to measure the image quality of a watermarkedimage which is given by:

$$PSNR = 10 \times log_{10} \frac{255^2}{MSE} \ (dB) \tag{12}$$

According to the definitions in statistics, the mean squared error (MSE) between the original and watermarked images is defined by

$$MSE = \frac{1}{M \times N} \sum_{i=1}^{M} \sum_{j=1}^{N} (H_{i,j} - H'_{i,j})^2 \tag{13}$$

Where $H_{i,j}$ and $H'_{i,j}$ indicate the pixel values in the location (i, j) of the original host image and the watermarked image, respectively, while M ×N is the image size. In this study, reliability was measured as the bit error rate (BER) of extracted watermark through this formula:

$$BER = \frac{B}{M \times N} \times 100 \tag{14}$$

Where, B is the number of erroneously detected bits, and $M \times N$ is the extracted watermark image dimensions. The PSNR for the watermarked image is 46.44 dB, and the BER of the extracted watermark is zero. Therefore, there is no obvious perceptual distortion between watermarked image and original one; the embedded watermark does not degrade the quality of original host image.

5.2   Robustness to Attacks

To test the robustness of our proposed method, we applied several attacks to the watermarked image. In the experiments, both geometric and non geometric attacks are considered. Fig. 4 shows an example of a watermarked image attacked with the listed attacks. The corresponding best extracted watermarks for denoted attacks are shown in Figs. 5.The test results,BER and PSNR computed for standard images are shown in Table 1 and 2.

6   Concluding Remarks

Our proposed method is a novel watermarking scheme for image authentication based on multiple chaotic systems. The scheme is specially designed for image, thus, enabling various network multimedia applications. Quantum chaos is applied to design the selection scheme for watermark embedding and jacobian elliptic map is used to encryption of watermark logo. This algorithm tries to address the shortcoming of watermarking such as small key space, watermarking speed and level of security.

Without the correct initial condition, the watermark cannot be successfully detected. In general, the method is suitable for image authentication with application in law, commerce, defense, medical databases and journalism. The security of watermarking is greatly improved when chaos is administered. The goal is to realize a watermarking method with a private code. Further studies must be started to develop watermarking methods with a public key.

References

1. Cox, I.J., Matthew, L.M., Jeffrey, A.B., et al.: Digital Watermarking and Steganography, 2nd edn. Morgan Kaufmann Publishers (Elsevier), Burlington, MA (2007)
2. Huang, C.H., Wua, J.L.: Fidelity-guaranteed robustness enhancement of blind-detection watermarking schemes. Information Sciences 179, 791–808 (2009)
3. Liu, Y., Zhao, J.: A new video watermarking algorithm based on 1-D DFT and Radon transform. Signal Processing 90, 626–639 (2010)
4. Wei, H., Yuan, M., Zhao, J., Kou, Z.: Research and Realization of Digital Watermark for Picture Protecting. In: First International Workshop on Education Technology and Computer Science, vol. 1, pp. 968–970. IEEE (2009)
5. Li, X.: A New Measure of Image Scrambling Degree Based on Grey Level Difference and Information Entropy. In: 2008 International Conference on Computational Intelligence and Security, vol. 1, pp. 350–354 (2008)
6. Shen, Z.W., Liao, W.W., Shen, Y.N.: Blind watermarking algorithm based on henon chaos system and lifting scheme wavelet. In: Proceedings of the 2009 International Conference on Wavelet Analysis and Pattern Recognition, Baoding, pp. 308–313 (2009)
7. Barni, M., Bartolini, F., Piva, A.: Improved wavelet based watermarking through pixel-wise masking. IEEE Trans Image Process 10, 783–791 (2001)
8. Peres, A.: Quantum Theory: Concepts and Methods 24
9. Tefas, A., Nikolaidis, A., Nikolaidis, N., Solachidis, V., Sekeridou, S., Pitas, I.: Markov chaotic sequences for correlation based watermarking schemes. Chaos, Solitons & Fractals 17, 567–573 (2003)
10. Nikolaidis, S., Pitas, I.: Comparison of different chaotic maps with application to image watermarking. In: Proceedings of IEEE International Symposium on Circuits and Systems, Geneva, pp. 509–512 (2002)
11. Eckart, C., Young, G.: The approximation of one matrix another of lower rank. Psycometrika 1, 211–218 (1936)
12. Run, R.-S., Horng, S.-J., Lai, J.-L., Kao, T.-W., Chen, R.-J.: An improved SVD-based watermarking technique for copyright protection. Expert Systems with Applications (July 28, 2011) (in press, uncorrected Proof), DOI: 10.1016/j.eswa.2011.07.059, ISSN 0957-4174
13. Lai, C.-C.: An improved SVD-based watermarking scheme using human visual characteristics. Optics Communications 284(4), 938–944 (2011), DOI: 10.1016/j.optcom.2010.10.047, ISSN 0030-4018
14. Ling, H.-C., Phan, R.C.-W., Heng, S.-H.: On an optimal robust digital image watermarking based on SVD using differential evolution algorithm. Optics Communications 284(19), 4458–4459 (2011), DOI: 0.1016/j.optcom.2011.05.019, ISSN 0030-4018
15. Dogan, S., Tuncer, T., Avci, E., Gulten, A.: A robust color image watermarking with Singular Value Decomposition method. Advances in Engineering Software 42(6), 336–346 (2011), doi:10.1016/j.advengsoft.2011.02.012, ISSN 0965-9978
16. Devancy, R.L.: An Introduction to Chaotic Dynamical Systems. Addison Wesley (1982)

Incorporating First-Order Unification into Functional Language via First-Class Environments

Shin-ya Nishizaki

Department of Computer Science, Tokyo Institute of Technology
2-12-1-W8-69, O-okayama, Meguro-ku, Tokyo, 152-8552, Japan
nisizaki@cs.titech.ac.jp

Abstract. Unification is a useful process by which one attempts to find a substitute satisfying a given set of equations. Among several kinds of unification algorithms, the unification for equations between first-order terms is known to be decidable and to satisfy the completeness. A unification mechanism plays an important role in logic programming languages, such as Prolog. In this paper, we propose an approach to incorporating a unification mechanism into a functional programming language via first-class environments. The first-class environment is a reflective feature in a programming language, which enables us to reify environments, to handle them as first-class values such as integers and Boolean values, and to reflect the reified environment as an environment at a meta-level. By identifying resulting substitutions of unification problems as first-class environments, we can introduce unification into functional programming languages. In this paper, we first give the syntax of a simple functional language with unifications. Second, we give its operational semantics in the style of Kahn's natural semantics. Finally, we introduce some related works and show the future direction of our works.

Keywords: functional programming language, first-order unification, first-class environment, unification.

1 Introduction

1.1 First-Class Environment and Environment Calculus

In program, variables are bound to certain values and refereed in expressions. The correspondence between the variables and their values at some point in time is called an *environment*. In the semantics of programming languages, this is usually formalized by a partial function whose domain is a finite set of variables and whose codomain is a set of denotable values.

In a programming language Scheme [13], we can use two kinds of runtime objects – continuations and environments – as first-class citizens; that is, it is possible to pass such values as parameters and to return them as results. The availability of first-class continuations and environments increases the expressiveness of the programming

V.V. Das and P.M. El-Kafrawy (Eds.): SPIT 2012, LNICST 117, pp. 19–25, 2014.
© Institute for Computer Sciences, Social Informatics and Telecommunications Engineering 2014

language. In some versions of Scheme, the following primitives enable environments to be treated as first-class citizens:

- **the-environment** is a zero-ary procedure returning a representation of the current environment in which the expression itself is evaluated;
- **eval** is a binary procedure mapping the representation of an expression and the representation of an environment into the value of this expression in this environment.

An environment does not appear explicitly in a functional program's computation expressed as reduction sequences. An environment is usually represented as a list of pairs of variables and their bound denotation, which forms an implicit computational structure of the lambda-calculus.

The substitution is used as a meta-level mechanism to describe the beta-reduction of the lambda-calculus, but it is not an object-level mechanism of the lambda-calculus, since it is not an explicit operation in the lambda-calculus. The idea of using explicit substitutions [1,5–7] is an interesting approach to make substitutions work at object-level in the lambda-calculus, and explicit substitutions are formalized as object-level substitutions using an environment in the $\lambda\sigma$-calculus.

Although explicit substitutions allow us to treat an environment at object-level in the $\lambda\sigma$-calculus, there is still a crucial difference between the object-level environments of the $\lambda\sigma$-calculus and the first-class environments of Scheme. In the $\lambda\sigma$-calculus, it is not possible to pass substitutions as parameters. For instance, the following term is not permissible in the $\lambda\sigma$-calculus. $\lambda sub.(x[sub])$, where an explicit substitution is passed to the argument *sub*. The point to be stressed is that, in the $\lambda\sigma$-calculus the syntactic class of explicit substitutions is precisely distinguished from its terms. If we introduce first-class environments into the $\lambda\sigma$-calculus, we should allow $\lambda env.(x[env])$ as a permissible term in such an extended lambda-calculus. Roughly speaking, the lambda-calculus with first-class environments is an extended lambda-calculus that allows environments as additional permissible terms.

1.2   Embedding Unification into a Functional Programming Language via a First-Class Environment

Unification [2,15] is processing by which one attempts to solve the satisfiability problem given as a set of equations. The goal of unification is to find a substitution which makes each equation hold by applying to both sides. There are various kinds of unification depending on syntactic structures of terms. Unification is widely used in automated reasoning, logic programming and programming language type system implementation. In this paper, we focus on the *first-order unification* [2,15], which solves unification problems for first-order terms. Variables in first-order terms are not assumed to have functional values but individuals, similar to first-order predicate logic.

2   The Lambda Calculus with Unifications, λunify

In this section, we introduce the syntax of a theoretical programming language, λunify, which is an untyped lambda calculus into which we have incorporated first-order unification.

A set **Var** of *variables* and a set **FunSym** of *constructors* (or sometimes *function symbols*) are given in advance of the following definition of the λunify's syntax. As the first-order predicate logic and the equational logic [2], to each function symbol f, a non-negative integer, called *arity*, is assigned. This is written as arity(f). The symbols x, y, z are typically used for variables and f, g, h for function symbols.

Definition 1 (Expression of λunify). The *expressions* of λunify are inductively defined by the following grammar:

$$e ::= x \mid \lambda x.e \mid (e_1\ e_2) \mid id \mid (e_1/x) \cdot e_2 \mid (e_1 \circ e_2) \mid f(e_1, \ldots, e_n)$$
$$\mid \{e_1 = e'_1, \ldots, e_m = e'_m\} \text{ orelse } e$$

The first three kinds of expression are called a variable, a *lambda-abstraction*, and a *function application*, respectively, and these are assumed to have similar meanings to the traditional lambda calculus[4]. The next three expressions are called the *identity environment*, an *environment extension*, and an *environment composition* respectively, and are the same as the environment lambda-calculi's [9,10]. The last two kinds of expression are called a *construnctor term* and a *unificand* respectively. The constructor terms are similar to the first-order terms in the predicate logic. A unificand

$$\{e_1 = e'_1, \ldots, e_m = e'_m\} \text{ orelse } e$$

has the following intuitive meaning:

- Try the first-order unification of a set of equations $\{\ e_1 = e_1', \ldots, e_m = e_m'\ \}$
  - If the unification succeeds, the unifier is regarded as a value of a first-class environment.
  - Otherwise, the expression e is evaluated and its value is returned.

This intuitive meaning will be formalized as the operational semantics presented in the later section. We sometimes use an abbreviation

$$\overline{\{e_m = e'_m\}} \text{ orelse } e$$

for

$$\{e_1 = e'_1, \ldots, e_m = e'_m\} \text{ orelse } e$$

3   Operational Semantics of λunify

In this paper, the operational semantics of the calculus λunify is given in the style of the *natural semantics* proposed by G. Kahn[8].

In the original natural semantics, the semantic relation takes two input arguments: the first argument is an expression to be assigned a meaning, and the second an environment that gives a meaning to each free variable occurring in the expression.

$$\langle Expression,\ Environment \rangle \Downarrow Denotation$$

Both the input arguments of the semantics relation of λunify are expressions. More precisely, the second argument is an expression denoting an environment. Though the lambda calculus cannot represent environments as expressions, our calculus can handle first-class environments and represent environments as expressions.

Definition 2 (Values). The set **Value** of *values* is defined inductively by the following grammar. Meta-variables $v, v', v_1, \ldots, v_n$ stand for values.

$$v ::= x \mid x \circ w \mid f(v_1, \ldots, v_n) \mid (u\ v) \mid (\lambda x.e) \circ v \mid id \mid (v/x) \cdot v'$$

Metavariable w and u stand for elements of subsets of **Value**, which are defined inductively by the following grammar:

$$w ::= x \mid x \circ w \mid f(v_1, \ldots, v_n) \mid (u\ v)$$
$$u ::= x \mid x \circ w \mid f(v_1, \ldots, v_n) \mid (u\ v)$$
$$\mid id \mid (v/x) \cdot v'$$

Definition 3 (Semantic Relation). The ternary relation $\langle e, v \rangle \Downarrow v'$ among a term e and values v, v' is defined inductively by the following rules.

$$\frac{}{\langle x, (v/x) \cdot v' \rangle \Downarrow v}\ \textbf{VarHit} \qquad \frac{\langle x, v \rangle \Downarrow v''}{\langle x, (v/y) \cdot v' \rangle \Downarrow v''}\ \textbf{VarSkip}$$

$$\frac{}{\langle x, id \rangle \Downarrow x}\ \textbf{VarId} \qquad \frac{v \neq id \quad v \neq (v_1/x) \cdot v_2}{\langle x, v \rangle \Downarrow x \circ v}\ \textbf{VarPending}$$

$$\frac{\langle e_i, v \rangle \Downarrow v_i\ (i = 1, \ldots, n)}{\langle f(e_1, \ldots, e_n), v \rangle \Downarrow f(v_1, \ldots, v_n)}\ \textbf{Constr} \qquad \frac{}{\langle \lambda x.e, v \rangle \Downarrow (\lambda x.e) \circ v}\ \textbf{Lam}$$

$$\frac{\langle e_1, v \rangle \Downarrow (\lambda x.e_1') \circ v_1 \quad \langle e_2, v \rangle \Downarrow v_2 \quad \langle e_1', (v_2/x) \cdot v_1 \rangle \Downarrow v}{\langle (e_1\ e_2), v \rangle \Downarrow v'}\ \textbf{Beta}$$

$$\frac{\langle e_1, v \rangle \Downarrow v_1 \quad v_1 \neq (\lambda x.e_1') \circ v_1'' \quad \langle e_2, v \rangle \Downarrow v_2}{\langle (e_1\ e_2), v \rangle \Downarrow (v_1\ v_2)}\ \textbf{AppPending}$$

$$\frac{}{\langle id, v \rangle \Downarrow v}\ \textbf{Id}$$

$$\frac{\langle e_1, v \rangle \Downarrow v_1 \quad \langle e_2, v \rangle \Downarrow v_2}{\langle (e_1/x) \cdot e_2, v \rangle \Downarrow (v_1/x) \cdot v_2} \ \mathbf{Extn} \qquad \frac{\langle e_2, v \rangle \Downarrow v_2 \quad \langle e_1, v_2 \rangle \Downarrow v_1}{\langle e_1 \circ e_2, v \rangle \Downarrow v_1} \ \mathbf{Comp}$$

$$\frac{\begin{cases} \langle e_i, v \rangle \Downarrow v_i \\ \langle e_i', v \rangle \Downarrow v_i' \\ \mathbf{Unify}(\{\overline{v_n = v_n'}\}) = [\overline{x_m \mapsto v_m''}] \end{cases}}{\langle \{\overline{e_n = e_n'}\} \ \mathbf{orelse}\ e, v \rangle \Downarrow (v_1''/x_1) \cdots (v_m''/x_m) \cdot v} \ \mathbf{UnifySuccess}$$

$$\frac{\begin{cases} \langle e_i, v \rangle \Downarrow v_i \\ \langle e_i', v \rangle \Downarrow v_i' \\ \mathbf{Unify}(\{\overline{v_n = v_n'}\}) = \mathbf{failure} \\ \langle e, v \rangle \Downarrow v' \end{cases}}{\langle \{\overline{e_n = e_n'}\} \ \mathbf{orelse}\ e, v \rangle \Downarrow v'} \ \mathbf{UnifyFailure}$$

Definition 4 (Unification Procedure). *Unification procedure* **Unify** is defined by the following equations, which takes a finite set of expressions as an argument and returns either a substitution (or a *unifier*) or a failure signal **failure**.

$$\mathbf{Unify}(\{\ \}) = [\ ],$$
$$\mathbf{Unify}(\{v = v, \overline{v_n = v_n'}\}) = \mathbf{Unify}(\{\overline{v_n = v_n'}\}),$$
$$\mathbf{Unify}(\{x = y, \overline{v_n = v_n'}\}) = [x \mapsto \sigma(y)] \cup \sigma$$
$$\mathbf{where}\ \sigma = \mathbf{Unify}(\{\overline{v_n[x \mapsto y] = v_n'[x \mapsto y]},\})$$
$$\mathbf{Unify}(\{x = v, \overline{v_n = v_n'}\}) = \mathbf{if}\ x\ occurs\ in\ v\ \mathbf{then\ raise\ failure\ else}$$
$$[x \mapsto \sigma(x)] \cup \sigma$$
$$\mathbf{where}\ \sigma = \mathbf{Unify}(\{\overline{v_n[x \mapsto v] = v_n'[x \mapsto v]}\}),$$
$$\mathbf{Unify}(\{v = x, \overline{v_n = v_n'}\}) = \mathbf{Unify}(\{x = v, \overline{v_n = v_n'}\}),$$
$$\mathbf{Unify}(\{f(\overline{v_n^1}) = f(\overline{v_n^2}), \overline{v_n = v_n'}\}) = \mathbf{Unify}(\{\overline{v_n^1 = v_n^2}, \overline{v_n = v_n'}\}),$$
$$\mathbf{Unify}(\{\overline{v_n = v_n'}\}) = \mathbf{raise\ failure}.$$

4   Example of λunify

In order to give fruitful examples, we extend the language λunify by adding several basic constructs such as conditionals and the recursive operator. In the lambda calculus, it is known that such constructs are encoded. For example, the recursive fixed-point operator can be represented as

$$Y_{cbv} = \lambda f.(\lambda x.\lambda y.(f(xx)y)(\lambda x.\lambda y.(f(xx)y))$$

in the call-by-value lambda calculus. In this paper, we introduce it as a primitive construct with the following rule.

$$\frac{\langle (M(Y_{cbv}\ M)), v \rangle \Downarrow v'}{\langle (Y_{cbv}\ M), v \rangle \Downarrow v'}$$

We also introduce the conditional branch and the comparison operator as primitive operators similar to the recursive operator.

$$\frac{\langle e_1, v \rangle \Downarrow \textbf{true}\quad \langle e_2, v \rangle \Downarrow v_2}{\langle \textbf{if } e_1 \textbf{ then } e_2 \textbf{ else } e_3, v \rangle \Downarrow v_2}\quad \frac{\langle e_1, v \rangle \Downarrow \textbf{false}\quad \langle e_3, v \rangle \Downarrow v_3}{\langle \textbf{if } e_1 \textbf{ then } e_2 \textbf{ else } e_3, v \rangle \Downarrow v_3}$$

$$\frac{\langle e_1, v \rangle \Downarrow v'\quad \langle e_2, v \rangle \Downarrow v'}{\langle e_1 = e_2, v \rangle \Downarrow \textbf{true}}\quad \frac{\langle e_1, v \rangle \Downarrow v_1'\quad \langle e_2, v \rangle \Downarrow v_2'\quad v_1' \neq v_2'}{\langle e_1 = e_2, v \rangle \Downarrow \textbf{false}}$$

For describing richer examples in this section, we introduce the constant symbols **nil** and **0**, which are function symbols **succ** and **cons** of arity 1 and 2, respectively.

By using the unification mechanism of λunif, we can describe destructing of the data structures. For example, a function that returns the length of a list given as an argument is represented as follows.

$$Y_{cbv}(\lambda len.\lambda l.\ (\textbf{if } l = \textbf{nil then 0 else } (\textbf{succ}(len\ l_1))$$
$$\circ\ (\{l = \textbf{cons}(a_1, l_1)\}\ \textbf{orelse}\ id))$$

The following is a detailed explanation of the term 'λunify'.

— This term gives a recursive definition of the list-length function, using the fixed-point operator Y_{cbv}.
— Before solving the unificand { $l = \textbf{cons}(a_1, l_1)$ }, the variable l is assumed to be bound to a list. After the unification, the variables a_1 and l_1 are bound to the head and the tail of the list, respectively.
— The conditional expression (**if** $l =$ **nil then** 0 **else** (**succ** (len, l_1)) is evaluated under the environment obtained by evaluating the unificand.

We give another example of a function which searches for an item in the list; if found, it returns the item's position; otherwise, it returns (the length of the list)+1.

$$Y_{cbv}(\lambda f.\lambda l.\ (\textbf{if } a_1 = \textbf{0 then 1 else } (\textbf{succ}(f\ l_1))$$
$$\circ\ (\{l = \textbf{cons}(a_1, l_1)\}\ \textbf{orelse}\ (0/a_1) \cdot id))$$

5   Concluding Remarks

In this paper, we proposed a functional programming language with a unification mechanism. We incorporated the unification by using first-class environments. We first gave the syntax of the language, and second, we gave its operational semantics in the style of Kahn's natural semantics. We finally introduced some related works and showed the future direction of our works.

Discussions. There are several studies in which the unification is embedded into programming languages. In the paradigm of functional programming, one such study is *Qute* by Sato and Sakurai[12]. In their language, the beta-reduction and the unification computation is tightly combined. The unification is processed as needed by the beta-reduction. The characteristic feature of Qute is parallel execution of the beta-reduction and the unification processing. However, handling of the variable scope is more complicated than that of λunify.

One of the future research directions of λunify is parallel execution of beta-reduction and unification processing, keeping the simple scoping feature of λunify.
In logic programming languages such as Prolog[14], the unification is the most fundamental mechanism of handling data. However, the meaning of variables in the logic programming languages is different to the other kinds of programming language. On the other hand, we succeeded in introducing unification into **λenv** keeping the standard meaning of the variables.

In this work, we focused on the first-order unification. The other kinds of unification such as higher-order unification[3], which enables us to unify the lambda terms. If we incorporate the higher-order unification into λunify, it enables us to describe programs which handle data with variable-bindings more easily. We would apply λunify to proof checking software such as the theorem prover Isabelle [11].

Acknowledgement. This work was supported by Grants-in-Aid for Scientific Research (C) (24500009). I would like to express my gratitude to Takayuki Higuchi for his collaboration and fruitful discussions in the early stage of this work.

References

1. Abadi, M., Cardelli, L., Curien, P.-L., Lévy, J.-J.: Explicit substitutions. Journal of Functional Programming 1(4), 375–416 (1991)
2. Baarer, F., Nipkow, T.: Term Rewriting and All That. Cambridge University Press (1999)
3. Baader, F., Snyder, W.: Unification theory. In: Robinson, J., Voronkov, A. (eds.) Handbook of Automated Reasoning, pp. 447–533. Elsevier Science Publishers (2001)
4. Barendregt, H.P.: The Lambda Calculus. Elsevier (1984)
5. Curien, P.L.: An abstract framework for environment machines. Theor. Comput. Sci. 82, 389–402 (1991)
6. Curien, P.L., Hardin, T., Lévy, J.-J.: Confluence properties of weak and strong calculi of explicit substitutions. J. ACM 43(2), 363–397 (1996)
7. Dowek, G., Hardin, T., Kirchner, C.: Higher-order unification via explicit substitutions, extended abstract. In: Proceedings of the Symposium on Logic in Computer Science, pp. 22–39. Springer (1987)
8. Kahn, G.: Natural Semantics. In: Brandenburg, F.J., Wirsing, M., Vidal-Naquet, G. (eds.) STACS 1987. LNCS, vol. 247, pp. 22–39. Springer, Heidelberg (1987)
9. Nishizaki, S.: Simply typed lambda calculus with first-class environments. Publications of Reseach Institute for Mathematical Sciences Kyoto University 30(6), 1055–1121 (1995)
10. Nishizaki, S.: Polymorphic environment calculus and its type inference algorithm. Higher-Order and Symbolic Computation 13(3), 239–278 (2000)

Software Defined Integrated RF Frontend Receiver Design

Sriramachandra Murthy Budaraju and M.A. Bhagyaveni

College of Engineering-Guindy, Anna University, Chennai, India
murthybs@bsnl.co.in, bhagya@annauniv.edu

Abstract. Software Defined Radio (SDR) technology uses a generic hardware platform supported by software modules to accommodate different communication standards, frequency bands and modulation schemes. In today's world, integration of various mobile communication standards like Code Division Multiple Access (CDMA), Global System for Mobile communication (GSM), Wideband CDMA (WCDMA) and Worldwide Interoperability for Microwave Access (WIMAX) is the need of the hour. This paper deals with the concepts and procedures involved in designing software defined integrated radio frequency (RF) frontend receiver which can be configured to support different technologies like GSM, CDMA and WCDMA. In a three band case, a new band pass sampling algorithm is proposed to evaluate valid sampling frequency ranges and corresponding intermediate frequencies for multiple standards. The simulation results show that the algorithm developed and the software defined integrated RF frontend receiver design proposed in this paper give good performance.

Keywords: Band Pass Sampling, Base Transceiver Station, Interoperability, Modulation, Numerically Controlled Oscillator, Reconfigurable architecture and Software Defined Radio.

1 Introduction

Software Defined Radio (SDR) is a term adopted by the international Software Defined Radio Forum to describe radios that provide software control of a variety of modulation techniques, variable bandwidth, security functions and waveform requirements of current and evolving standards. The main aim of SDR is to design a reconfigurable hardware which can support different technologies just by changing the software. Quite often this is done with general purpose Digital Signal Processors (DSP) or Field Programmable Gate Arrays (FPGA).

In this paper, a reconfigurable SDR based integrated RF frontend receiver design is given for multiple standards, i.e. GSM, CDMA and WCDMA. The main challenge in designing reconfigurable frontend receiver is to find out valid sampling frequency and corresponding intermediate frequencies. The band pass sampling algorithm for three band case is given in this paper and valid sampling frequency ranges are obtained for these standards. The intermediate frequencies for the system considered are calculated and given.

V.V. Das and P.M. El-Kafrawy (Eds.): SPIT 2012, LNICST 117, pp. 26–33, 2014.

2   Band Pass Sampling

The central idea behind the SDR architecture is to place analog to digital and digital to analog convertors as near to the antenna as possible, leaving the implementation of the most radio functionality to a programmable micro or signal processor. One way to accomplish this in a radio receiver front end is by directly down converting the desired radio frequency (RF) signal to a target intermediate frequency (IF) using band pass sampling. In band pass sampling method, initially, all possible orders of spectral replicas in the spectrum of the sampled signal are determined. For each case, valid sampling frequency range in terms of parameters such as bandwidth, centre frequency, the upper/lower cutoff frequency of RF signals is derived. The challenge is to determine a valid sampling frequency closest to the bandwidth of RF signal that will translate the band pass signal into sampled bandwidth without aliasing. The value of the IF for the down converted signals is given as follows [2].

$$f_{IF} = \begin{cases} rem\ (f_c, f_s) & if\ \left\lfloor (f_c/(f_s/2)) \right\rfloor\ is\ even \\ f_s - rem\ (f_c, f_s) & if\ \left\lfloor (f_c/(f_s/2)) \right\rfloor\ is\ odd \end{cases} \tag{1}$$

Where, f_c is the centre frequency of the RF signal, f_s is the sampling frequency and rem (f_c, f_s) is reminder of f_c / f_s.

2.1   Procedure to Determine Valid Sampling Frequency Range

Consider three RF signals with frequency ranges given by f_{L1} - f_{H1}, f_{L2} - f_{H2} and f_{L3} - f_{H3}, with bandwidths as B_1, B_2 and B_3 and centre frequencies as f_1, f_2 and f_3 respectively. The centre frequencies are related by $f_2 = R_1 f_1$ and $f_3 = R_2 f_2$, where R_1 and R_2 are positive real numbers calculated and used in the algorithm.

For the sampled signal to be without aliasing, the spectrum of each signal must not straddle any integer multiple of $f_s/2$. Therefore, the positive spectra of the three signals '1', '2' and '3' must lie inside some segments n_1, n_2 and n_3 respectively. Since n_1 is the number of segment where spectrum '1' is located, the largest value of n_1 is determined by $n_1 = \left\lfloor (f_{L1}/f_s) \right\rfloor$.

For a three band case, the bandwidth of a segment should at least accommodate all non overlapping replicas (replicas '1', '-1', '2', '-2', '3', and '-3'). This means that $f_s \geq 2(B_1 + B_2 + B_3)$. Therefore, the value of n_1 is upper bounded by

$$n_1 \leq \left\lfloor \left(\frac{f_{L1}}{2(B_1 + B_2 + B_3)} \right) \right\rfloor \tag{2}$$

In addition, since spectrum of '1' is in segment n_1, we can write

$$n_1 f_s \langle f_1 \langle (n_1 + 1) f_s \tag{3}$$

Multiplying (3) by R_1/f_s and using the relation of $f_2 = R_1 f_1$, we get

$$R_1 n_1 \langle (f_2 / f_s) \langle R_1 (n_1 + 1) \tag{4}$$

Taking 'floor' function on (4) leads to

$$\lfloor (R_1 n_1) \rfloor \langle n_2 \langle \lfloor (R_1 (n_1 + 1)) \rfloor \tag{5}$$

Similarly, we get

$$\lfloor (R_2 n_2) \rfloor \langle n_3 \langle \lfloor (R_2 (n_2 + 1)) \rfloor \tag{6}$$

Table 1. Boundary constraints for a three band case

Case	Boundary Constraint	
	Spectrum '1' or '2'	Spectrum '2' or '3'
1	$f_{L1} \geq n_1 f_s$	$f_{H2} \leq (n_2 + \frac{1}{2}) f_s$
2	$f_{L1} \geq (n_1 + \frac{1}{2}) f_s$	$f_{H2} \leq (n_2 + 1) f_s$
3	$f_{L1} \geq n_1 f_s$	$f_{L2} \geq (n_2 + \frac{1}{2}) f_s$
4	$f_{L1} \geq (n_1 + \frac{1}{2}) f_s$	$f_{L2} \geq n_2 f_s$
5	$f_{H1} \leq (n_1 + 1) f_s$	$f_{H2} \leq (n_2 + \frac{1}{2}) f_s$
6	$f_{H1} \leq (n_1 + \frac{1}{2}) f_s$	$f_{H2} \leq (n_2 + 1) f_s$
7	$f_{H1} \leq (n_1 + 1) f_s$	$f_{L2} \geq (n_2 + \frac{1}{2}) f_s$
8	$f_{H1} \leq (n_1 + \frac{1}{2}) f_s$	$f_{L2} \geq n_2 f_s$
9	$f_{L2} \geq n_2 f_s$	$f_{H3} \leq (n_3 + \frac{1}{2}) f_s$
10	$f_{L2} \geq (n_2 + \frac{1}{2}) f_s$	$f_{H3} \leq (n_3 + 1) f_s$

Table 2. The valid ranges of sampling frequency

Case	Range of valid f_s
1	$\dfrac{f_{H2}}{(n_2 + \frac{1}{2})} \leq f_s \leq \min(\dfrac{f_{L1}}{n_1}, \dfrac{f_{L2} - f_{H1}}{n_2 - n_1}, \dfrac{f_{L3} - f_{H2}}{n_3 - n_2})$
2	$\dfrac{f_{H2}}{(n_2 + 1)} \leq f_s \leq \min(\dfrac{f_{L1}}{n_1 + \frac{1}{2}}, \dfrac{f_{L2} - f_{H1}}{n_2 - n_1}, \dfrac{f_{L3} - f_{H2}}{n_3 - n_2})$
3	$\dfrac{f_{H1} + f_{H2}}{(n_1 + n_2 + 1)} \leq f_s \leq \min(\dfrac{f_{L1}}{n_1}, \dfrac{f_{L2}}{n_2 + \frac{1}{2}}, \dfrac{f_{L3}}{n_3 + 1})$
4	$\dfrac{f_{H1} + f_{H2}}{(n_1 + n_2 + 1)} \leq f_s \leq \min(\dfrac{f_{L1}}{n_1 + \frac{1}{2}}, \dfrac{f_{L2}}{n_2}, \dfrac{f_{L3}}{n_3 - \frac{1}{2}})$
5	$\max(\dfrac{f_{H1}}{n_1 + 1}, \dfrac{f_{H2}}{n_2 + \frac{1}{2}}, \dfrac{f_{H3}}{n_3}) \leq f_s \leq \dfrac{f_{L1} + f_{L2}}{(n_1 + n_2 + 1)}$
6	$\max(\dfrac{f_{H1}}{n_1 + \frac{1}{2}}, \dfrac{f_{H2}}{n_2 + 1}, \dfrac{f_{H3}}{n_3 + \frac{1}{2}}) \leq f_s \leq \dfrac{f_{L1} + f_{L2}}{(n_1 + n_2 + 1)}$
7	$\max(\dfrac{f_{H1}}{n_1 + 1}, \dfrac{f_{H2} - f_{L1}}{n_2 - n_1}, \dfrac{f_{H3} - f_{L2}}{n_3 - n_2}) \leq f_s \leq \dfrac{f_{L2}}{(n_2 + \frac{1}{2})}$
8	$\max(\dfrac{f_{H1}}{n_1 + \frac{1}{2}}, \dfrac{f_{H2} - f_{L1}}{n_2 - n_1}, \dfrac{f_{H3} - f_{L2}}{n_3 - n_2}) \leq f_s \leq \dfrac{f_{L2}}{n_2}$
9	$\dfrac{f_{H3}}{(n_3 + \frac{1}{2})} \leq f_s \leq \min(\dfrac{f_{L2}}{n_2}, \dfrac{f_{L3} - f_{H2}}{n_3 - n_2}, \dfrac{f_{H3} - f_{L1}}{n_3 - n_1})$
10	$\dfrac{f_{H3}}{(n_3 + 1)} \leq f_s \leq \min(\dfrac{f_{L2}}{n_2 + \frac{1}{2}}, \dfrac{f_{L3} - f_{H2}}{n_3 - n_2}, \dfrac{f_{H3} - f_{L1}}{n_3 - n_1})$

The boundary constraints and ranges of valid sampling frequency for some of the possible cases are given in Table 1 and 2 respectively. Some of the valid sampling frequency ranges for a three band case are calculated and given in Table 3. The corresponding IFs are calculated using (1) and given in Table 4.

Table 3. Valid sampling frequency ranges for three band case

Standard	Channel Range (MHz)	Sampling Frequency Range (MHz)
CDMA-IS 95 GSM-900 WCDMA	824-825.25 895-895.2 1920-1925	12.919463-12.924812
		13.099206-13.122137
		13.336822-13.358209
		13.461654-13.46890
		13.528689-13.535433
		13.563636-13.568905
		13.961386-13.963636
		14.109589-14.117647

Table 4. Sampling frequency and down converted IF

Sampling Frequency (MHz)	IF1 (MHz)	IF2 (MHz)	IF3 (MHz)
12.924812	2.5630	3.2880	3.2970
13.099206	0.6250	4.3540	3.0833
13.358209	3.5840	0.10	1.0821
13.4689	3.0221	6.1526	3.5527
13.528689	0.6250	2.2065	1.4262
13.568905	3.0782	0.4477	4.2845
13.963636	0.7705	1.4273	4.4818
14.117647	5.8015	5.6882	2.50

3   Software Defined Integrated RF Frontend Receiver

Digital front end of a BTS is shown in the figures 1 and 2. The configurable part in an SDR is its digital front end. The digital front end consists of digital band pass filters, ADC, Numerically Controlled Oscillator (NCO) and anti aliasing filters. Numerically controlled Oscillator (NCO) is the digital version of local oscillator. This paper focuses on the sampling frequency for the ADC which in turn determines the down converted IF and the NCO frequency.

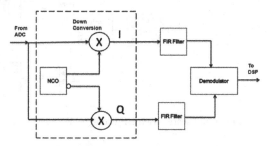

Fig. 1. Digital Frontend Receiver

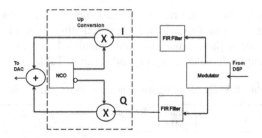

Fig. 2. Digital Frontend Transmitter

Software defined integrated RF frontend receiver architecture for GSM, CDMA-IS95A and WCDMA technologies for the uplink band is shown in Fig. 3. In the absence of actual input signal, we simulate the incoming signal using the Gaussian noise generator. The output of the generator is filtered into required uplink bands of CDMA (824-849 MHz), GSM (890-915 MHz) and WCDMA (1920-1980 MHz) using digital band pass filters.

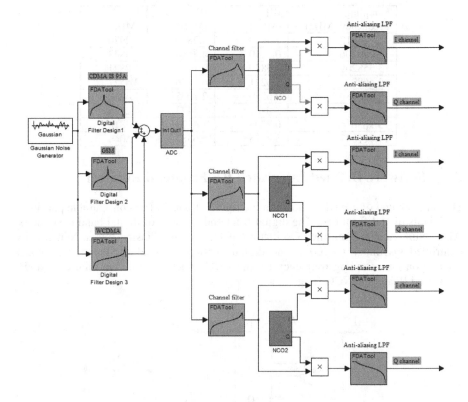

Fig. 3. Software based RF Frontend Receiver

The outputs from the digital filters are added and given to the ADC block. The ADC block also carries out the functions of amplification and gain control in addition to the analog to digital conversion. The sampling frequency of ADC is determined by the band pass sampling algorithm as given in sec.2. Direct down conversion of these RF signal bands to the respective baseband frequency is carried out using digital down converter. The carrier frequency for Numerically Controlled Oscillator (NCO) is taken from the valid Intermediate Frequencies as calculated in sec.2. These digital down convertors will give the output as the CDMA, GSM and WCDMA baseband signals. These baseband signals are then fed to the respective demodulator.

4   Simulation and Results

For simulation, we chose the frequencies as 890-890.2 MHz for GSM, 824-825.25 MHz for CDMA and 1920-1925 MHz for WCDMA. The sum of these three signals is given as input signal to the ADC whose sampling frequency is selected from the frequency ranges given in Table 3. We have considered 13.568905 MHz as the sampling frequency and the results are obtained. The input signal to the ADC consisting of the spectrum of CDMA, GSM and WCDMA bands is shown in Fig. 4. The corresponding intermediate frequencies are given in Table 4 as 3.0782 MHz, 0.4477 MHz and 4.2845 MHz for CDMA, GSM and WCDMA standards respectively. These down converted IFs are generated by NCO, NCO1 and NCO2. The baseband spectra of GSM, CDMA, and WCDMA are shown in figures 5, 6 and 7 respectively. These results show that the band pass sampling algorithm developed and the Software Defined Integrated RF Frontend Receiver Design proposed in this paper give good performance.

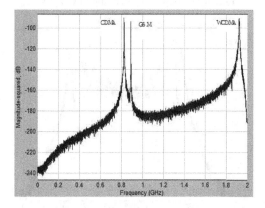

Fig. 4. The spectrum of simulated GSM, CDMA and WCDMA bands

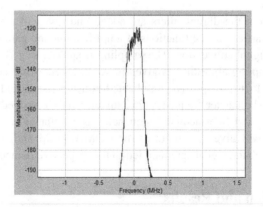

Fig. 5. The baseband spectrum of GSM

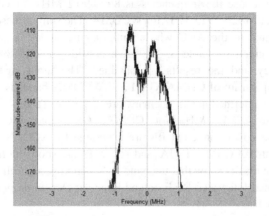

Fig. 6. The baseband spectrum of CDMA

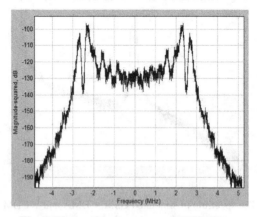

Fig. 7. The baseband spectrum of WCDMA

5 Conclusion

In this paper, a new receiver model for the Software Defined Integrated RF Frontend Receiver to interoperate amongst GSM, CDMA and WCDMA is given. This architecture multiplies the cell capacity by a factor of three. The band pass sampling algorithm developed in this paper for a three band case can be extended for N bands. The Software Defined Integrated RF frontend receiver model developed in this paper can be upgraded to interoperate amongst N standards. In a similar way, the transmitter model also can be developed.

References

1. Mitola, J.: The software radio architecture. IEEE Communication Magazine 33(5) (May 1995)
2. Akos, D.M., Stockmaster, M., Tsui, J.B.Y., Caschera, J.: Direct bandpass sampling of multiple distinct RF signals. IEEE Trans. Commun. 47(7), 983–988 (1999)
3. Tseng, C.-H., Chou, S.-C.: Direct down conversion of multiple RF signals using Bandpass Sampling. In: IEEE International Conference on Communications, vol. 3, pp. 2003–2007 (2003)
4. Bae, J., Park, J.: An Efficient Algorithm for Bandpass Sampling of Multiple RF Signals. IEEE Signal Processing Letters 13(4) (April 2006)
5. Bose, S., Khaitan, V., Chaturvedi, A.: A Low-Cost Algorithm to Find the Minimum Sampling Frequency for Multiple Bandpass Signals. IEEE Signal Processing Letters 15 (2008)
6. Prithviraj, V., Manikandan, K., Prasanna, C., Saranesh, S., Subramanian, R.: Front end design of Software defined BTS for interoperability between GSM and CDMA. In: VITAE 2009, Alborg, Denmark (May 2009)
7. Vasudevan, S.K., Sivaraman, R., Alex, Z.C.: Software Defined Radio Implementation. International Journal of Computer Applications 4(8) (August 2010)
8. Kim, H.-J., Kim, J.-U., Kim, J.-H., Wang, H., Lee, I.-S.: The Design Method and Performance Analysis of RF Subsampling Frontend for SDR/CR Receivers. IEEE Transactions on Industrial Electronics 57(5) (May 2010)

Acknowledgement-Based Trust Framework
for Wireless Sensor Networks

X. Anita[1], J. Martin Leo Manickam[2], and M.A. Bhagyaveni[1]

[1] Anna University, Chennai, India
anitaextee@yahoo.co.in
bhagya@annauniv.edu
[2] St. Joseph's College of Engineering, Chennai, India
josephmartin_74@yahoo.co.in

Abstract. Most of the existing trust-based routing schemes requires the support of promiscuous mode of operation and gathers large number of recommendations from the neighbors for trust derivation. In this paper, we propose a new Two-way Acknowledgement-based Trust framework with individual (2-ACKT-I) acknowledgements which calculates the direct trust using a link layer acknowledgement and a two-hop acknowledgement from a downstream neighbor. The simulation results demonstrate that 2-ACKT-I scheme significantly outperforms the conventional multihop routing schemes and promiscuous mode-based trust scheme in terms of packet delivery ratio and network lifetime.

Keywords: Trust, routing protocol, WSN, black hole, malicious attack.

1   Introduction

Wireless Sensor Networks (WSNs) consists of densely deployed tiny sensor nodes to monitor the real world environment by sensing, processing and communicating about the sensor field [1]. Due to the use of insecure communication channel, the WSNs are prone to varied types of attacks [2-5]. Several trust-based routing schemes are proposed in the literature to thwart the network layer attacks. Trust is the level of confidence in an entity and classified as direct and indirect trust [6]. The direct trust derivation requires promiscuous mode of operation which demands the sensor to be in the idle listening state till the next hop neighbor forwards the packet and hence, consume more energy. Moreover, the promiscuous mode of operation does not always provide sufficient evidence on the behavior of a monitored node. A monitored node may not be able to relay the packet due to the low quality of the wireless link. Alternatively, the indirect trust is derived based on the recommendations gathered from the neighbors. The large number of recommendations gathered from the neighbors increases the overhead and energy consumption in the network. Hence, the design objective of the proposed Two-way Acknowledgement based Trust (2-ACKT-I) framework with individual acknowledgements is to

V.V. Das and P.M. El-Kafrawy (Eds.): SPIT 2012, LNICST 117, pp. 34–40, 2014.
© Institute for Computer Sciences, Social Informatics and Telecommunications Engineering 2014

- To increase the network lifetime by avoiding the promiscuous mode of operation of sensors and thereby allowing the sensors to be in sleep mode as directed by the MAC,
- To reduce the memory requirement by representing the trust with lower number of bits, and
- To reduce the control overhead by minimizing the number of recommendations gathered in the network.

This paper is organized as follows: Section 2 describes the related work. Section 3 presents the proposed 2-ACKT-I protocol and performance analysis is presented in Section 4. The conclusions and future scope are followed in the Section 5.

2   Related Work

Many trust-based routing schemes proposed for WSNs uses either direct observation or recommendations or a combination of both to derive trust on its neighbors. Ganeriwal et al. proposed RFSN [7] scheme employs a watchdog mechanism and bayesian formulation to represent the trust based on the recommendations received from the neighbors. It will not cope with uncertain situation when the attacks are much more planned considering the weaknesses in different building blocks of the framework. Bourkerche et al. proposed ATRM [8] scheme uses the mobile agents in each node for trust management in clustered WSNs. It assumes the existence of a trusted authority to generate and launch mobile agents and so it is vulnerable to single point of failure. Most of the trust management schemes do not address the various resource constraint requirements of WSN but GTMS [9] proposed by Riaz Ahmed et al. has overcome some of these constraints. Each node calculates trust based on direct or indirect observations. Trust value is represented as an unsigned integer and saves memory space. The drawback of GTMS is that it demands high energy and more memory space for cluster heads (CHs). Moreover, it also assumes a trusted BS which is immune to security threats. Hosam A. Rahhal et al. proposed a TCLM [10] scheme for WSN and the trust are calculated by a cross-layer concept i.e by using ACKs from datalink layer and TCP layer. The trust value is represented in the range [0,1] as real numbers which requires more memory. The aforementioned trusted routing schemes uses promiscuous mode of operation for monitoring a neighboring node which incurs more energy in a resource constrained WSNs.

3   The 2-ACKT-I Routing Protocol

3.1   Assumptions

The 2-ACKT-I protocol is designed with the following assumptions:
- all nodes behave legitimately during route discovery stage,
- a peer-to-peer network with all SNs having unique identity,

- all nodes are homogenous with regard to storage capacity, processing speed and energy, and
- no collaborative attackers present.

The 2-ACKT-I protocol consists of the four components such as neighbor monitoring, trust computation, trust representation and 2-ACK routing protocol as shown in the Fig.1.

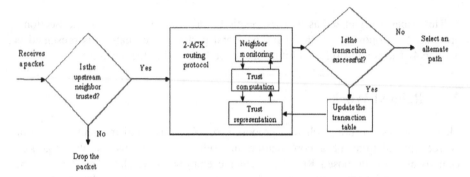

Fig. 1. Block diagram of 2-ACKT-I routing protocol

3.2   Neighbor Monitoring

The neighbor monitoring component in a trust-based routing scheme must ensure that the neighbor has successfully received the packet and it has forwarded the packet honestly to its neighbor by following the underlying routing protocol. Consider the topology shown in the Fig. 2.

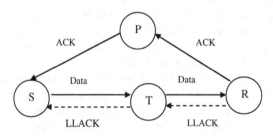

Fig. 2. Neighbor Monitoring

Let us assume that the subject (S) unicasts a data packet to its neighbor target (T). Being a legitimate node, target will forward the packet to its next hop sponsor (R) by following the underlying routing protocol. For accurate derivation of trust, the subject must ensure the occurrence of the following two events:

(1)   Target has successfully received the packet sent by it, and
(2)   Target has forwarded the packet to its downstream neighbor R faithfully following the protocol.

In 2-ACKT scheme, the occurrence of event (1) is ensured by using the link layer acknowledgement (LLACK) generated from the IEEE 802.15.4 MAC protocol.

The occurrence of event (2) is ensured by unicasting a two-hop ACK to the subject through the alternate path R-P-S as shown in the Fig. 2 where P is the third party neighbor. The alternate path is determined during the route discovery stage by exploiting the dense nature of the sensor network as discussed in the section 3.4. The subject on receiving a LLACK from the target and subsequently an acknowledgement from sponsor through the alternate path will consider that transaction as successful one else it is considered to be failed.

3.3   Trust Computation and Representation

The observed successful and failed transactions are stored in the transaction table. The fields in the transaction table of the subject are as follows:

<node id, number of successful transactions (T_s), number of failed transactions (T_f), trust level (T_L)>

where *node id* is the address of the neighbor namely target, *number of successful transactions* is incremented by 1 when individual acknowledgement is received, *number of failed transactions* is incremented by 1 when it has not received the ACK in a given timeout, and *trust level* can take an integer value from 0 to 7 as shown in the Fig. 3. The trust value is computed based on the observed number of successful and failed transaction entries in the transaction table as given by

$$T_V = \left(\frac{T_s + \varepsilon}{T_s + T_f} \right) * 100 \tag{1}$$

where ε is a constant. The computed T_V lies in the range [0,100] and it is not directly stored in the transaction table as it consumes more memory. It is mapped to one of the possible trust level (T_L) as shown in the Fig. 3. T_L can take an integer value which lies in the range [0,7] and requires memory space of 3 bits. A target is considered to be trusted when $T_L > 3$. Any request or response from an untrusted target will not be considered during route discovery and packet forwarding stages.

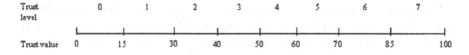

Fig. 3. Trust Representation

3.4   2-ACK Routing Protocol

When a SN desires to report an event to the BS for which a valid route is not found, it initiates a route discovery process by broadcasting a route request (RREQ) to its neighbor. The RREQ contains the following fields:

*<source_address,   source_seq_#,   broadcast_id,   destination_seq_#,   hop_cnt,
upstream_neighbor_address>*

The pair *<source_address, broadcast_id>* uniquely identifies a RREQ. *broadcast_id* is incremented whenever the source issues a new RREQ. *upstream_neighbor_address* is the address of the neighbor from which it receives the RREQ. On receiving a RREQ packet from a neighbor, the intermediate SN verifies whether the packet is received from a trusted neighbor by checking the transaction table. If the neighbor SN is found to be trustworthy, each neighbor either satisfies the RREQ by sending a route reply (RREP) packet to the source or rebroadcasts the RREQ to its own neighbor after incrementing the *hop_cnt* and updating the *upstream_neighbor_address*. Subject address is derived from the *upstream_neighbor_address* in the received RREQ. A node may receive multiple copies of same RREQ packet from various neighbors. If a node receives redundant RREQ packet i.e with same *broadcast_id* and *source_address* as in the processed RREQ, then it does not rebroadcast the packet but it verifies the *upstream_neighbor_address* in the received RREQ. If the *upstream_neighbor_address* is same, then the node records the address of the neighbor from which it has received the redundant copy of RREQ to establish the alternate path to the subject. This neighbor is referred as third party neighbor as it relays RREQ with same *broadcast_id*, *source_address* and *upstream_neighbor _address* as in already processed RREQ. Once the RREQ reaches the BS or an intermediate SN with a fresh enough route, the BS or an intermediate SN responds by unicasting an RREP packet back to the neighbor from which it first received the RREQ. Each route table entry contains the following information:

*<destination address, next hop, number of hops, destination sequence number, active
neighbors for this route, third party neighbors for this route, expiration time for the
route table entry>.*

Each SN maintains a route table entry for each destination of interest.

4   Results and Discussion

The performance of 2-ACKT-I protocol is studied using the ns-2 simulator. The malicious nodes manifest black hole attack [2]. We took a simulation area of 300 X 300 m, with six hundred nodes placed in random. The transmission range is 45 m. The IEEE 802.15.4 is the MAC layer protocol used to evaluate the performance of the proposed trust model under attack conditions. We have also implemented the promiscuous mode-based trust (PMT-AODV) scheme in AODV [11] routing protocol. The 2-ACKT-I, PMT-AODV and AODV protocols are tested against exactly the same scenario and connection pattern. In AODV, the discovered route to the BS may consist of malicious nodes. As a result, the packet loss in AODV is 61.9 percent higher than 2-ACKT-I protocol as shown in Fig. 4(a). The malicious nodes are effectively identified and eliminated in the discovered route and hence results in lower packet loss in 2-ACKT-I and PMT-AODV protocols. This has a positive effect on the packet delivery ratio (PDR) of the 2-ACKT-I and PMT-AODV protocols as shown in the Fig. 4(b). 2-ACKT-I routing protocol augments the PDR of the AODV routing protocol by up to 28.57 percent. The performance of 2-ACKT-I and PMT-AODV are almost the same. In 2-ACKT-I routing protocol, the sponsor sends ACK to the subject through the third party for every data packet received from the target. As a result, the control overhead of 2-ACKT-I is 45.44 percent higher than AODV protocol. In PMT-AODV, all the neighboring sensor nodes overhear the control packets as well as the data packets to compute trust. As a result, the control overhead is 16.07 percent higher than 2-ACKT-I as shown in Fig. 4(c). The simulation is performed with an initial energy of 0.5 joules to calculate the network lifetime. The higher energy consumption for trust evaluation of 2-ACKT-I and PMT-AODV protocol results in lower network lifetime of 3.79 percent and 5.34 percent respectively over AODV routing protocol as shown in Fig. 4(d). The lower overhead and non-promiscuous mode of operation for trust evaluation in 2-ACKT-I protocol keeps the network lifetime 1.61 percent higher than that of PMT-AODV.

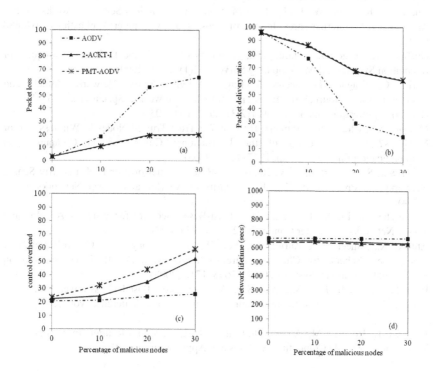

Fig. 4. Performance Comparison of 2-ACKT-I, PMT-AODV and AODV routing protocols

5   Conclusion

Security is an important problem that can significantly degrade the performance of resource constrained WSNs. In this paper, we have proposed a new 2-ACKT-I framework for trust evaluation in WSNs. The simulation results show that the proposed protocol has better performance than the conventional multihop and trust-based routing protocols in terms of packet delivery ratio, control overhead and network lifetime. In this paper, the malicious attacks are manifested by individual sensor nodes. However, there exists a much wider spectrum of security threats involving collaborative attackers. Hence, we plan to design a comprehensive trust-based security solution that thwarts collaborative attackers in a resource constrained WSNs.

References

1. Chen, X., Makki, K., Yen, K., Pissinou, N.: Sensor Network Security: A Survey. IEEE Communications Surveys & Tutorials 11(2), 52–73 (2009)
2. Wang, Y., Attebury, G., Ramamurthy, B.: A Survey of Security Issues in Wireless Sensor Networks. IEEE Communication Surveys and Tutorials 8(2), 2–23 (2006)
3. Yu, Y., Li, K., Zhou, W., Li, P.: Trust Mechanisms in Wireless Sensor Networks: Attack Analysis and Countermeasures. Journal of Network and Computer Applications, 867–880 (2012)
4. Hoffman, K., Zage, D., Rotaru, C.N.: A Survey of Attack and Defense Techniques for Reputation Systems. ACM Computing Surveys 42(1), 1–31 (2009)
5. Karlof, C., Wagner, D.: Secure Routing in Wireless Sensor Networks: Attacks and Countermeasures. Journal on Elsevier's Ad Hoc Networks, Special Issue on Sensor Network Applications and Protocols 1(2-3), 293–315 (2003)
6. Momani, M., Challa, S., Alhmouz, R.: Can We Trust Trusted Nodes in Wireless Sensor Networks? In: Proceedings of the International Conference on Computer and Communication Engineering, pp. 1227–1232 (2008)
7. Ganeriwal, S., Srivatsava, M.B.: Reputation-Based Framework for High Integrity Sensor Networks. In: Proc. ACM Workshop Security of Ad Hoc and Sensor Networks, p. 66 (2004)
8. Boukerche, A., Li, X., EL-Khatib, K.: Trust-Based Security for Wireless Ad Hoc and Sensor Networks. Computer Comm. 30, 2413–2427 (2007)
9. Ahmed, R., Jameel, H., d'Auriol, B.J., Lee, H., Lee, S., Song, Y.-J.: Group-Based Trust Management Scheme for Clustered Wireless Sensor Networks. IEEE Transactions on Parallel and Distributed Systems 20(11), 1698–1712 (2009)
10. Rahhali, H.A., Ali, I.A., Shaheen, S.I.: A Novel Trust-Based Cross-Layer Model for Wireless Sensor Networks. In: 28th National Radio Science Conference, vol. C5, pp. 1–10 (2011)
11. Perkin, C.E., Royer, E.M.: Ad Hoc On Demand Distance Vector Routing. In: Second IEEE Workshop on Mobile Computing, Systems and Applications, pp. 90–100 (1999)

Complexity of Checking Strong Satisfiability of Reactive System Specifications

Masaya Shimakawa, Shigeki Hagihara, and Naoki Yonezaki

Department of Computer Science,
Graduate School of Information Science and Engineering,
Tokyo Institute of Technology.
2-12-1-W8-67 Ookayama,
Meguro-ku, Tokyo 152-8552, Japan
{masaya,hagihara,yonezaki}@fmx.cs.titech.ac.jp

Abstract. Many fatal accidents involving safety-critical reactive systems have occurred in unexpected situations, which were not considered during the design and test phases of the systems. To prevent these accidents, reactive systems should be designed to respond appropriately to any request from an environment at any time. Verifying this property during the specification phase reduces the development costs of safety-critical reactive systems. This property of a specification is commonly known as realizability. It is known that the complexity of the realizability problem is 2EXPTIME-complete. On the other hand, we have introduced the concept of strong satisfiability, which is a necessary condition for realizability. Many practical unrealizable specifications are also strongly unsatisfiable. In this paper, we show that the complexity of the strong satisfiability problem is EXPSPACE-complete. This means that strong satisfiability offers the advantage of lower complexity for analysis, compared to realizability.

Keywords: Reactive System, Verification of Specification, Complexity, Linear Temporal Logic.

1 Introduction

A reactive system is a system that responds to requests from an environment in a timely fashion. The systems used to control elevators or vending machines are typical examples of reactive systems. Many safety-critical systems, such as the systems that control nuclear power plants and air traffic control systems, are also considered reactive systems.

In designing a system of this kind, the requirements are analyzed and then described as specifications for the system. If a specification has a flaw, such as inappropriate case-splitting, a developed system may fall into unintended situations. Indeed, many fatal accidents involving safety-critical reactive systems have occurred in unexpected situations, which were not considered during the design and test phases of the systems. It is therefore important to ensure that a specification does not possess this kind of flaw[6].

V.V. Das and P.M. El-Kafrawy (Eds.): SPIT 2012, LNICST 117, pp. 41–50, 2014.
© Institute for Computer Sciences, Social Informatics and Telecommunications Engineering 2014

More precisely, a reactive system specification must have a model that can respond in a timely fashion to any request at any time. This property is called realizability, and was introduced in [1, 12]. In [12], A. Pnueli and R. Rosner showed that a reactive system can be synthesized from a realizable specification.

On the other hand, in [8, 9], we introduced the concept of strong satisfiability, which is a necessary condition for realizability. Many practical unrealizable specifications are also strongly unsatisfiable[9]. In [5], we presented a method for checking whether or not a specification satisfies strong satisfiability. We also proposed techniques for identifying the flaws in strongly unsatisfiable specifications in [4]. Another approach for checking strong satisfiability was introduced in [17].

However, there has been no discussion of the complexity of the strong satisfiability problem, which is an important consideration, since such knowledge would be useful for obtaining an efficient verification procedure for strong satisfiability. In this paper, we show that the complexity of the strong satisfiability problem is EXPSPACE-complete. Since it is known that the complexity of the realizability problem is 2EXPTIME-complete, this means that strong satisfiability offers the advantage of lower complexity for analysis, compared to realizability.

The remainder of this paper is organized as follows. In Section2, we introduce the concepts of a reactive system, linear temporal logic(LTL) as a specification language, and strong satisfiability, which is a necessary condition for the realizability of a reactive system specification. In Section3, we show that the strong satisfiability problem for a specification written in LTL is EXPSPACE-complete. In Section4, we discuss the complexity of the strong satisfiability problem in relation to that of the satisfiability problem and the realizability problem. We present our conclusions in Section5.

2   Specifications for Reactive Systems and Their Properties

2.1   Reactive Systems

A reactive system (illustrated in Fig. 1) is a system that responds to requests from an environment in a timely fashion.

Fig. 1. A reactive system

Definition 1 (Reactive System). *A reactive system RS is a triple $\langle X, Y, r \rangle$, where X is a set of events caused by an environment, Y is a set of events caused by the system, and $r : (2^X)^+ \to 2^Y$ is a reaction function.*

We refer to events caused by the environment as 'input events,' and those caused by the system as 'output events.' The set $(2^X)^+$ is the set of all finite sequences of sets of input events. A reaction function r relates sequences of sets of previously occurring input events with a set of current output events.

2.2 Language for Describing Reactive System Specifications

The timing of input and output events is an essential element of reactive systems. Modal logics are widely used in computer science. Among these, temporal logics have often been applied to the analysis of reactive systems, following the application of such logics to program semantics by Z. Manna and A. Pnueli[7]. A propositional linear temporal logic (LTL)[11] with an 'until' operator is a suitable language for describing the timing of events. In this paper, we use LTL to describe the specifications of reactive systems. We treat input events and output events as atomic propositions.

Syntax. Formulae in LTL are inductively defined as follows:
- Atomic propositions are formulae; i.e., input events and output events are formulae.
- $f \wedge g$, $\neg f$, $\mathbf{X}f$, $f\mathbf{U}g$ are formulae if f and g are formulae.

  Intuitively, $f \wedge g$ and $\neg f$ represent the statements 'both f and g hold' and 'f does not hold,' respectively. The notation $\mathbf{X}f$ means that 'f holds at the next time,' while $f\mathbf{U}g$ means that 'f always holds until g holds.' The notations $f \vee g$, $f \to g$, $f \leftrightarrow g$, $f \oplus g$, $f\mathbf{R}g$, $\mathbf{F}f$, and $\mathbf{G}f$ are abbreviations for $\neg(\neg f \wedge \neg g)$, $\neg(f \wedge \neg g)$, $\neg(f \wedge \neg g) \wedge \neg(\neg f \wedge g)$, $\neg(f \leftrightarrow g)$, $\neg(\neg f \mathbf{U} \neg g)$, and $(\neg \bot)\mathbf{U}f$, $\neg \mathbf{F} \neg f$ respectively, where $\bot$ is an atomic proposition representing 'falsity.'

Semantics. A behavior is an infinite sequence of sets of events. Let i be an index such that $i \geq 0$. The i-th set of a behavior σ is denoted by $\sigma[i]$. When a formula f holds on the i-th set of a behavior σ, we write $\sigma, i \models f$, and inductively define this relation as follows:

- $\sigma, i \models p$ iff $p \in \sigma[i]$
- $\sigma, i \not\models \bot$
- $\sigma, i \models f \wedge g$ iff $\sigma, i \models f$ and $\sigma, i \models g$
- $\sigma, i \models \neg f$ iff $\sigma, i \not\models f$
- $\sigma, i \models \mathbf{X}f$ iff $\sigma, i + 1 \models f$
- $\sigma, i \models f\mathbf{U}g$ iff $\exists j \geq 0.((\sigma, i + j \models g)$ and $\forall k(0 \leq k < j. \ \sigma, i + k \models f))$

We say that σ satisfies f and write $\sigma \models f$ if $\sigma, 0 \models f$. We say that f is satisfiable if there exists a σ that satisfies f.

2.3   Properties of Reactive System Specifications

It is important for reactive system specifications to satisfy realizability. Realizability requires that there exist a reactive system such that for any input events with any timing, the system produces output events such that the specification holds.

Definition 2 (Realizability). *A specification Spec is realizable if the following holds:*

$$\exists RS \forall \tilde{\imath}(behave_{RS}(\tilde{\imath}) \models Spec),$$

where $\tilde{\imath}$ is an infinite sequence of sets of input events; i.e., $\tilde{\imath} \in (2^X)^\omega$. $behave_{RS}(\tilde{\imath})$ is the infinite behavior of $\tilde{\imath}$ caused by RS, defined as follows. If $\tilde{\imath} = i_0 i_1 ...$,

$$behave_{RS}(\tilde{\imath}) = (i_0 \cup o_0)(i_1 \cup o_1) \ldots ,$$

where o_i is a set of output events caused by RS; i.e., $o_i = r(i_0 ... i_i)$, and $\cup$ denotes the union of two sets.

The following property was shown to be a necessary condition for realizability in [8].

Definition 3 (Strong satisfiability). *A specification Spec is strongly satisfiable if the following holds:*

$$\forall \tilde{\imath} \exists \tilde{o}(\langle \tilde{\imath}, \tilde{o} \rangle \models Spec),$$

where $\tilde{o}$ is an infinite sequence of sets of output events; i.e., $\tilde{o} \in (2^Y)^\omega$. If $\tilde{\imath} = i_0 i_1 ...$ and $\tilde{o} = o_0 o_1 ...$, then $\langle \tilde{\imath}, \tilde{o} \rangle$ is defined by $\langle \tilde{\imath}, \tilde{o} \rangle = (i_0 \cup o_0)(i_1 \cup o_1) ....$

Intuitively, strong satisfiability is the property that if a reactive system is given an infinite sequence of sets of future input events, the system can determine an infinite sequence of sets of future output events. Strong satisfiability is a necessary condition for realizability; i.e., all realizable specifications are strongly satisfiable. Conversely, many practical strongly satisfiable specifications are also realizable.

Example 1. Let us consider a simple example of a control system for a door. The initial specification is as follows.

1. The door has two buttons: an open button and a close button.
2. If the open button is pushed, the door eventually opens.
3. While the close button is pushed, the door remains shut.

The events 'the open button is pushed' and 'the close button is pushed' are both input events. We denote these events by x_1 and x_2, respectively. The event 'the door is open (closed)' is an output event. We denote this event by y (resp., $\neg y$). The initial specification is then represented by $Spec_1$: $\mathbf{G}((x_1 \rightarrow \mathbf{F}y) \wedge (x_2 \rightarrow \neg y))$ in LTL. This specification is not strongly satisfiable, and consequently unrealizable, due to the fact that there is no response that satisfies $Spec_1$ for the environmental behavior in which the close button is still being pushed after the open button has been pushed. Formally, for $\tilde{\imath} = \{x_1, x_2\}\{x_2\}\{x_2\}...$, $\exists \tilde{o}(\langle \tilde{\imath}, \tilde{o} \rangle \models Spec_1)$ does not hold. Hence $\forall \tilde{\imath} \exists \tilde{o}(\langle \tilde{\imath}, \tilde{o} \rangle \models Spec_1)$ does not hold.

However, suppose the constraint 3 in the initial specification can be weakened to 3':
3'. If the close button is pushed, the door eventually closes.

Then the modified specification is represented by $\mathbf{G}((x_1 \rightarrow \mathbf{F}y) \wedge (x_2 \rightarrow \mathbf{F}\neg y))$, and this is both strongly satisfiable and realizable.

3   Complexity of Checking Strong Satisfiability

In this section, we show that the strong satisfiability problem (i.e., whether or not a specification written in LTL satisfies strong satisfiability) is EXPSPACE-complete. In other words, (1) the strong satisfiability problem is in the class EXPSPACE (the class of problems solvable in $O(2^{p(n)})$ amount of space by a deterministic Turing machine, where $p(n)$ is a polynomial function), and (2) all the problems in EXPSPACE are reducible to the strong satisfiability problem.

3.1   Upper Bound

First, we show that the strong satisfiability problem is in EXPSPACE. We demonstrate a procedure for checking strong satisfiability which uses $O(2^{p(n)})$ amount of space. This procedure is a modified version of the technique introduced in [5].

A *non-deterministic Büchi automaton* is a tuple $A = \langle \Sigma, Q, q_0, \delta, F \rangle$, where Σ is an alphabet, Q is a finite set of states, q_0 is an initial state, $\delta \subseteq Q \times \Sigma \times Q$ is a transition relation, and $F \subseteq Q$ is a set of final states. A run of A on an ω-word $\alpha = \alpha[0]\alpha[1]...$ is an infinite sequence $\gamma = \gamma[0]\gamma[1]...$ of states, where $\gamma[0] = q_0$ and $(\gamma[i], \alpha[i], \gamma[i+1]) \in \delta$ for all $i \geq 0$. We say that A accepts α, if there is a run γ on α such that $In(\gamma) \cap F \neq \emptyset$ holds, where $In(\gamma)$ is the set of states that occur infinitely often in γ. The set of ω-words accepted by A is called the language accepted by A, and is denoted by $L(A)$.

Let $Spec$ be a specification written in LTL. We can check the strong satisfiability of $Spec$ via the following procedure.

1. We obtain a non-deterministic Büchi automaton $A = \langle 2^{X \cup Y}, Q, q_0, \delta, F \rangle$ such that $L(A) = \{\sigma \mid \sigma \models Spec\}$ holds.
2. Let $A' = \langle 2^X, Q, q_0, \delta', F \rangle$ be a non-deterministic Büchi automaton obtained by restricting A to only input events, where $\delta' = \{(q, i, q') \mid \exists o\, (q, i \cup o, q') \in \delta\}$. Note that $L(A') = \{\tilde{\imath} \mid \exists \tilde{o}\, \langle \tilde{\imath}, \tilde{o} \rangle \in L(A)\}$ holds due to the definition of δ'.

3. We check whether or not A' is universally acceptable (which means that $L(A') = (2^X)^{\omega}$). If it is universally acceptable, we conclude that *Spec* is strongly satisfiable. If it is not universally acceptable, we conclude that *Spec* is not strongly satisfiable.

A can be constructed within $O(2^{|Spec|})$ amount of space, and the size of A is also $O(2^{|Spec|})$[16]. Since A' is obtained by projection, A' can be constructed within $O(|A|)$ amount of space, and the size of A' is $O(|A|)$. The universality problem for a Büchi automaton is in PSPACE[15], and Step 3 is accomplished within $O(p(|A'|))$ amount of space. Therefore, we can check strong satisfiability in $O(2^{|Spec|})$ amount of space, and we can conclude that the strong satisfiability problem is in EXPSPACE.

Theorem 1. *The strong satisfiability problem for specifications written in LTL is in the complexity class EXPSPACE.*

3.2   Lower Bound

In this section, we show that the strong satisfiability problem is EXPSPACE-hard, by providing polynomial time reduction from the EXP-corridor tiling problem[3] to the strong satisfiability problem. It is well known that the EXP-corridor tiling problem is EXPSPACE-complete.

Definition 4 (EXP-corridor tiling problem). *The EXP-corridor tiling problem is as follows: For a given $(T, H, V, t_{init}, t_{final}, m)$ where T is a finite set of tiles, $H, V \subseteq T \times T$ are horizontal and vertical adjacency constraints, $t_{init}, t_{final} \in T$ are the initial and final tiles, and $m \in N$, determine whether or not there exists $k \in N$, and an assignment function $f : [0,...,(2^m - 1)] \times [0, k] \to T$, such that the following conditions are satisfied:*

1. $f(0, 0) = t_{init}$
2. $f(2^m - 1, k) = t_{final}$
3. *for any* $0 \le i < 2^m - 1, 0 \le j \le k, (f(i, j), f(i + 1, j)) \in H$ *holds.*
4. *for any* $0 \le i \le 2^m - 1, 0 \le j < k, (f(i, j), f(i, j + 1)) \in V$ *holds.*

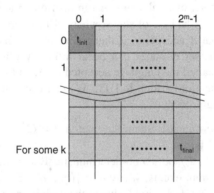

Fig. 2. The EXP-corridor tiling problem

As Fig. 2 shows, the tiling grid has $2^m \times \omega$ points. Intuitively, this problem asks: "for a given tiling grid, does there exist k such that a tile can be assigned to each point (i, j) for which $0 \le i < 2^m$ and $0 \le j \le k$, satisfying the conditions 1-4?" The condition 1 is the condition for the initial tile, and states that the initial tile t_{init} is assigned to the leftmost and topmost point. The condition 2 is the condition for the final tile, and states that the final tile t_{final} is assigned to the rightmost and bottommost point. The condition 3 is the condition for horizontal lines, and states that each tile and the tile to its right satisfy the horizontal adjacency constraint H. The condition 4 is the condition for vertical lines, and states that each tile and the tile beneath it satisfy the vertical adjacency constraint V.

We provide polynomial time reduction from the EXP-corridor tiling problem to the complement of the strong satisfiability problem. That is, for the EXP-corridor tiling problem $(T, H, V, t_{init}, t_{final}, m)$, we construct a formula φ_{tiling} such that $\exists \vec{i} \forall \vec{o}(\langle \vec{i}, \vec{o} \rangle \models \neg \varphi_{tiling})$ holds if and only if the answer to the tiling problem $(T, H, V, t_{init}, t_{final}, m)$ is affirmative.

In this reduction, we relate "there exists a tiling assignment" in the tiling problem to "there exists an infinite sequence of sets of input events." Furthermore, "the tiling assignment satisfies the conditions" is related to "the corresponding infinite sequence of sets of input events does not satisfy φ_{tiling} for any infinite sequence of sets of output events."

Input events.   To relate an infinite sequence of sets of input events to a tiling assignment, we introduce the following input events.
- x_t for each $t \in T$: "the tile t is placed on the point (i, j)" is related to "the input events x_t occur at the time $i + (2^m) \cdot j$."
- *end*: "tiling assignment concludes at the point (i, j)" is related to "*end* occurs at the time $i + (2^m) \cdot j$."
- $c_0, \ldots, c_{m-1}$: These are m bit counters that count the amount of time. By checking these counters, we can identify a column of the tiling grid.

Output events. We introduce the following output events.
- $y_0, \ldots, y_{m-1}$: These are used to identify a column.

The formula φ_{tiling}. The formula φ_{tiling} is the negation of the conjunction of the formulae (1)-(6) mentioned below. Here we use the following abbreviations:

$$\dot{c} = 0 \equiv \bigwedge_{0 \le i < m} \neg c_i$$

$$\dot{c} = 2^m - 1 \equiv \bigwedge_{0 \le i < m} c_i$$

$$\dot{c} = \dot{y} \equiv \bigwedge_{0 \le i < m} (c_i \leftrightarrow y_i)$$

– The constraint for m bit counters $c_0, \ldots, c_{m-1}$.

$$\left(\bigwedge_{0 \leq i < m} \neg c_i \right) \wedge \left(\bigwedge_{0 \leq i < m} \mathbf{G}\left((c_i \oplus \bigwedge_{0 \leq j < i} c_j) \leftrightarrow \mathbf{X} c_i \right) \right) \tag{1}$$

This represents the statement "the value of $\dot{c}$ is 0 initially, and is incremented on every pass," which means that "$\dot{c}$ is a counter."
– The relation between a tile and a point of the grid.

$$\bigwedge_{t \in T} \mathbf{G}(x_t \rightarrow \bigwedge_{t' \neq t} \neg x_{t'}) \wedge \mathbf{G}(\neg end \rightarrow \bigvee_{t \in T} x_t) \tag{2}$$

This represents the statement "at most one tile is assigned to each grid point, and if tiling is not finished, some tile must be assigned."
– The constraint for the condition 1.

$$x_{t_{init}} \tag{3}$$

This represents the statement "the initial tile t_{init} is placed on the point (0, 0)."
– The constraint for the condition 2.

$$\neg end \, \mathbf{U}(\neg end \wedge \dot{c} = 2^m - 1 \wedge x_{t_{final}} \wedge \mathbf{XG} \, end) \tag{4}$$

This represents the statement "the final tile t_{final} is placed on some point in column 2^m - 1, and tiling is finished."
– The constraint for the condition 3.

$$\mathbf{G}(\dot{c} \neq 2^m - 1 \wedge \neg end \rightarrow \bigvee_{(t,t') \in H} (x_t \wedge \mathbf{X} x_{t'})) \tag{5}$$

This represents the statement "if tiling is not finished and the current point is not in the (2^m-1)-th column (i.e., a point exists to the right of it), then the tile at the current point and the tile to the right satisfy the condition H."
– The constraint for the condition 4.

$$\left(\bigwedge_{0 \leq i < m} \mathbf{G}(y_i \leftrightarrow \mathbf{X} y_i) \right) \rightarrow$$
$$\mathbf{G}((\dot{c} = \dot{y} \wedge \mathbf{XF}(\neg end \wedge \dot{c} = 0)) \rightarrow \bigvee_{(t,t') \in V} (x_t \wedge \mathbf{X}((\dot{c} \neq \dot{y}) \mathbf{U}(\dot{c} = \dot{y} \wedge x_{t'})))) \tag{6}$$

This represents the statement "if the value of y is never changed, for any current point in the column indicated by y, if tiling is not finished at the point just below the current point, the tile at the current point and the tile beneath it satisfy the condition V." Here "the tile at the current point and the tile beneath it satisfy the condition V" is specified by "$(t, t') \in V$ such that t is placed on the current point and t' is placed on the point whose column follows that of the current point by y." Hence $(\forall \dot{y}(\ldots \models (6))$ represents the statement "for any column, tiles in the column satisfy the condition V," which means "any tiles satisfy the condition V."

Theorem 2. *The strong satisfiability problem for specifications written in LTL is EXPSPACE-hard.*

Proof. As mentioned above, we can construct a formula φ_{tiling} such that the answer to the EXP-corridor tiling problem is affirmative if and only if the corresponding φ_{tiling} is not strongly satisfiable. The size of φ_{tiling} is polynomial in the size of the problem $(T, H, V, t_{init}, t_{final}, m)$, and φ_{tiling} can be constructed in polynomial time. Therefore, the EXP-corridor tiling problem is reducible to the complement of the strong satisfiability problem. Since the EXP-corridor tiling problem is EXPSPACE-complete, the complement of the strong satisfiability problem is EXPSPACE-hard, and the strong satisfiability problem is co-EXPSPACE-hard. Since EXPSPACE=co-EXPSPACE, the strong satisfiability problem is also EXPSPACE-hard.

4   Discussion

In this section, we discuss the complexity of the strong satisfiability problem in relation to that of the satisfiability problem and the realizability problem. It is well known that the complexity of the satisfiability problem for specifications written in LTL is PSPACE-complete[14], and the complexity of the realizability problem for specifications written in LTL is 2EXPTIME-complete[13]. PSPACE is the complexity class of problems solvable in $O(p(n))$ amount of space by a deterministic Turing machine, and 2EXPTIME is the complexity class of problems solvable in $O(2^{\wedge}(2^{\wedge}(p(n))))$ amount of time by a deterministic Turing machine. The relationship between these classes is as follows:

$$\text{PSPACE} \subsetneq \text{EXPSPACE} \subseteq \text{2EXPTIME}$$

Therefore, the strong satisfiability problem is more difficult than the satisfiability problem, and is easier than or of equal difficulty to the realizability problem.

5   Conclusion

In this paper, we showed that the strong satisfiability problem is EXPSPACE-complete. This indicates that the strong satisfiability problem is more difficult than the satisfiability problem, and is easier than or of equal difficulty to the realizability problem.

  In future work, we will investigate the complexity of stepwise satisfiability and strong stepwise satisfiability, which are properties of reactive system specifications that were introduced in [8]. Furthermore, we will discuss the complexity of the strong satisfiability problem for subsystems of LTL that are syntactically restricted. If we succeed in finding a subsystem for which specifications can be verified efficiently, verification of reactive system specifications will become more practical. For realizability, subsystems of LTL were given in [2, 10]. We will find another subsystem by taking strong satisfiability into account. The results presented in this paper will provide important guidelines for this future work.

Acknowledgments. This work was supported by a Grant-in-Aid for Scientific Research(C) (24500032).

References

1. Abadi, M., Lamport, L., Wolper, P.: Realizable and unrealizable specifications of reactive systems. In: Ronchi Della Rocca, S., Ausiello, G., Dezani-Ciancaglini, M. (eds.) ICALP 1989. LNCS, vol. 372, pp. 1–17. Springer, Heidelberg (1989)
2. Alur, R., La Torre, S.: Deterministic generators and games for ltl fragments. ACM Trans. Comput. Logic 5(1), 1–25 (2004)
3. Boas, P.V.E.: The convenience of tilings. In: Complexity, Logic, and Recursion Theory, pp. 331–363. Marcel Dekker Inc. (1997)
4. Hagihara, S., Kitamura, Y., Shimakawa, M., Yonezaki, N.: Extracting environmental constraints to make reactive system specifications realizable. In: Proc. of the 16th Asia-Pacific Software Engineering Conference, pp. 61–68. IEEE (2009)
5. Hagihara, S., Yonezaki, N.: Completeness of verification methods for approaching to realizable reactive specifications. In: Proc. of 1st Asian Working Conference on Verified Software. UNU-IIST Technical Report, vol. 348, pp. 242–257 (2006)
6. Jackson, D.: Automating first-order relational logic. In: Proceedings of the 8th ACM SIGSOFT International Symposium on Foundations of Software Engineering: Twenty-First Century Applications, SIGSOFT 2000/FSE-8, pp. 130–139. ACM (2000)
7. Manna, Z., Pnueli, A.: Axiomatic approach to total correctness of programs. Acta Informatica 3(3), 243–263 (1974)
8. Mori, R., Yonezaki, N.: Several realizability concepts in reactive objects. In: Information Modeling and Knowledge Bases (1993)
9. Mori, R., Yonezaki, N.: Derivation of the input conditional formula from a reactive system specification in temporal logic. In: Langmaack, H., de Roever, W.-P., Vytopil, J. (eds.) FTRTFT 1994 and ProCoS 1994. LNCS, vol. 863, pp. 567–582. Springer, Heidelberg (1994)
10. Piterman, N., Pnueli, A., Sa'ar, Y.: Synthesis of reactive(1) designs. In: Emerson, E.A., Namjoshi, K.S. (eds.) VMCAI 2006. LNCS, vol. 3855, pp. 364–380. Springer, Heidelberg (2006)
11. Pnueli, A.: The temporal semantics of concurrent programs. Theoretical Computer Science 13, 45–60 (1981)
12. Pnueli, A., Rosner, R.: On the synthesis of a reactive module. In: Proceedings of the 16th ACM SIGPLAN-SIGACT Symposium on Principles of Programming Languages, pp. 179–190 (1989)
13. Rosner, R.: Modular Synthesis of Reactive Systmes. Ph.D. thesis, Weizmann Institute of Science (1992)
14. Sistla, A.P., Clarke, E.M.: The complexity of propositional linear temporal logics. J. ACM 32(3), 733–749 (1985)
15. Sistla, A.P., Vardi, M.Y., Wolper, P.: The complementation problem for Büchi automata with applications to temporal logic. Theor. Comput. Sci. 49(2-3), 217–237 (1987)
16. Tauriainen, H.: On translating linear temporal logic into alternating and nondeterministic automata. Research Report A83, Helsinki University of Technology, Laboratory for Theoretical Computer Science, Espoo, Finland (2003)
17. Yoshiura, N.: Decision procedures for several properties of reactive system specifications. In: Futatsugi, K., Mizoguchi, F., Yonezaki, N. (eds.) ISSS 2003. LNCS, vol. 3233, pp. 154–173. Springer, Heidelberg (2004)

Towards a Systematic Approach
for Heterogeneous Web Service Messages

Ibrahim Ahmed Al-Baltah, Abdul Azim Abdul Ghani,
Wan Nurhayati Wan Ab. Rahman, and Rodziah Atan

Faculty of Computer Science and Information Technology
University Putra Malaysia
Abou_amel@yahoo.com,
{azim,wannur,rodziah}@fsktm.upm.edu.my

Abstract. Establishing semantic interoperability between the heterogeneous messages of Web services has been a critical issue since the emergence of Web service. So far, many approaches that are aimed at solving semantic conflicts to achieve semantic interoperability of heterogeneous messages of Web service have been proposed. However, despite the significant contributions of the current approaches, semantic conflicts remain the critical problem that prevents exchanging the data between heterogeneous messages seamlessly. In this paper, we propose a new systematic approach to solve semantic conflicts of heterogeneous messages. The proposed approach revolves around three steps; semantic conflict identification, detection and solution.

Keywords: SOA, Web service, semantic conflicts, message-level conflicts, message-level mediation.

1 Introduction

Service oriented architecture (SOA) is a new paradigm that recently emerged as a logical way for designing systems to provide services; these services have published and discoverable interface [1-2]. Web services are currently the most promising SOA based implementation technology [2-4]. SOA using Web services is considered as the latest approach that aims at providing interoperability between heterogeneous systems [5].

Web services are built based on the concept of messages exchange. However, the process of exchanging the messages between Web services is always hampered by the heterogeneities that exist between heterogeneous messages. These heterogeneities result from using different meanings and representations of the same data. In practice, semantic conflicts may arise at two levels; ontology-level and message-level. Semantic conflict at ontology-level arises when the sender and receiver Web services are described into two different ontologies with different concepts. While semantic conflict at message-level is related to the actual implementation of the sender and receiver Web services. However, the focus of this paper is on solving message-level conflicts.

V.V. Das and P.M. El-Kafrawy (Eds.): SPIT 2012, LNICST 117, pp. 51–56, 2014.

Thus, establishing successful semantic interoperability between heterogeneous messages is not an easy task. This requires bringing the source and the target message into the meaning agreement. Meaning agreement means that the output of the source message and the input of the target message should agree about the meaning of the data that being exchanged between them. Despite Web service standards and technologies (e.g., WSDL, SOAP, UDDI, SAWSDL), semantic conflict is still far to be solved using these technologies, because these technologies ignore data semantics [6].

Considerable efforts have been done to solve semantic problem that arises between heterogeneous Web service messages such as [7-10]. So far, the problem of semantic interoperability between heterogeneous Web service messages has not been sufficiently and effectively addressed. Thus, this paper aims at proposing a new systematic approach for addressing this problem. The proposed approach includes semantic conflicts identification, detection and solution.

The rest of this paper is organized as follows. Section 2 briefly discusses semantic conflicts at message-level. Section 3 presents the proposed approach. Section 4 reviews some of the related works. Finally, section 5 concludes this paper and provides some suggestions on the future work.

2   Message-Level Conflicts

Web services are provided by different organizations using different techniques. Every organization has its own polices, strategies and vocabularies. From Web service providers' view, the same term is always interpreted differently by Web services [7]. Thus, message-level conflict is related to the Web service implementation itself. The main components of the message of Web service are schema and data.

Thus, message-level conflicts would arise in data-level and schema-level of the message. Data-level conflicts arise due to multiple interpretations and representations of the same data [11-12], while schema-level conflicts arise due to the multiple structures of the message schema. However, message sender and receiver should have agreed on the meaning of the data in advance before exchanging the message can take place. Thus, this condition is very important to be met to achieve semantic interoperability in Web services messages [13].

3   The Proposed Approach

In this section, we present our new systematic approach for achieving semantic interoperability between heterogeneous messages. The proposed approach has three main steps; semantic conflicts identification (classification), detection and solution. Figure 1 illustrates the logical flow of the proposed approach. However, due to space limitations, we briefly discussed these three steps:

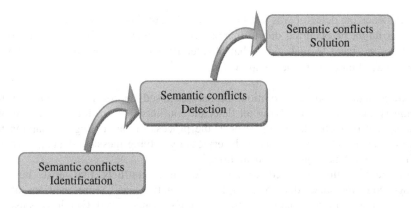

Fig. 1. The proposed systematic approach

Step 1: Semantic conflicts identification. Semantic conflicts identification is the process of identifying the likely conflicts that may arise between the heterogeneous messages under consideration. Semantic conflicts should be identified and categorized properly in the way that no contradiction between them. This is due to the fact that these conflicts play as the crucial seeds for the next steps (detection and solution), and the success of the next steps relies on the success of the semantic conflicts identification. Identifying these conflicts should be based on clear definition for each semantic conflicts, and then classify them accordingly.

Several considerable efforts have been proposed for identifying and classifying semantic conflicts in different domains, i.e., in heterogeneous databases [14-15], in heterogeneous XML data source [16], and in message-level heterogeneities of Web service [10]. In this context, we believe that identifying suitable classification for semantic conflicts is very important and useful to be used as a guideline for detecting and solving conflicts that occur between heterogeneous messages.

Moreover, such classification is helpful to divide the whole semantic conflicts problem into distinct sub-problems, which require relevant detectors and mediators. Unfortunately, this step is still done manually by the experts of the domain under consideration at design time.

Step 2: Semantic conflicts detection. The identified conflicts from the identification step should be automatically detected in this step. The main target of this step is to detect all identified conflicts at run time to facilitate the solution process. The semantic conflict classification that would be produced from the first step will be encoded, i.e., into rules at design time. Then these rules will be executed at run time to detect the conflicts at run time. In another hand, semantic conflict classification might be encoded into ontology at design time, and then this ontology will be used at run time as a key player for semantic conflicts detection, i.e. the work that has been done [17] in the area of database.

The result from the detection process is either detected or undetected conflict. Detected conflict means that the given conflicts from the identification step has been detected at run time and it will be forwarded to the next step (solution). Undetected conflict means the detector was unable to detect the conflict that was identified in step 1. This is might be occurred due to inappropriate conflict identification or encoding. Therefore, we have to make sure that all identified conflicts are detected properly before forwarding them to the solution step.

Step 3: Semantic conflicts solution. In our proposed approach, semantic conflict solution is the process of solving all detected conflicts that are forwarded from the previous step (detection). In this respect, the process of facilitating exchanging the messages between heterogeneous Web services by solving message data and schema conflicts is called message-level mediation.

Message-mediation is used to solve semantic conflicts that arise between heterogeneous messages due to multiple interpretations and representations of the same data, and multiple structures of the message schema as well. Ontology is used as a key player in message-level mediation to provide semantics of the data that being mediated. Thus, the process of message-level mediation includes identifying the used ontology and specifying the mapping between the heterogeneous messages and the used ontology. Mappings are created between the elements of the output and input of Web services messages and the shared ontology [18] at design time. Two types of mappings are required to perform message-level mediation:

- Mapping the output message elements to the corresponding ontology concepts.
- Mapping the input message elements to the corresponding ontology concepts.

Once the required mappings are specified, the participating Web services can interoperate by using these mappings [10].

4   Related Works

Recently, there have been a significant number of approaches on handling semantic conflicts. In these approaches, the process of handling semantic conflicts is different from some approaches to another. On one hand, some approaches start with identifying (classifying) and end with solving semantic conflicts. Such as [10] proposed a solution for semantic conflicts at message level. Their solution involves around classifying semantic conflicts that occur at message level and then solving these conflicts using data mediation technique. However, they only focus on solving semantic conflicts at schema-level of the message. A solution for Web service federations was proposed in [19]. The process of the proposed solution involves around identifying and then solving message data level conflicts.

On another hand, some approaches handled semantic conflicts by detecting and solving semantic conflicts. Such as [6] proposed a technique to detect and reconcile semantic heterogeneity that arise only on message data-level during Web service composition. This approach involves the use of COIN ontology which as a lightweight ontology. The key idea for detecting semantic conflicts was based on extracting all modifiers of ontology concept, then comparing the modifiers values if they are not equal that means context conflicts is thus determined. However, the correct interoperability in this approach is based on the modifiers availability of the ontology concepts [7].

Furthermore, some approaches focused only on the solution step. Such as, [18] proposed data mediation approach to solve message level heterogeneities by transforming the input and output messages to reference model. The transformation repository in their study is still lack of some transformation types, which means that some of semantic conflicts cannot be solved using their approach.

Another approach called context-based mediation was proposed in [7] for solving message data-level conflicts. Even though the problem of semantic conflicts has been addressed from different perspectives and using different strategies, the same problem remains as a challenge for establishing semantic interoperability between heterogeneous Web service messages.

To this end, we can see clearly the difference between the current approaches in terms of the solution process and the capability of solving the problem. Therefore, the steps of our systematic approach are structured in a logical way. This logical structure gives our approach the capability for solving semantic conflicts efficiently and effectively.

5 Conclusion

In this paper, we presented a new systematic approach for solving semantic conflicts of heterogeneous messages. This approach is revolves around three main steps semantic conflicts identification, detection and solution. Semantic conflict identification is the process of collecting and identifying the conflicts from the domain under consideration. Semantic conflict detection is the process of detecting the conflicts that have been identified in the first step. Semantic conflicts solution is the process of solving the conflicts that have been detected.

As future work, we aim at looking into the following issues. First, provide a specific semantic conflict classification, which capture all likely conflicts that may occur in Web service at message level. Second, implement semantic conflicts detector and resolver based on the given classification.

Acknowledgment. This work is funded in part by Malaysia Ministry of Higher Education fundamental research grant number 02-12-10-1007FR.

References

1. Channabasavaiah, K., Holley, K., Tuggle, E.: Migrating to a Service-Oriented Architecture. IBM Developer Works 16 (2003)
2. Papazoglou, M.P., Traverso, P., Dustdar, S., Leymann, F.: Service-Oriented Computing: State of the Art and Research Challenges. Computer 40, 38–45 (2007)
3. Al-Moayed, A., Hollunder, B.: Quality of Service Attributes in Web Services. In: 5th International Conference on Software Engineering Advances, pp. 367–372 (2010)

4. Nezhad, H.R.M., Benatallah, B., Casati, F., Toumani, F.: Web Services Interoperability Specifications. Computer 39, 24–32 (2006)
5. Kien, T.N., Erradi, A., Maheshwari, P.: WSMB: a Middleware for Enhanced Web Services Interoperability. In: First International Conference on Interoperability of Entreprise Software and Applications (Interop-ESA 2005), Geneva, Switzerland (2005)
6. Li, X., Madnick, S., Zhu, H., Fan, Y.: Reconciling Semantic Heterogeneity in Web Services Composition. In: The International Conference on Information Systems (ICIS 2009), pp. 1–17 (2009)
7. Mrissa, M., Ghedira, C., Benslimane, D., Maamar, Z., Rosenberg, F., Dustdar, S.: A Context-Based Mediation Approach to Compose Semantic Web Services. ACM Trans. Internet Technol. 8, 4 (2007)
8. Zaremba, M., Herold, M., Zaharia, R., Vitvar, T.: Data and Process Mediation Support for B2B Integration. In: Evaluation of Ontology-based Tools and the Semantic Web Service Challenge, in Conjunction with ESWC 2008 (2008)
9. Xitong, L., Stuart, M., Hongwei, Z., Yushun, F.: An Approach to Composing Web Services with Context Heterogeneity. In: IEEE International Conference on Web Services (ICWS 2009), Los Angeles, CA, USA, pp. 695–702 (2009)
10. Nagarajan, M., Verma, K., Sheth, A., Miller, J.: Ontology Driven Data Mediation in Web Services. International Journal of Web Services Research 4, 104–126 (2007)
11. Peristeras, V., Loutas, N., Goudos, S.K., Tarabanis, K.: A Conceptual Analysis of Semantic Conflicts in Pan-European E-Government Services. Journal of Information Science 34, 877–891 (2008)
12. Park, J., Ram, S.: Information Systems Interoperability: What Lies Beneath? ACM Trans. Inf. Syst. 22, 595–632 (2004)
13. Pokraev, S., Reichert, M., Steen, M., Wieringa, R.: Semantic and Pragmatic Interoperability: A Model for Understanding. In: Open Interoperability Workshop on Enterprise Modeling and Ontology for Interoperability, pp. 1–5 (2005)
14. Ram, S., Park, J., Kim, K., Hwang, Y.: A Comprehensive Framework for Classifying Data and Schema-Level Semantic Conflicts in Geographic and Non-Geographic Databases. In: 9th Workshop on Information Technologies and Systems, Charlotte, NC, pp. 185–190 (1999)
15. Naiman, C.F., Ouksel, A.M.: A Classification of Semantic Conflicts in Heterogeneous Database Systems. Journal of Organizational Computing 5, 167–167 (1995)
16. Pluempitiwiriyawej, C., Hammer, J.: A Classification Scheme for Semantic and Schematic Heterogeneities in XML Data Sources. Technical report 00-004, University of Florida, Gainesville, FL (2000)
17. Sudha, R., Jinsoo, P.: Semantic Conflict Resolution Ontology (SCROL): an Ontology for Detecting and Resolving Data and Schema-Level Semantic Conflicts. IEEE Transactions on Knowledge and Data Engineering 16, 189–202 (2004)
18. Bouras, T., Gouvas, P., Mentzas, G.: Dynamic Data Mediation in Enterprise Application Integration. In: eChallenges e-2008 Conference, Stockholm, Sweden, pp. 917–924 (2008)
19. Aragão, V.R., Fernandes, A.A.A.: Conflict Resolution in Web Service Federations. In: Jeckle, M., Zhang, L.-J. (eds.) ICWS-Europe 2003. LNCS, vol. 2853, pp. 109–122. Springer, Heidelberg (2003)

Software Development
for Autonomous Unmanned Aerial Vehicle

Rania Elgohary

Information System Department, Faculty of Computer and Information Sciences,
Ain Hams University, Cairo, Egypt
dr.raniaelgohary@fcis.asu.edu.eg

Abstract. Throughout the software development process, artifacts are created and modified .The emerging area of intelligent unmanned aerial vehicle (UAV) research has shown rapid development in recent years. This paper aims at developing the late life-cycle fixes are generally costly more expensive than corrections in the early phases. Defect detection in the software artifacts is not only related to the requirement specification phase but it is also required in all phases of software development life cycle. It should be achieved as early as possible in every phase to make sure that propagation of the accumulated defects is decreases as much as possible. The objective of this paper is to describe the design and implementation of a small semiautonomous UAV. This research aims at improving the efficiency of the whole software development process by providing a low-cost micro-electro mechanical system-based flight control system for small UAVs that can be used for autonomous exploration in unknown urban environments. In particular the hardware and software architectures used in the design are developed. The proposed design was tested in a series of flights to urban obstacle setup where the UAV successfully provided vital, accurate, sensitive, and on time information to many receptors. The impact of this design appears in its efficacy when used by specialists to send vital reports to the competent authorities to deal with a catastrophe or a conjuncture in a speedy organized way in the presence of live up-to-date information.

Keywords: Micro-Electronic Mechanical System (MEMS), Unmanned Air Vehicle (UAV),Software Development, Autonomous Control.

1 Introduction

Software development life cycle (SDLC) is a structure imposed on the development of a software product. Research has shown that late life-cycle fixes are generally costly more expensive than corrections in the early phases. UAVs are complex systems involving multiple engineering disciplines consisting of the following major subsystems: Planning, Guidance, Navigation and Flight Control. Over the last few years, several improvements have been presented in the field of UAV [1]. Typically, tasks include photogrammetric survey pipeline inspection, dam surveillance, and

V.V. Das and P.M. El-Kafrawy (Eds.): SPIT 2012, LNICST 117, pp. 57–64, 2014.

inspection of flooded areas infrastructure maintenance, terrain monitoring, fire fighting, and volcano observations within the category of UAVs. The different flying characteristics of a helicopter with respect to fixed-wing systems require more effort for the manual control via radio link. High piloting skills are needed for manual hovering, for keeping the ideal position and altitude along a pre-planned path. Moreover, the operation range of a manually piloted helicopter is limited to the line-of-sight or the skill of the pilot to detect and follow its orientation. This paper proposes a low cost efficient software development model that proposes a solution for UAV software development cycle and control problems. The model helps to identify a problem or a catastrophe location accurately rather than building expectations or performing blind search for the problem location. The expected results would have their impact on the Geographic Information Systems (GIS) technology and the use of Artificial Intelligence (AI) in UAVs.

2   Related Work

Unmanned Aerial Vehicle systems (UAV) become very attractive for various commercial, industrial, public, scientific and military operations. Latest developments in the field of navigation systems have led to miniaturized boards which integrate GPS, enabling to fly UAVs in an autonomous way. These new technologies allow low cost navigation systems to be integrated in helicopters' models, though the advantage of small size positioning and orientation sensors come with low prices. Nevertheless, the combination of GPS/INS sensors with image data for navigation represents a key factor to achieve more precise and reliable results with respect to manually controlled UAVs. Previous work has focused on the engineering side of UAVs and ignored the software development cycle included in this process.   One of the important developments is the Draganflyer X6 UAV helicopter, designed by Draganfly Innovations Inc. [2] for aerial photography and ideography. TiaLinx designed and developed the most advanced imaging technology and integrated sensor clusters for the high-end security and surveillance applications [3]. Other UAVs like the fixed wing UAVs currently used by the military are large, expensive, special purpose vehicles with limited autonomy [10]. At the other end of the spectrum, there are small UAVs (less than six foot wingspan) and micro air vehicles (MAV) (less than one foot wingspan) [4, 5, 6, and 7]. This paper proposes a software development model that utilizes an innovative design with differential thrust inspired by the above mentioned systems. This design was used in a system that allows the helicopter to maneuver in a quick and accurate way. Furthermore, the GPS holds hands free function while the helicopter maintains its position in the air. Constant GPS readings are sent back to the handheld controller as part of the real-time telemetry display.

3   The Proposed Model AGCUAV

The software design and the screen layout are based on operator experiences and customer demands for a self-explanatory environment, which allows monitoring all relevant UAV information and makes it easy to learn and memorize the UAV operation(s) for Autonomous Geographical control for unmanned Aerial vehicle AGCUAV. Mission planning is done by a graphical user interface, including moving map capabilities and waypoint editing by simple mouse clicks. The actual flight trajectory and the reference flight trajectory are both displayed on a map. Commands by the joystick or by the waypoint mission planner will directly be uploaded to the flight controller and will be executed immediately [8]. The developed environment can be used to operate helicopters and fixed wing aircraft. Furthermore, the implemented operations can be used in many applications, such as aerial photography, aerial surveillance or many kinds of aerial inspection [9]. The identification of a catastrophe location accurately can lead to higher probabilities in saving people and other physical parties. The proposed model (AGCUAV) uses a small UAV that controls the plane from a distance through the use of a laptop to carry out critical tasks. The model also uses a Global Positing Systems (GPS) navigation to increase the capacity to control the plane by calculating the ratio of Coordinates from the Aircraft Accurately. In addition, the model uses a GIS, which consists of a map of the site where the plane flies to determine the optimum air way and identifies difficulties in order to avoid it with the help of the used hardware. This paper presents a comprehensive analysis of the content of UAV data utilized in a multi-layer architecture model of 2D flight situation. Moreover, the paper describes the virtual instrument interface design that reflects the basic method of GUI (Graphical User Interface), and discusses the Ground Control Station (GCS) for Autonomous UAV Architecture.

3.1 GCS for Autonomous UAV Architecture

UAV has typically been used in civil and military fields all over the world. Based on the UAV mission of autonomous flight, GCS including hardware and software, becomes important equipment to be developed. A well functioning GCS should consist of three parts: a portable ground station hardware system, a virtual instrument panel for the attitude information and flight path showing all kinds of error alert. Through the whole test on the ground and in the sky, GCS can show the remote sensing information precisely and send the control command in time. This can be used later to assist in the function of autonomous cruise task for UAV.

The proposed model consists of three main modules in figure 1. The first module is the interface, which actually comprises two interfaces: (a) GCS System shown in figure 1: used for control on the plane by establishing interface design as the gadgets in the cabin crew on real planes to make controlling planes much easier to use; (b) GIS: creates a map to the enterprise location and creates this map in much detail to define the conjuncture location and the plane coordinates easily. The second module is the data collection, which is concerned with managing the collection of data from the instruments as cameras that collect data about conjuncture location and GPS that collect data about the coordinates, airway, and angle of the plane. This data is used to enrich the software by adding/updating data. The third module is the instrument, which is an encapsulation of all of the instruments used to collect raw data the developed system would have the ability to provide video images through the use of a variety of cameras, including high resolution digital still camera, high definition video camera, low light high resolution black and white video or an infra red camera. The system should also be designed with controls that ease its use and with a very minimal training. It should also provide an extremely stable aerial platform that aids to capture photographs and videos. Finally, a remote controller was required to control a battery operated helicopter that can be equipped with a high resolution still camera (with remote zoom, shutter control and tilt), high definition video, and low light black and white video or infrared camera. This model defines the required instruments, their tasks and the interaction between them. This model is integrated in the framework shown in figure 2.

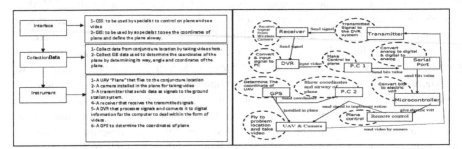

Fig. 1. The architecture of GCS model   **Fig. 2.** The system framework

4   The Proposed System Components Development

4.1   Hardware Development

The proposed system in Figure 3 includes a highly-integrated wireless transmission links, which are lighter than traditional links. The flight control provides altitude hold control and GPS navigation based on gain scheduling proportional-integral-derivative control. Flight tests to survey the grass quality of a large lawn show that the small UAV, which can fly autonomously according to a series of pre-arranged waypoints with a controlled altitude while the wireless video system transmits images of the surveillance target to GCS. All devices used in the proposed system are developed as The Cam and sound sensor with transmitter and receiver UAV vision, the digital video recorder (DVR), AV receiver, the devices used in the plane control, and all the devices used in the plane control, Electro-gyroscope, Three-ax accelerometers and the Global Positioning System (GPS) provided long term stability with high accuracy. The coordinates that denote the location of an infestation was identified via a satellite circling the earth and transmitting signal called a pseudo random code. Each signal was encoded with information used to determine a receiver's location. The signal transmission included the time the signal was sent and the satellite's location in space. Moreover RADAR SYSTEMS is developed where the radiated power is largely dependent on the antenna aperture. Increasing the radiated power will increase the range of the radar but unless it is accompanied by LPI it will also announce the presence of the radiating aircraft to sensors on another one that still does not have you in its radar range.

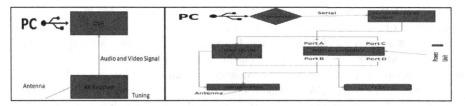

Fig. 3. Hardware Phase\control\Display System

This paper emphasizes three parts to build a well-functioning GCS: a portable ground station hardware system, a virtual instrument panel for the altitude information and flight path showing all kinds of error alert. Through the whole test on the ground and in the sky, GCS shows the remote sensing information precisely and sends the control command in time. Table 1shows the related technical specifications.

Table 1. Technical specifications of the helicopter model

Max Speed	40 km/h
Max Flight Range	50 m
Max High	30 m
Max Takeoff Weight	300gm
Battery Life	15 min

4.2 The Software Development

The verification and validation processes are an essential and integral part of the software development process. Many Software Quality Assurance SQA standards have set guidelines for these processes. The software testing in this paper can be offers verification of the software under test and its validation at several levels. The complexity of software projects is increasing rapidly and in turn both cost and time of the testing process have become a major proportion of the software development process. The functional requirements of the proposed model AGCUAV, in the context of the current research work, are **Feature Detection:** this includes detecting the predominant features such as corners, edges and blobs in an image and generating a feature descriptor associated to each feature, **Feature Matching:** matching the features between successive images and generate the correspondence set, **Compute Motion Parameters** :vehicle (or camera) motion is computed from the correspondence set to generate the homograph matrix containing the six state parameters (position and orientation) of the vehicle. **Predict and Correction:** this involves predicting and correcting the next state parameters of the vehicle to steer the vehicle to the desired trajectory. The correction is essential as errors may get accumulated in the due course of time during navigation from one way-point to the other. The prediction and the correction are achieved using a state estimator or a navigational filter resulting in reaching the destination via (known) way-points. These functional requirements are illustrated in details in Figure 4. Figure 4 represents the steps of the system workflow between system actors, control station system specialist and GPS & GIS specialist The workflow of this system is illustrated as follows: the system owner finds conjuncture in any location in his area work when he finds this he must request a report for altitude problem from the control station system specialist to send an report to the system owner about the altitude problem. The control station system specialist needs to define the conjuncture location position from GIS & GPS specialist to send a plane (UAV) to the conjuncture location accurately. When the GIS & GPS specialist defines the conjuncture location then he sends it to control station system specialist to define the distance, height, and other things in flight operations. The control station system specialist needs to define airway from GIS (maps) for the work area to starting takeoff. The working between the control station system specialist and the GPS & GIS specialist is parallel. Finally, when the plane arrives to the conjuncture location, the control station system specialist records a video about the conjuncture location. Then the control station system sends this video to the system owner to send human agent to handle this problem. Computer-based testing can be classified into six levels according to its testing objectives, each of which focuses on a particular class of errors. The following is a discussion of these levels and their corresponding test objectives in both hardware and software testing. The scope of activity diagrams is individual use cases. Checking the consistency of activity diagrams with the specifications is out of the paper's scope. Suppose that the operations in the activity diagram are consistent with the requirements specifications of the use case are represented in the activity diagram Figure 4 and the sequence of tasks with interactions the system actors are represented in Figure 5.

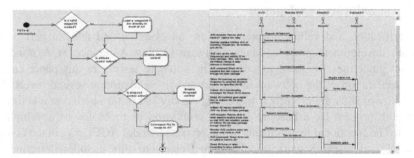

Fig. 4. AGCUAV activity diagram   **Fig. 5.** The system sequence diagram

4.3   Hardware Testing and Development

This section explains how one simulates and improves the hardware problems. For this purpose, a UAV helicopter with a remote control and a computer with maximum weight of takeoff were used. The aircraft was supported with helium balloon system, So two balloons were installed, one in front of the plane, and the second in the back of the plane where the installation of a column of carbon fiber was placed down the plane. The installation of the camera was on the top of carbon fiber for clarity of the vision. The use of the balloon helped to reduce the weight of the aircraft due to high balloon filled with helium gas, light weight. This modified the efficiency of the engine and provided the torque in the plane take off and the flight operation is increased. Moreover, for the flight stability and balance the weight of UAV was reduced as mentioned above. For the sensitivity of transaction in UAV, an R-2R Circuit was designed in order to convert digital signals to electrical power.

4.4   Software Testing and Development

This paper improves the quality of the verification and validation V&V processes by enhancing the performance and efficiency of the testing process through automating the test cases generation process. The V&V processes play a tremendous role in improving the overall quality of the software. The proposed model presents an architecture that creates from activity diagrams a special table and a directed flow graph that are used in conjunction with the category partition method to generate a final reduced set of test cases. The generated test cases can be sent to any requirements management tool to be traced against the requirements. Experimental evaluation is presented to prove that the model saves time, space and consequently cost, improving by that the overall performance of the testing process. It is therefore imperative to reduce the cost and improve the effectiveness of software testing by automating the testing process. The testing effort is divided into three parts: test case generation, test execution, and test evaluation.

5   Simulation Scenarios

This section presents results of both simulation and hardware tests. The scenario consists of a small autonomous ground vehicle operating on level ground; while a ground vehicle driving on a flat surface has the navigation system was performing. The following scenario would occur: When a conjuncture occurs, the UAV will fly to the location of conjuncture the system records the place then sends it back to the GCS system .This enlightens the rescue team and helps them to be more prepared. This paper presents a system able to provide vital information (accurate, sensitive and on time) to many receptors. This will allow the specialists to send vital reports to the competent authorities to deal with the catastrophe or the conjuncture in a very speedy way.

6   Conclusion

This paper presents the software development life cycle of a low-cost autonomous helicopter model called "AGCUAV". The paper illustrates the development and testing of each cycle. Fixing faults early in the development process are much more cost effective than trying to consider those defects in the later cycles of the development process. The presented model AGCUAV provides a low cost solution for autonomous control challenges that helps the end user to do his task in an easy and efficient way. The AGCUAV model shares limitations with most computer embedded systems: limited space, limited power resources, increasing computation requirements, complexity of the applications, and time to market requirements. The proposed AGCUAV model orbits around four key elements: enhanced hardware architecture, a service/subscription based software architecture and an abstraction communication layer. This improved system may be use by specialists to send vital reports to the competent authorities to deal with the catastrophe or the conjuncture. The work done in this paper can be extended by adding high quality hardware, such as thermostat and sensitive detection of explosives that are sensitive to smoke, auto-piloting and autonomous adaptation to unexpected events are suggested.

References

1. Beard, D., Kingston, M., Quigley, D., Snyder, R., Christiansen, W., Johnson, T.: McLain: Autonomous Vehicle Technologies for Small Fixed-Wing UAVs. Journal of Aerospace Computing, Information and Communication 2 (2005)
2. Gibralta, E.: DRAGANFLY - RC/UAV with Infra-Red & HD Video. SteelMac Limited, Unit 27 New Harbors (2010)
3. Brecher, A., Noronha, V., Herold, M.: Unmanned Aerial Vehicles (UAVs) in Transportation. In: Specialist Workshop (2005)
4. McCormack, E.: Unmanned Aerial Vehicles: The Use of Small Unmanned Aircraft by the Washington State Department of Transportation. Research report, Agreement T4118, Task 04 (2008)
5. Coifman, B., McCord, M., Mishalani, R., Redmill, K.: Surface Transportation Surveillance from Unmanned Aerial Vehicles. In: Proceedings of the 83rd Annual Meeting of the Transportation Research Board (2004)
6. Eisenbeiss, H.: A Mini Unmanned Aerial Vehicle (UAV): System Overview and Image Acquisition. In: International Workshop on Processing and Visualization Using High-Resolution Imagery (2004)
7. Seok, J., Ro, K., Dong, L.: Lessons Learned: Application of Small UAV for Urban Highway Traffic Monitoring. In: 45th AIAA Aerospace Sciences Meeting and Exhibit (2005)
8. Soon, J., Tomlin, C.: Design and Implementation of a Low Cost, Hierarchical and Modular Avionics Architecture for the DragonFly UAVs. In: Proceedings of AIAA Guidance, Navigation, and Control Conference (2002)
9. Zelinski, S., Koo, T., Sastry, S.: Hybrid System Design for Formations of Autonomous Vehicles. In: IEEE Conference on Decision and Control (2003)
10. Anderson, E., Beard, R., McLain, T.: Real Time Dynamic Trajectory Smoothing for Uninhabited Aerial Vehicles. In: IEEE Transactions on Control Systems Technology (2005)
11. Rudek, R., Rudek, A., Skworcow, P.: An optimal sequence of tasks for autonomous learning systems. In: 16th International Conference on Methods and Models in Automation and Robotics, MMAR (2011)

Comparative Study between CFO and SCFO in OFDM Systems

Mohamed Tayebi and Merahi Bouziani

Laboratory of Telecommunications and Digital Signal Processing
University of Sidi Bel Abbes, 22000, Algeria
tayebi_med@hotmail.com

Abstract. OFDM has emerged at the beginning of the second half of last century. Its applications are diverse and extend to different wireless and optical communication systems. It is well known that OFDM is very sensitive to frequency shifts. The imperfections of the local oscillators of the transmitter and receiver affects the carrier, while the Doppler-effect affects the carrier, also the sub-carriers of the OFDM signal. This gives rise to inter-carrier interference (ICI) responsible for the degradation of system performance. In this paper we have studied OFDM in a radio mobile channel. We proposed a new model that includes the offsets generated by the Doppler-effect at different sub-carriers. We compared it with the existing model which considers only the carrier frequency offset and we calculated the error between the two mathematical models.

Keywords: Orthogonal frequency division multiplexing (OFDM), carrier frequency offset (CFO), sub carriers frequency offset (SCFO), Doppler-effect, Inter carriers Interferences (ICI), carrier to interferences ratio (CIR).

1   Introduction

The pair FFT / IFFT was the missing piece in digital communications. Its use has allowed the emergence of OFDM [1]. The OFDM has earned a special place in various wireless networks like HIPERLAN/2 and IEEE 802.11a. Recently, she found its applications in the optical domain [2]-[3]. The use of the OFDM is limited in part by its great sensitivity to frequency offsets. They destroy the orthogonality and gives rise to inter-carrier interference. These discrepancies are mainly due to imperfections of the local oscillators of the transmitter and receiver [4]. The Doppler effect present in the radio mobile channel accentuates this shifts [5]. The offset due to the Doppler-effect affects the carrier. In a recent study [7], a new model was proposed. It includes all the offset of the subcarriers of the OFDM signal. In the model proposed in [6], the Doppler-effect is supposed to affect the carrier, it then generates the carrier frequency offset CFO. In the model proposed in [7], the Doppler effect affects not only the carrier but also the subcarriers of the OFDM signal. It then generates the subcarriers frequency offset SCFO. Our work consists in compare and deduce the resulting error between the two models. We gave the analytical expression for this error and then we

V.V. Das and P.M. El-Kafrawy (Eds.): SPIT 2012, LNICST 117, pp. 65–69, 2014.
© Institute for Computer Sciences, Social Informatics and Telecommunications Engineering 2014

make a number of simulation to clarify the results. This work is structured as follows, in section 2, we study the carrier frequency offset (CFO) and the subcarriers frequency offset (SCFO). In section 3, we analysis the inter-carrier interference generated by the two models. Section 4 compare performances of both models and calculate the error introduced on the CIR. Finally, section 5 concludes the paper.

2   Analysis of Frequency Shifts

The frequency shifts in an OFDM signal is caused by two different parameters, the Doppler-effect and the imperfections of local oscillators. The total normalized offset is then [7]:

$$\varepsilon_t = \varepsilon(1 + \beta) \pm k \frac{v}{c} cos\alpha = \varepsilon_p + k\beta \quad with \quad (\beta = \pm \frac{v}{c} cos\alpha) \tag{1}$$

The normalized value of the carrier frequency offset created by the imperfections and Doppler-effect is noted ε_p, while ε_t represents the normalized value of total offset. The relative velocity between the transmitter and receiver is represented by v, α represents the angle formed by the velocity vector and the direction of electromagnetic wave, c is the speed of light and k the subcarrier index. If we neglect the offset created by the Doppler-effect on all subcarrier, we introduce an error which is equal to:

$$Error = \pm k \frac{v}{c} cos\alpha = k\beta \tag{2}$$

This error is proportional to the subcarrier index k.

3   Analysis of Inter-carrier Interference

The OFDM signal affected by a frequency offset is written as[7]:

$$y(n) = \sum_{k=0}^{N-1} X(k) \exp\left(j2\pi \frac{n}{N}(k + \varepsilon_t)\right) \tag{3}$$

Where $X(k)$ is the transmitted signal. By replacing ε_t by its value, the equation becomes:

$$y(n) = \exp\left(j2\pi \frac{n\varepsilon_p}{N}\right) \times \sum_{k=0}^{N-1} X(k) \exp\left((j2\pi \frac{nk}{N})(1 + \beta)\right) \tag{4}$$

The carrier frequency offset creates a phase shifts of the signal $y(n)$, while the Doppler-effect expand it (or compress it). At the output of the FFT, we obtain the symbols $Y(k)$, its expression is given by the relation [7]:

$$Y(k) = \frac{1}{N}\sum_{n=0}^{N-1}\sum_{k=0}^{N-1} X(k)\exp\left(j2\pi\frac{n}{N}(k - m + k\beta + \varepsilon_p)\right) \qquad (5)$$

$$= \sum_{k=0}^{N-1} X(k)S_{km}(k - m) \qquad (6)$$

After some manipulations $S_{km}(k - m)$ is then written [7]:

$$S_{km}(k - m) = \frac{sin\pi(k - m + k\beta + \varepsilon_p)}{Nsin\frac{\pi}{N}(k - m + k\beta + \varepsilon_p)}\exp\left(j\pi(k - m + k\beta + \varepsilon_p)\right) \qquad (7)$$

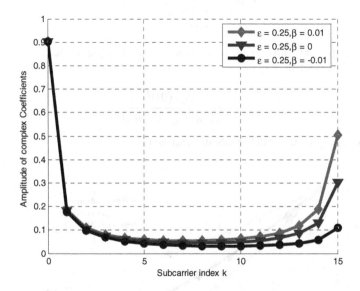

Fig. 1. Amplitudes of complex coefficients depending on the subcarrier index k for different values of the relative speed

The amplitudes of the complex coefficients depend on the difference $(k - m)$, the subcarrier index k and the relative speed β. In the model where we only consider the carrier frequency offset, the complex coefficients have the value [6]:

$$S(k - m) = \frac{sin\,\pi(k - m + \varepsilon_p)}{Nsin\frac{\pi}{N}(k - m + \varepsilon_p)}\exp j\pi\left(1 - \frac{1}{N}\right)(k - m + \varepsilon_p) \qquad (8)$$

La figure 1 plot the complex coefficients for different values of relative speed. The error is given by the relation:

$$Error = \left| \frac{sin\pi(k - m + k\beta + \varepsilon_p)}{Nsin\frac{\pi}{N}(k - m + k\beta + \varepsilon_p)} \right| - \left| \frac{sin\,\pi(k - m + \varepsilon_p)}{Nsin\frac{\pi}{N}(k - m + \varepsilon_p)} \right| \qquad (9)$$

Note that this error increased when the subcarrier index increases.

4   Errors Analysis

Performance is measured in terms of CIR. The useful signal is calculated for $k = m$, while the interference is computed for $k \neq m$. For the model with CFO, CIR is expressed [6]:

$$CIR = \frac{|S(0)|^2}{\sum_{\substack{k=0 \\ k\neq m}}^{N-1} |S(k - m)|^2} \qquad (10)$$

It is the same for any sub-carrier. If we consider the Doppler-effect affects all sub-carriers, the CIR is written[7]:

$$CIR = \frac{|S_{kk}(0)|^2}{\sum_{\substack{k=0 \\ k\neq m}}^{N-1} |S_{km}(k - m)|^2} \qquad (11)$$

The CIR is not the same for differents sub-carriers[7].

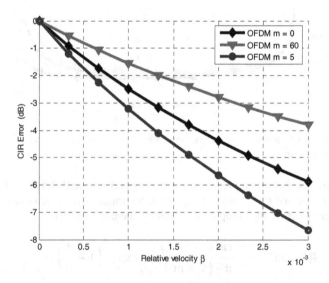

Fig. 2. Plot of the error on the CIR as a function of relative speed

We derive the error on the CIR, it is equal to:

$$Error = 10log_{10}\left(\frac{|S_{ll}(0)|^2}{\sum_{\substack{k=0\\k\neq m}}^{N-1}|S_{lk}(k-m)|^2}\right) - 10log_{10}\left(\frac{|S(0)|^2}{\sum_{\substack{k=0\\k\neq m}}^{N-1}|S(k-m)|^2}\right) \quad (12)$$

This error is plotted in figure 2, its value varies from 3.8 to 7.65 dB.

5   Conclusion

In this paper, we studied the OFDM in a mobile radio channel. The frequency shifts were studied in more detail. In fact, we took into account the offset of the different subcarriers of the OFDM signal created by the Doppler-effect. A new mathematical model is considered. Then, we compared the proposed model with the existing model which considers only the carrier frequency offset as a source of inter-carrier interference. This comparison has mounted that there is a difference between the two models. In terms of CIR, this difference varies between 3.8 and 7.65 dB.

References

1. Weinstein, S., Ebert, P.: Data transmission by frequency-division multiplexing using the discrete Fourier transform. IEEE Trans. Commun. 19, 628–634 (1971)
2. Armstrong, J.: OFDM for Optical communications. Journal of Lightwave Technology 27(3) (February 1, 2009)
3. Yang, Q., He, Z., Yang, Z., Yu, S., Yi, X., Shieh, W.: Coherent optical DFT-Spread OFDM transmission using orthogonal band multiplexing. OPTICS EXPRESS 20(3), 2379–2385 (2012)
4. Sathananthan, K., Tellambura, C.: Performance analysis of an OFDM system with carrier frequency offset and phase noise. In: IEEE Vehicular Technology Conference, VTC 2001 Fall, Atlantic City, NJ, USA, October 7-11, vol. 4, pp. 2329–2332 (2001)
5. Capoglu, R., Li, Y., Swami, A.: Effect of Doppler Spread in OFDM-Based UWB Systems. IEEE Transactions on Wireless Communications 4(5) (September 2005)
6. Zhao, Y., Haggman, S.-G.: Intercarrier interference self-cancellation scheme for OFDM mobile communication systems. IEEE Trans. Commun. 49, 1185–1191 (2001)
7. Tayebi, M., Bouziani, M.: Performance of OFDM in radio mobile channel. In: Elmoataz, A., Mammass, D., Lezoray, O., Nouboud, F., Aboutajdine, D. (eds.) ICISP 2012. LNCS, vol. 7340, pp. 142–148. Springer, Heidelberg (2012)

Microarray Time Series Modeling and Variational Bayesian Method for Reverse Engineering Gene Regulatory Networks

M. Sánchez-Castillo[1], I.M. Tienda Luna[2], D. Blanco-Navarro[1],
and M.C. Carrión-Pérez[1]

[1] Department of Applied Physics, University of Granada, 18071, Spain
[2] Department of Electrical and Computer Engineering, University of Granada, 18071, Spain
{mscastillo,isabelt,dblanco,mcarrion}@ugr.es

Abstract. Gene expression is a complex process controlled by underling biological interactions. One model that tries to explain these relationships at a genetic level is the gene regulatory networks. Uncovering regulatory networks are extremely important for live sciences to understand how genes compete and are associated. Despite measurement methods have been successfully developed within the microarray technique, the analysis of genomic data is difficult due to the vast amount of information considered. We address here the problem of modeling the gene regulatory networks by a novel linear model and we propose a Bayesian approach to learn this structure from microarray time series.

Keywords: microarray, gene regulatory networks, VBEM algorithm.

1   Introduction

Microarray experiments have supposed a breakthrough into genomic research. With this technique, the expression of thousand of genes may be quantified simultaneously. Genomic studies demand help from computer science community to process and analyze such a vast amount of information. One topic of special interest is the study of genetic interactions. Uncovering that kind of relationships is extremely important to understand how genes compete and are associated to produce complex responses and co-operative effects, information which can be used in many fields such as disease treatment and new drug design.

One model that tries to explain genetic interactions is the gene regulatory network (GRN). In a GRN it is considered that the expression of a gene, known as child, depends on others presented in the network, known as parents. We address here the problem of modeling and inferring the GRN from microarray time series. Specifically, this paper revises the linear model presented in [1] and proposes a new one that fits better microarray data. Additionally, a variational Bayesian method based on new model is proposed.

V.V. Das and P.M. El-Kafrawy (Eds.): SPIT 2012, LNICST 117, pp. 70–75, 2014.

2   Gene Regulatory Networks Modeling

Gene regulatory networks are characterized by two important aspects [2]. First is the connectivity, also referred as network topology, which represents the linkage pattern of the network. This logical structure have been modeled in [1] by a set of binary latent variables, denoted by

$$\mathbf{x}_i = [x_i(1),\ldots,x_i(G)]^T \in \{0,1\}^{G \times 1} \tag{1}$$

where $x_i(j) = 1$ specifies that the j-th gene is a parent of the i-th gene or $x_i(j) = 0$ otherwise. Second, genetic networks also specifies regulatory effects between elements, i.e. strength and type of interaction. This scheme has been described in [1] by an additional set of weights, denoted by

$$\boldsymbol{\omega}_i = [\omega_i(1),\ldots,\omega_i(G)]^T \in \Re^{G \times 1} \tag{2}$$

with $\omega_i(j) > 0$ for gene activation and $\omega_i(j) < 0$ for gene inhibition.

3   Linear Models for Microarray Time Series Fitting

Consider a microarray data set $\mathbf{Y} \in \Re^{G \times (N+1)}$ with G genes and $N+1$ time samples, such as $[\mathbf{Y}]_{i,n} = y_i(n)$ the observed expression level: relative mRNA abundance of the i-th gene at the n-th time sample. Assuming a Markov process, a first order autoregressive (AR1) model have been proposed in [1]. This approach expressed microarray data as a linear combination of the observations and the variables describing the gene regulatory network, plus independent and identically distributed (IID) Gaussian white noise, as

$$y_i(n) = \sum_{j=1}^{G} y_i(n-1)\omega_i(j)x_i(j) + e_i(n) \tag{3}$$

with

$$p(e_i(n)) = N(e_i(n)|0, \sigma_i^2), \forall n. \tag{4}$$

However, this model establishes relationships between the observed expression levels, $y_i(n)$, which are supposed to be noisy. It would be much more realistic to establish these relationships between the real expression level, denoted by $z_i(n) = y_i(n) - e_i(n)$. Therefore, we propose a novel approach where genetic relationships are established between the real expression levels instead of its noisy observation, leadding to a first order autoregressive moving-average (AR1MA1) model as

$$y_i(n) = \sum_{j=1}^{G} y_j(n-1)\omega_i(j)x_i(j) - \sum_{j=1}^{G} e_j(n-1)\omega_i(j)x_i(j) + e_i(n). \tag{5}$$

4   Variational Bayesian Expectation-Maximization Framework

Consider $\mathbf{y}_i$ the set of observations, $\mathbf{x}_i$ the set of latent or hidden variables and $\mathbf{\theta}_i$ the set of unknowns parameters for the i-th variable. The posterior distribution could be derived from the priors and the likelihood as

$$p(\mathbf{x}_i, \mathbf{\theta}_i | \mathbf{y}_i) = \frac{p(\mathbf{y}_i | \mathbf{x}_i, \mathbf{\theta}_i) p(\mathbf{x}_i, \mathbf{\theta}_i)}{p(\mathbf{y}_i)} \tag{6}$$

with $p(\mathbf{y}_i)$ the marginal likelihood obtained by marginalization as

$$p(\mathbf{y}_i) = \int p(\mathbf{y}_i | \mathbf{x}_i, \mathbf{\theta}_i) p(\mathbf{x}_i, \mathbf{\theta}_i) d\mathbf{x}_i d\mathbf{\theta}_i. \tag{7}$$

Finding an analytical solution for the marginal likelihood and posterior distributions usually is a difficult task. An alternative to compute the posterior distribution by marginalization have been presented by Beal et al. in [3]. Instead of integrating out the unknowns, variational Bayes computes a lower bound of the logarithm of the marginal likelihood. In virtue of Jensen's inequality, lower bound can be expressed by a functional depending on a free distribution as,

$$\log p(\mathbf{y}_i) \geq F[q(\mathbf{x}_i, \mathbf{\theta}_i)] = \int q(\mathbf{x}_i, \mathbf{\theta}_i) \log \frac{p(\mathbf{y}_i, \mathbf{x}_i, \mathbf{\theta}_i)}{q(\mathbf{x}_i, \mathbf{\theta}_i)} d\mathbf{x}_i d\mathbf{\theta}_i. \tag{8}$$

Optimization of (8) is a problem that may be solved by variational calculus. Alternatively, based on a mathematical convenience, variational Bayesian choose a free distribution that factorizes into conjugate families as

$$q(\mathbf{x}_i, \mathbf{\theta}_i | \xi) \approx q(\mathbf{x}_i | \xi_{\mathbf{x}_i}) q(\mathbf{\theta}_i | \xi_{\mathbf{\theta}_i}) \tag{9}$$

with $\xi = \{\xi_{\mathbf{x}_i}, \xi_{\mathbf{\theta}_i}\}$ hyperparameters that characterizes the conjugate families.

For conjugate models, the computation of the posterior becomes into a set of posterior hyperparameters learning rules. Therefore, variational Bayesian Expectation-Maximization (VBEM) methods consist of the following two steps, in which one of the free distributions is optimized whilst the other one is fixed as

$$q\left(\mathbf{x}_i | \hat{\xi}_{\mathbf{x}_i}^{(t+1)}\right) \propto e^{\left\langle \log p(\mathbf{y}_i | \mathbf{x}_i, \mathbf{\theta}_i) \right\rangle_{q\left(\mathbf{\theta}_i | \hat{\xi}_{\mathbf{\theta}_i}^{(t)}\right)} + p(\mathbf{x}_i)} \tag{10}$$

$$q\left(\mathbf{\theta}_i | \hat{\xi}_{\mathbf{\theta}_i}^{(t+1)}\right) \propto e^{\left\langle \log p(\mathbf{y}_i | \mathbf{x}_i, \mathbf{\theta}_i) \right\rangle_{q\left(\mathbf{x}_i | \hat{\xi}_{\mathbf{x}_i}^{(t+1)}\right)} + p(\mathbf{\theta}_i)} \tag{11}$$

Subsequetnly, the lower bound is updated and VBEM algorithm iterates until the difference after two consecutive steps satisfies a convergence criterion as

$$\left| \frac{F\left[q\left(\mathbf{x}_i,\mathbf{\theta}_i\middle|\hat{\xi}^{(t+1)}\right)\right] - F\left[q\left(\mathbf{x}_i,\mathbf{\theta}_i\middle|\hat{\xi}^{(t)}\right)\right]}{F\left[q\left(\mathbf{x}_i,\mathbf{\theta}_i\middle|\hat{\xi}^{(t+1)}\right)\right]} \right| \leq \varepsilon. \tag{12}$$

5   VBEM Method Applied to the AR1MA1 Model

Given a generative model as the AR1MA1 one in (5), we are going to consider the binary variables describing the topology of the network $\mathbf{x}_i$ as latent variables whilst the weights and noise variance $\mathbf{\theta}_i = \{\mathbf{\omega}_i, \sigma_i^2\}$ are interpreted as model parameters. On the other hand, data will be a microarray time series for the i-th gene as $\mathbf{y}_i = [y_i(1),\dots,y_i(N)]^{\mathrm{T}}$. Taking into account (4) and (5), the likelihood function may be expressed as

$$p(\mathbf{y}_i|\mathbf{x}_i,\mathbf{\theta}_i) = N\left(\mathbf{y}_i\middle|\mathbf{RD}_{\mathbf{\omega}_i}\mathbf{x}_i, \frac{\sigma_i^2}{\gamma_i}\mathbf{1}^N\right) \tag{13}$$

with $\mathbf{D}_{\mathbf{\omega}_i}$ a diagonal matrix with vector $\mathbf{\omega}_i$, $\mathbf{R} = \mathbf{T}\mathbf{Y}^{\mathrm{T}}$, $\mathbf{T} = \begin{bmatrix}\mathbf{1}^N\middle|\mathbf{0}\end{bmatrix} \in \mathfrak{R}^{G\times(N+1)}$ and

$$\gamma_i = \gamma_i(\mathbf{x}_i,\mathbf{\omega}_i) = \left(1 + \mathbf{\omega}_i^{\mathrm{T}}\mathbf{D}_{\mathbf{\omega}_i}\mathbf{D}_{\mathbf{x}_i}\mathbf{x}_i\right)^{-1}. \tag{14}$$

According to (9), probability distributions must be chosen from families that factorizes into hidden variables and parameters. We are going to choose priors from the same families as in method proposed in [1] as

$$q(\mathbf{x}_i) = N\left(\mathbf{x}_i\middle|\mathbf{\mu}_{\mathbf{x}_i},\mathbf{\Sigma}_{\mathbf{x}_i}\right) \tag{15}$$

$$q(\mathbf{\omega}_i,\sigma_i^2) = N\left(\mathbf{\omega}_i\middle|\mathbf{\mu}_{\mathbf{\omega}_i},\sigma_i^2\mathbf{\Sigma}_{\mathbf{\omega}_i}\right)IG\left(\sigma_i^2\middle|\alpha_i,\beta_i\right) \tag{16}$$

a Gaussian and Normal scaled Inverse Gaussian distribution with $\xi_{\mathbf{x}_i} = \{\mathbf{\mu}_{\mathbf{x}_i},\mathbf{\Sigma}_{\mathbf{x}_i}\}$ and $\xi_{\mathbf{\omega}_i} = \{\mathbf{\mu}_{\mathbf{\omega}_i},\mathbf{\Sigma}_{\mathbf{\omega}_i},\alpha_i,\beta_i\}$ the hyperparameters to be learned from data.

Likelihood function in (13) does not satisfies the requirements for the conjugate model. Specifically, dependence of variance scale (14) on the unknowns does not allows to define conjugate priors. As a suboptimal solution, we propose a fixed point approach where scale effect of γ_i is approximated according to the most probable of $\mathbf{x}_i$ and $\mathbf{\omega}_i$, given by its means as

$$\bar{\gamma}_i \approx \gamma_i\left(\mathbf{\mu}_{\mathbf{x}_i},\mathbf{\mu}_{\mathbf{\omega}_i}\right) = \left(1 + \mathbf{\mu}_{\mathbf{\omega}_i}^{\mathrm{T}}\mathbf{D}_{\mathbf{\mu}_{\mathbf{\omega}_i}}\mathbf{D}_{\mathbf{\mu}_{\mathbf{x}_i}}\mathbf{\mu}_{\mathbf{x}_i}\right)^{-1}. \tag{17}$$

6   Results and Discussion with Synthetic Data

We have applied the proposed VBEM algorithm to synthetic data sets. Specifically two VBEM methods were considered: (*i*) based on the AR1 model proposed in [1], refereed as AR1-VBEM method and (*ii*) based on the new AR1MA1 proposed model, refereed as AR1MA1-VBEM method. To compare the performance, various sets have been generated with $G = 50$ genes, $N = 50$ time samples and different levels of noise with a signal-to-noise ratio SNR $\in (1,80)$. Each data set have been generated by simulation using the priors and likelihood as in section 5 with subjective priors. According to biological knowledge, sugessting that in a real regulatory network each gene has a limited number of parents, we have set up the netkork topology for having 15 parents (about the 30% of the total number of genes). The inference procedure has been repeated one hundred times for having a satatistically significant result.

In Figure 1 we have plotted the performance of each method as an error percentage versus the noise level. The most undesireable performance would correspond to a random assignment with constant error rate around the 50%. We have considered as a satisfactory result an error rate lower than percentile 5%. It can be noticed that AR1MA1-VBEM method outperforms the AR1-VBEM one, producing satisfactory error rates at lower levels of noise.

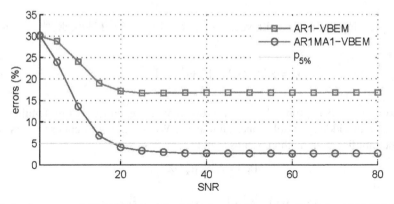

Fig. 1. Performance of AR1-VBEM method (stroke with box tokens) and the AR1MA1-VBEM one (stroke with circle tokens). AR1MA1-VBEM method outperforms the AR1-VBEM one with an error rate under percentile 5% for SNR > 20.

In binary decission, however, another kind of statistics are more suitable for analyzing these results [4]. We are going to consider the receiver operating characteristic (ROC) curve that represents the hits or true postive rate (TPR) versus the false postive or error rate (FPR). Random performance would correspond to a line through the origin with unitary slope, referred as the no-discrimination (ND) line. The area under the ROC curve (AUROCc) summarizes this analysis, with values between 0.5 for the ND line and a maximum value equal to 1.0 corresponding to the best performance.

In Figure 2 we have plotted the AUROCc for both VBEM methods at different levels of noise. Results show that AR1MA1-VBEM method outperforms the AR1-VBEM one, with values closer to one at for higher SNR.

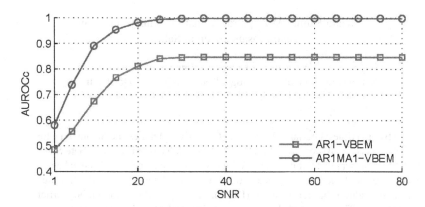

Fig. 2. AUROCc versus the level of noise for the AR1-VBEM method (stroke with box tokens) and the AR1MA1-VBEM one (stroke with circle tokens). AR1MA1-VBEM outperforms AR1-VBEM with higher AUROCc at any level of noise and values closer to one for higher SNR.

References

1. Tienda-Luna, I.M.: Constructing Gene Networks Using Variational Bayesian Variable Selection. Articial Life 14(1), 65–79 (2008)
2. Ribeiro, A.: A General Modeling Strategy for Gene Regulatory Networks with Stochastic Dynamics. J. Comput. Biol. 13(9), 1630–1639 (2006)
3. Beal, M.J., Ghaharamani, Z.: The Variational Bayesian EM Algorithm for Incomplete Data with Application to Scoring Graphical Model Structures. Bayesian Statistics 7 (2003)
4. Huang, Y.: Reverse engineering gene regulatory network, a survey of statistical models. SPMAG 26(1), 76–97 (2009)

A New Nanoscale DG MOSFET Design with Enhanced Performance – A Comparative Study

Sushanta Kumar Mohapatra, Kumar Prasannajit Pradhan,
and Prasanna Kumar Sahu

Department of Electrical Engineering,
National Institute of Technology, Rourkela-769008, Odisha, India

Abstract. Triple Material (TM) Double Gate (DG) Metal Oxide Semiconductor Field Effect Transistor (MOSFET) with high-k dielectric material as Gate Stack (GS) is presented in this paper. A lightly doped channel has been taken to enhance the device performance and reduce short channel effects (SCEs) such as drain induced barrier lowering (DIBL), sub threshold slope (SS), hot carrier effects (HCEs), channel length modulation (CLM). We investigated the parameters like Surface Potential, Electric field in the channel, SS, DIBL, Transconductance (g_m) for TM-GS-DG and compared with Single Material (SM) DG and TM-DG. The simulation and parameter extraction have been done by using the commercially available device simulation software ATLAS^{TM}.

Index Terms: MOSFET, silicon-on-insulator (SOI), DG, SCEs, Gate Stack (GS) engineering, TM-DG, ATLAS^{TM} device simulator.

1   Introduction

To scale the planar bulk MOSFET into nanometre regime, significant challenges and difficulties come across to control the SCEs. Various new structures have been reported to reduce the SCEs in SOI devices. The DG MOSFET is one of the promising candidates because of its two gates which control the channel from both sides and electrostatically superior to a single gate MOSFET which allows additional gate length scaling due to good control of SCEs [1],[6],[7].

In SOI devices the leakage current (I_{off}) can be controlled by different architectures. The required threshold voltage (V_T) can be achieved by keeping channel un-doped and altering the gate work function. Thus MOSFETs can be fabricated with lightly doped channels resulting in high carrier mobility [8],[10]. The DG MOSFETs also suffer from considerable short channel behaviour in the sub 100 nm regime. A new device structure TM-DG MOSFET is developed to improve the device immunity against the SCEs and therefore improve the device reliability in high performance circuit applications. This new structure gives improving SCEs such as DIBL, HCEs, reducing channel length modulation (CLM). It also improves the drive current, SS, leakage current and g_m. Three different laterally contacted materials with different work function have been taken for gate electrode of the device. Material

V.V. Das and P.M. El-Kafrawy (Eds.): SPIT 2012, LNICST 117, pp. 76–81, 2014.

work functions will be selected in such a way that work function near the source is highest and near the drain is lowest for n-channel MOSFET. As a result, the electric field and electron velocity along the channel suddenly increase near the interface of the two gate materials, resulting in increased gate transport efficiency. The low work function near the drain side reduces the peak electric field and reduces the HCEs when compared to single material gate structure [2], [3], [4], [5].

Day by day the gate oxide thickness t_{ox} is decreasing and approaching physical limits (<2nm), for which quantum mechanical tunnelling induces severe gate leakage current through the dielectric. In our work the high dielectric material taken over thin SiO_2 layer [10], [11], [12]. We investigate the SCEs of TM-DG MOSFET in comparison with the conventional DG MOSFET. We also have taken TM-GS-DG MOSFET with the high dielectric material Si_3N_4. Our results demonstrated that the proposed TM-GS-DG MOSFET exhibits good current characteristics and reduced SCEs such as DIBL, HCEs and CLM compared to the conventional DG MOSFET and TM-DG MOSFET.

2   Device Structure

Schematic structures of TM-DG and TM-GS-DG MOSFET are shown in Fig.1 and Fig.2 with M1, M2, and M3 of gate lengths L_{G1}, L_{G2}, L_{G3} respectively. We have studied only n-type MOSFET in our analysis. The work function for the gate materials is assumed as 4.8ev for SM-DG and 4.8ev, 4.6ev, 4.4ev for TM-DG. The gate length (L_G) =60nm for SM and for TM gate material length ratio (1:1:1) was taken. The channel thickness t_{Si} =10nm and oxide thickness t_{SiO2}=3nm for SM, TM_DG and t_{SiO2}=1nm, t_{Si3N4}=2nm for TM-GS-DG is made in these devices. Source/Drain doping $N_D=10^{20}$ cm^{-3} with variation of channel doping $N_a=10^{15}$cm^{-3} to 10^{18} cm^{-3} considered.

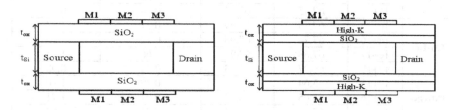

Fig. 1. Schematic of SM and TM-DG   **Fig. 2.** Schematic of TM-GS-DG MOSFET
MOSFET

3   Simulation

In the simulation the model used comprises the inversion layer Lombardi constant voltage and temperature (CVT) mobility model that takes into account the effect of parallel and perpendicular fields, along with doping and temperature dependent parts of the mobility. The Shockley–Read–Hall and Auger recombination models for minority carrier recombination have been used. Furthermore, we chose Gummel's method (or the decoupled method), along with Newton's method (or the fully coupled method), to solve the equations included in the CVT model [2], [13].

4 Results and Discussions

In Fig.3., I_{DS}-V_{GS} transfer characteristics on linear scale and log scales for three different device structures have been compared at V_{DS}=10 mV and 1.2 V. We have extracted SS and maximum drain current (Id) for three different structures by changing channel doping which is given in Table 1.

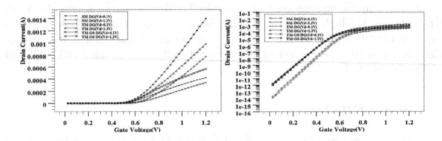

Fig. 3. Simulated drain current I_{DS} as a function of the gate voltage V_{GS} on (a) normal and (b) log scales for three structures at N_A= 1x10^{16}cm^{-3}

Table 1. Extracted Parameters from Fig.3

Structure		Subthreshold Slope		Max Drain Current	
Model	N_A(cm^{-3})	SS ,V_d=0.1V	SS , V_d=1.2V	I_{d1}(mA) ,V_d=0.1V	I_{d2}(mA),V_d=1.2V
SM-DG	1e+15	62.02	62.34	0.61	1.07
	1e+16	62.04	62.35	0.62	1.08
	1e+17	62.15	62.41	0.56	1.03
	1e+18	62.45	62.12	0.34	0.77
TM-DG	1e+15	67.75	67.99	0.71	1.24
	1e+16	67.74	67.98	0.72	1.25
	1e+17	67.68	67.92	0.66	1.21
	1e+18	66.97	67.43	0.42	0.98
TM-GS-DG	1e+15	65.64	65.73	0.89	1.70
	1e+16	65.65	65.74	0.91	1.71
	1e+17	65.63	65.75	0.84	1.67
	1e+18	65.27	65.51	0.57	1.40

In Fig 4.(a) The sensitivity of SS for different channel doping is demonstrated. The SS is lower for TM-GS-DG than TM-DG. The TM-GS-DG shows a higher drive current than the DG and TM-DG MOSFET with un-doped or lightly body doping (1x10^{15} and 1x10^{16}) which is examined in Fig. 4(b). The surface potential of the three devices with different V_{GS} and V_{DS} are given in Fig. 5(a). As seen from the figure barrier height for channel carriers at the edge of the source has less change with increase in drain voltage. It is clear from that Fig., the minimum channel potential lies under control of gate voltage.

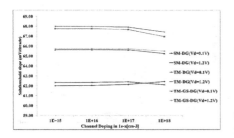 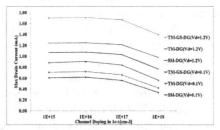

Fig. 4. (a) Variation of SS and (b) maximum drain current for different channel doping (N_A)

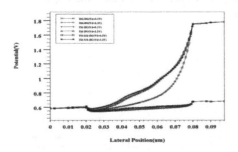 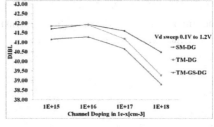

Fig. 5. (a)Surface Potential along the channel for different values of V_{GS} and V_{DS} (b) Variation of DIBL for different channel doping (N_A))

The minimum surface potential extracted as threshold voltage and DIBL are given in Table 2. The sensitivity of DIBL was examined for different channel doping as shown in Fig. 5(b). The figure shows among from the three device structures, TM-GS-DG gives lower DIBL which reduces the SCEs.

Table 2. Extraction of DIBL and Transconductance for different channel doping

Model	N_A(cm^{-3})	V_{t1}(V), V_d=0.1V	V_{t2}(V), V_d=1.2V	DIBL	g_{m1}, V_d=0.1V	g_{m2}, V_d=1.2V
SM-DG	1e+15	0.48	0.02	41.70	1.00	1.86
	1e+16	0.49	0.03	41.94	1.01	1.88
	1e+17	0.50	0.04	41.60	0.92	1.86
	1e+18	0.59	0.14	40.48	0.61	1.68
TM-DG	1e+15	0.43	-0.03	41.85	1.16	1.98
	1e+16	0.44	-0.02	41.91	1.16	2.00
	1e+17	0.44	-0.01	41.18	1.06	1.98
	1e+18	0.50	0.07	39.27	0.71	1.85
TM-GS-DG	1e+15	0.45	0.00	41.17	1.58	2.84
	1e+16	0.46	0.00	41.29	1.60	2.87
	1e+17	0.46	0.01	40.65	1.47	2.84
	1e+18	0.50	0.08	38.81	1.01	2.67

Fig.6. shows electric field in the lateral position of the three device structures with V_{DS} (0.1V and 1.2V). It is clearly visible from that figure the different in the value of work function of the gate material for TM-DG results two additional peaks. The peak value of the electric field at drain side is reduced for TM-GS-DG as compared to SM-DG and TM-DG, which minimises the HCE and impact ionisation. Fig.7 (a) shows the transconductance (g_m) for TM-GS-DG is higher as compared to SM and TM-DG in both the bias voltages. The increment of g_m leads to higher intrinsic gain which gives better RF application.

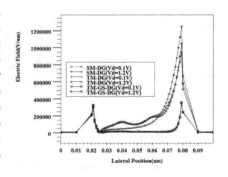

Fig. 6. E. Field for different V_{GS} and V_{DS}

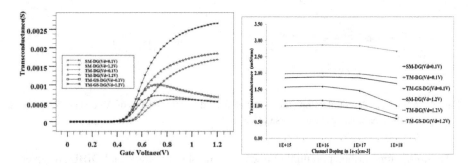

Fig. 7. (a)Variation of g_m as a function V_{GS} for three structures at $N_A= 1x10^{16}cm^{-3}$, (b).Variation of g_m as a function of N_A

The Table 2 is the extraction of g_m for different N_A and the Fig.7 (b) shows the variation of g_m as a function of the channel doping N_A. All three device structures give better g_m for lightly doped channel. The TM-GS-DG shows highest g_m in comparison to SM-DG and TM-DG. The GS engineering provides higher drain current (as shown in Fig.3) because of the reduced EOT which increases the gate capacitance. The increment of drain current increases the transconductance for GS architecture.

5   Conclusion

We provide a thorough investigation of the performance for gate engineering TM and TM-GS double gate MOSFETs as a function of device geometry as well as doping strategies. The design and simulation on NMOS electrical characteristics has been successfully done using commercially available device simulation software ATLAS[TM]. We can model the SM-DG, TM-DG and TM-GS-DG by altering the material work function Φ_m and the value of k. The TM-GS-DG shows a better control of gate on the channel that improves the SCEs and also increases the transconductance implies a high dc gain. Reduction of electric field at the drain end indicates a low HCE. From all above simulation results and extracted parameters the TM-GS-DG with less channel doping gives better performance from its counterpart SM-DG and TM-DG.

Acknowledgements. The authors would like to thank the department of Electronics and Telecommunication Engineering, Jadavpur University, West Bengal.

References

1. Das Gupta, A.: Multiple Gate MOSFETs: The Road to the future (2007)
2. Goel, K., Saxena, M., Gupta, M., Gupta, R.S.: Modeling and Simulation of a Nanoscale Three-Region Tri-Material Gate Stack (TRIMGAS) MOSFET for Improved Carrier Transport Efficiency and Reduced Hot-Electron Effects. IEEE Transaction on Electron Devices 53(7) (July 2006)
3. Razavi, P., Orouji, A.A.: Nanoscale Triple Material Double Gate (TM-DG) MOSFET for Improving Short Channel Effects. In: International Conference on Advances in Electronics and Micro-Electronics, pp. 11–14 (2008)
4. Tiwari, P.K., Dubey, S., Singh, M., Jit, S.: A two-dimensional analytical model threshold voltage of short-channel triple-material double-gate metal-oxide-semiconductor field-effect-transistors. Journal of Applied Physics 108, 074508 (2010)
5. Chen, M.-L., Lin, W.-K., Chen, S.-F.: A New Two-Dimensional Analytical Model for Nanoscale Symmetrical Tri-Material Gate Stack Double Gate Metal-Oxide-Semiconductor Field Effect Transistors. Japanese Journal of Applied Physics 48, 104–503 (2009)
6. Chaudhry, Kumar, M.J.: Controlling short-channel effects in deep submicron SOI MOSFETs for improved reliability: A review. IEEE Trans. Device Mater. Rel. 4(1), 99–109 (2004)
7. Nguyen, B.-Y., Celler, G., Mazuré, C.: A Review of SOI Technology and its Applications. 01-Nguyen-v4n2-AF 19.08.09 19:28, pp. 51–54
8. Young, K.K.: Short-channel effect in fully depleted SOI MOSFETs. IEEE Trans. Electron Devices 36(2), 399–402 (1989)
9. Gupta, S.K., Baidya, A., Baishya, S.: Simulation and Optimization of Lightly-Doped Ultra-Thin Triple Metal Double Gate (TM-DG) MOSFET with High-K Dielectric for Diminished Short Channel Effects. In: International Conference on Computer & Communication Technology, pp. 221–224 (2011)
10. Wong, B.P., Mittal, A., Cao, Y., Starr, G.: Nano-CMOS Circuit and Physical Design. A John Willy &Sons, INC. Publication (2005)
11. Dusastre, V., Heber, J., Pulizzi, F., Stoddart, A., Pamies, P., Martin, C.: The Interface is Still the Device. Nature Materials 11, 91 (2012)
12. Kasturi, P., Saxena, M., Gupta, M., Gupta, R.S.: Dual-Material Double-Layer Gate Stack SON MOSFET: A Novel Architecture for Enhanced Analog Performance—Part II: Impact of Gate-Dielectric Material Engineering. IEEE Transactions on Electron Devices 55(1) (January 2008)
13. DevicesimulatorATLAS usermanual. Silvaco Int., SantaClara, CA (May 2006), http://silvaco.com

Variable Block Based Motion Estimation Using Hexagon Diamond Full Search Algorithm (HDFSA) via Block Subtraction Technique

Ranjit Singh Sarban Singh, Jitvinder Dev Singh, and Lim Kim Chuan

Department of Computer Engineering,
Faculty of Electronics and Computer Engineering,
Universiti Teknikal Malaysia Melaka (UTeM)
Hang Tuah Jaya, 76100 Durian Tunggal
Melaka, Malaysia
ranjit.singh@utem.edu.my, jit_1986@yahoo.com

Abstract. Motion estimation is a process of estimating the pixels displacement between two successive frames. The most common motion estimation technique used in the modern world is the block based motion estimation method. There are two types of block based motion estimation method which is the fixed block size and variable block size. This paper introduces a newly developed variable block based Hexagon Diamond Full Search Algorithm which uses the variable block based motion estimation integrating the block subtraction technique. Three different variable block size of 16×16 pixels, 8×8 pixels and 4×4 pixels are introduced in this paper to estimate the different types of motions. In order to select a particular variable block size, the block subtraction technique is applied before the motion estimation process is conducted. The block subtraction technique is mainly used to select the variable block size based on the pixels changes that occur during the motion estimation process. In order to evaluate the performance of the variable block based Hexagon Diamond Full Search Algorithm, superior algorithms are used to compare its performance in terms of average Peak Signal to Noise Ratio (PSNR), average search points and elapsed processing time.

Keywords: Variable Block Based, Motion Estimation, Hexagon Diamond, Block Subtraction Technique.

1 Introduction

Motion estimation process is to exploits the temporal redundancy that exists between two consecutive frames [1]. The pixels displacements are either individually or in a small group is determined while exploiting the temporal redundancy [2]. The pixels displacement usually represents a motion vector at coordinate (x, y). There are few techniques used for motion estimation, such as the pel-recursive [3], frequency domain [4], and block based [5]. The most commonly used technique is the block based technique. This technique divides the frames into equal square macro blocks [1].

V.V. Das and P.M. El-Kafrawy (Eds.): SPIT 2012, LNICST 117, pp. 82–87, 2014.

The macro blocks are sized into 16 × 16 pixels, 8 × 8 pixels and 4 × 4 pixels block based on the algorithm development requirements. All the macro blocks are compared between the current frame and previous frame for motion estimation process [6-7].

In this paper, a new variable block based Hexagon Diamond Full Search Algorithm (HDFSA) is developed to estimate the motion estimation. The HDFSA algorithm applies the 16 × 16 pixels, 8 × 8 pixels and 4 × 4 pixels types of block sizes. The selection of the block size is based on the change that occurs in the pixels value through the block subtraction technique.

2   Proposed Method

As illustrated in Figure 1, the hexagon search pattern consists of seven search points with one search point is located the center point whereas the diamond search pattern consists of five search points with one search point is located the center point. The hexagon search pattern evaluates all the search points to determine the best Mean Absolute Difference (MAD). If the best MAD point is found at one of the six search points surrounding the center point, that point will be located as the new center point. The new hexagon search pattern will consists of three new search points and four old search point from the previous hexagon search pattern. If the best MAD point is found at the center search point of the hexagon search pattern in the first search step, the search pattern will change to the small diamond search pattern.

Figure 2 shows the full search pattern search points evaluation in a search window to find the best MAD to determine the best matched motion vector coordinate point. The methodology of the full search pattern is illustrated in Figure 2.

The hexagon diamond search pattern implements the 16 × 16 pixels and 8 × 8 pixels of block size whereas the full search step apply the 4 × 4 pixels block size. Before the selection of block size for motion estimation process, threshold value is obtained from the first frame and second frame from the 144 × 176 pixels input video sequence. The first frame and second frame is divided into 16 × 16 pixels block size using Equation 1.

$$\text{Block} = (1+BS*(i-1): BS*i, \ 1+BS*(j-1): BS*j) \tag{1}$$

Where r = 144 (horizontal pixels),
         c = 176 (vertical pixels),
         BS = 16 (block size),
         i = 1: (r / BS),
         j = 1: (c / BS).

Then the block subtraction technique is applied to subtract the extracted blocks from the first frame and second frame as shown in Figure 3. The subtraction process is initialized according to the location of the blocks for an example if the block in the second frame is located at coordinate (1, 1), then the block in the first frame also must be located at coordinate (1, 1).

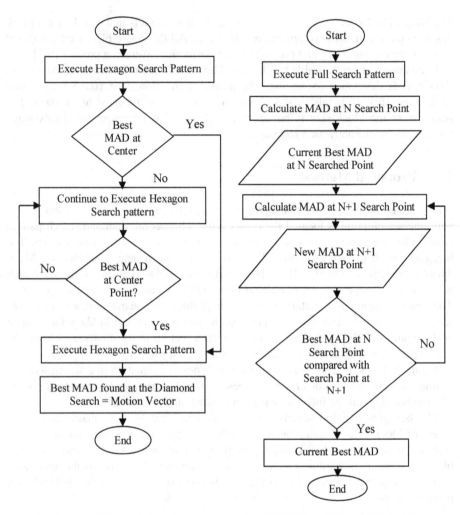

Fig. 1. Hexagon Diamond Search Pattern Methodology   **Fig. 2.** Full Search Pattern Methodology

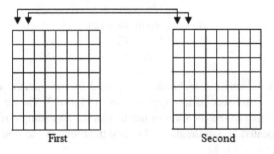

Fig. 3. Block Subtraction Technique

After completing the subtraction process, non-zero elements that exist in each block is calculated and arranged into a matrix form. The non-zero elements are scanned to determine the maximum and minimum value that exists in the matrix form. Those maximum and minimum values are used to calculate the threshold value to select a particular block size. The threshold value is usually divided into two sections as shown in Figure 4.

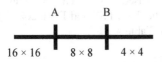

Fig. 4. Threshold Point for Block Size Selection

Table 1. Threshold Value

	Point A	Point B
Akiyo	61 ≤	≥ 123
Coastguard	203 ≤	≥ 225
Foreman	192 ≤	≥ 223
News	166 ≤	≥ 204

The total amount of non-zero elements for each block is used to select the block size based on evaluated threshold value. If the evaluated non-zero values fall at the left region of point A as shown in Figure 4, the block size will remains at 16 × 16 pixels. Thus, if the evaluated non-zero values fall at the right region of point B as shown in Figure 4, then the 16 × 16 pixels block size is divided into smaller block size of 4 × 4 pixels. Hence, if the evaluated non-zero values fall in between the point A and point B region as shown in Fig. 4, then the 16 × 16 pixels block size is divided into 8 × 8 pixels block size. The threshold value for point A and point B for the each respective video sequences is shown in Table 1.

3   Experimental Results and Analysis

The performance of the proposed variable block based HDFSA is evaluated based on the average Peak Signal to Noise Ratio (PSNR) value, average search point and elapsed processing time. Four different types of video sequence with frame size of 144 × 176 pixels are used in this experiment. The results recorded are for ten frames for each video sequence. The results for average PSNR value, average search points and elapsed processing time is presented in Table 2, Table 3 and Table 4 respectively. The results of the proposed variable block based HDFSA are compared with superior algorithms which are the Full Search, Three Step Search (TSS), Four Step Search (FSS), and Diamond Search (DS).

Table 2. Average PSNR value (dB)

	FS	TSS	FSS	DS	HDFSA
Akiyo	47.06	47.06	47.06	47.06	46.55
Coastguard	33.11	33.11	33.11	33.12	31.01
Foreman	26.40	26.28	26.29	24.54	24.83
News	37.65	37.67	37.66	37.22	36.91

Table 2 show that the newly developed variable block based HDFSA achieved a similar average PSNR value compared with the superior algorithms. The degradation of PSNR performance is mainly caused by the reduce of the search points. Table 3 shows the variable block based HDFSA manage to reduce the used of search points compared with the superior algorithms. This shows that the variable block based HDFSA is able to have similar image quality while reducing the number of search points as recorded in Table 2. However, variable block based HDFSA algorithm's elapsed processing time increased due to the application of variable block based search. This has caused the elapsed processing time increases compared with the TSS, FSS and DS algorithms but still lower compared with FS algorithm as shown in Table 4.

Table 3. Average Search Point

	FS	TSS	FSS	DS	HDFSA
Akiyo	225	25	18	14	9
Coastguard	225	25	18	14	9
Foreman	225	25	21	17	10
News	225	25	18	14	11

Table 4. Elapsed Processing Time (Seconds)

	FS	TSS	FSS	DS	HDFSA
Akiyo	1.89	1.07	1.07	1.04	1.37
Coastguard	2.17	1.06	1.05	1.03	1.58
Foreman	1.83	1.08	1.05	1.02	1.58
News	1.85	1.08	1.04	1.02	1.15

4   Discussion

Pixels are the main component used to represent information in an image in the form of color representation. A change in the pixels value indicates of motion or interference at a particular region of interest. If the pixels value remains unchanged this indicates that there is no motion or interference has occurred. Thus, block subtraction technique is integrated to further analyze the motion estimation for motion vector finding in a reference block based on the first frame and second frame.

The 16 × 16 pixels, 8 × 8 pixels and 4 × 4 pixels block sizes are used to evaluate the changes that occur in an image pixels value. The evaluation process only take place based on the type of motion complexity occurred during the threshold value measurement. The block size is adapted into the variable block based HDFSA based on the threshold value complexity shown in Table 1.

The result presented in Table 2, Table 3 and Table 4 shows each video sequence have its own motion complexity when the block subtraction technique is applied to measure the maximum and minimum of non-zero elements. Based on the threshold value presented in Table 1, initially the variable block based HDFSA search will conduct the search using the 16 × 16 pixels block size before switching to 8 × 8 pixels block size and finally to 4 × 4 pixels block size search for the motion vector estimation process.

The variable block based HDFSA algorithm is developed to determine or estimate the motion estimation based on the change in image pixels value. Experiment results and analysis is tabulated in section 3 after conducting the experiment. Based on the result, variable block based HDFSA algorithm proven able to measure the similar PSNR value while reducing the number of search points compared with DS algorithm as shown in Table 2 and Table 3. The elapsed processing time in Table 4 for variable block based HDFSA increase compared with DS, FSS and TS is due to the variable block methodology. Whereas the all the superior algorithms are developed and experimented using fixed block based methodology.

Also, this paper also emphasizes that the variable block based methodology can be used as motion estimation search methodology to estimation the motion translation for an area of interest.

5   Conclusion

The variable block based HDFSA is a newly developed algorithm which estimate or determine the motion estimation using the pixels value threshold measured using the block subtraction technique. This algorithm is able to produce similar average PSNR value compared with FS, TSS, FSS and DS while reducing the search point.

Acknowledgements. Funding for this project is provided by the Fundamental Research Grant Scheme (FRGS), Malaysia. This research has been conducted at Universiti Teknikal Malaysia Melaka. We would like to express our gratitude to Universiti Teknikal Malaysia Melaka whom funded this research.

References

1. Jitvinder, H.S.D.S., Ranjit, S.S.S., Anas, S.A., Lim, K.C., Salim, A.J.: Medical Image Pixel Extraction via Block Positioning Subtraction Technique for Motion Analysis. In: Osman, N.A.A., Abas, W.A.B.W., Wahab, A.K.A., Ting, H.-N. (eds.) 5th Kuala Lumpur International Conference on Biomedical Engineering 2011. IFMBE Proceedings, vol. 35, pp. 690–693. Springer, Heidelberg (2011)
2. Eduarda, R.M., Bruno, B.V., Cláudio, M.D., Bruno, Z., Sergio, B.: Multiprocessing Acceleration of H.264/AVC Motion Estimation Full Search Algorithm under CUDA Architecture. In: South Symposium on Microelectronics, pp. 41–44 (2011)
3. Estrela, V., Rivera, L.A., Bassani, M.H.S.: Pel-Recursive Motion Estimation Using the Expectation-Maximization Technique and Spatial Adaptation. In: WSCG Posters Proceedings. Union Agency-Science Press, Czech Republic (2003)
4. Fabrizio, J.: Dubuisson.: Motion Estimation using Tangent Distance. In: International Conference on Image Processing, pp. 489–492 (2007)
5. Boudlal, A., Nsiri, B., Aboutajdine, D.: Modeling of Video Sequences by Gaussian Mixture: Application in Motion Estimation by Block Matching Method. EURASIP Journal on Advances in Signal Processing, 1–7 (2010)
6. Ranjit, S.S.S., Jitvinder, H.S.D.S., Lim, K.C., Salim, A.J.: Motion Analysis for Real-Time Surveillance Video via Block Pixel Analysis Technique. In: International Conference on Signal, Image Processing and Applications, pp. 60–64 (2011)
7. Ranjit, S.S.S., Sim, K.S., Besar, R., Tso, C.P.: From Ultrasound Images To Block Based Region Motion Estimation. Biomedical Imaging and Intervention Journal (Biij) 5(3) (2009)

Circular Patch Antenna with 1D-EBG for X-Band

Amina Bendaoudi and Rafah Naoum

Laboratory of Telecommunication and Digital Signal Processing
University of Sidi Bel Abbès, 22000, Algeria
{amina_nes,rafah.naoum}@yahoo.fr

Abstract. This paper presents unidimensionnel electromagnetic band gap structure (1D-EBG) uses the circular patch antenna as an excitation source. Moreover, this paper presents a comparison between circular and square excitation source. The proposed model is simulated using Ansoft HFSS software and various antenna parameters are measured. Since, the resonance frequency of this structure is 12 GHz; these antennas are suitable for X-band [8.2 GHz; 12.4 GHz] and military applications. The results show the possibility of using a circular patch antenna as the excitation source with unidimensionnel electromagnetic band gap instead of a square patch antenna according to the same resonance frequency and with a reflection coefficient equal to -17.73dB and a directivity of 21.2dB.

Keywords: Circular patch antennas, Resonant EBG, Bragg Mirror, Directivity.

1   Introduction

The extensive, rapid and explosive growth in wireless communication technology and communication systems is prompting the extensive use of low profile, low cost, less weight and easy to manufacture antennas. All these requirements are efficiently realized by microstrip antennas. The applications of microstrip antennas are wide spread because of their advantages due to their conformal and simple planar structure [1], [2]. But the major disadvantage of microstrip antennas is its low directivity and do not have a good radiation patterns.

In the last decade, periodic EBG structures were the focus of much attention due to their promising applications in microwave circuit and antenna design. These EBG periodic structures exhibit wide band pass and band rejection properties at certain microwave frequencies. This unique property has been utilized in enhancing the performance of microstrip antennas and circuits [3-4]. The EBG can forbid the propagation for electromagnetic waves whatever their direction of propagation. The introduction of a defect within a structure 1D-EBG can open a frequency band of transmission and improves the reflection and the directivity significantly.

In reference [5], has been shown that an antenna can provide values of directivity exceeding 15 dB in the presence of an excitation source square patch type and thus allows to overcome the problem of power system required complex for feeding a network of patches. In this paper, we use a structure consisting of a Bragg mirror

V.V. Das and P.M. El-Kafrawy (Eds.): SPIT 2012, LNICST 117, pp. 88–94, 2014.
© Institute for Computer Sciences, Social Informatics and Telecommunications Engineering 2014

placed on top of a circular patch antenna. Therefore, the following work is divided into five sections: the first section is devoted to give an overview of the circular patch antenna. Second section gives a preface of the unidimensionnel electromagnetic band gap (1D-EBG) structure. Third section discusses the 1D-EBG design with a circular patch antenna as a probe. Forth section demonstrates the results of the paper as a whole and a comparison between both structures: square patch antenna with 1D-EBG and circular patch antenna with 1D-EBG is presented. Finally, a brief conclusion is presented in the fifth section.

2   The Design of Circular Patch Antenna

Patch antennas play a very significant role in today's world of wireless communication systems. A microstrip patch antenna is very simple in the construction using a conventional microstrip fabrication technique. The most commonly used microstrip patch antennas are rectangular and circular patch antennas [6]. Microstrip antenna can be defined as a structure that has a conducting patch printed on a grounded microwave substrate [7].

The resonant frequencies of the circular patch can be analyzed conveniently using the cavity model [8], [9], [10]. The cavity is composed of two perfect electric conductors at the top and bottom to represent the patch and the ground plane, and a cylindrical perfect magnetic conductor around the circular periphery of the cavity. Using the synthesis procedure as mentioned in [11], the resonant frequency of a circular patch can be computed as:

$$f_0 = \frac{c \cdot J_{mn}}{2\pi \, r \, \sqrt{\varepsilon_r}} \tag{1}$$

Where
r = radius of circular patch antenna.
ε_r= dielectric constant.
J_{mn} = mth zero of the derivative of the Bessel function or order n.
For dominant mode TM_{11}, J_{mn} = 1.84118 [12] which is extensively used in all kind of microstrip antennas.

3   Unidimensionnel Electromagnetic Band Gap Structure (1D-EBG)

The 1D-EBG are composed of a stacks periodic dielectric or metallic structures, it have properties of frequency filtering which is illustrated by changes depending on the frequency coefficients of reflection through a material EBG illuminated by a plane wave at normal incidence.

3.1   Creation of a Bragg Mirror

A multi-layered structure will be created, that almost completely reflects a perpendicular incoming wave for one specific frequency (f_0). Therefore, an adjustment to every layer is necessary in order to obtain a destructive interference of the transmitted waves. Every layer has to be $\lambda/4$ thick if the multi-layered structure is an alternation between layers of air and layers of a dielectric material [5].

The formulas which represent the thicknesses of the air layer and the layer of dielectric are the following:

$$e_{air} = \frac{c}{4 f_0} \tag{2}$$

$$e_{diel} = \frac{c}{4 f_0 \sqrt{\varepsilon_r}} \tag{3}$$

Where c is the celerity of light in vacuum.

3.2   Creation of a Resonant Cavity

The introduction of a defect in this structure (figure 1) results in a narrow transmission peak within the band gap. A defect layer of air is introduced, λ_0 thick, the wavelength corresponding with the center frequency f_0 of the band gap. This structure forms a resonant cavity, similar to the Fabry-Perot cavity [5].

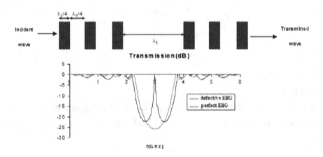

Fig. 1. Multi-layered structure with a defect and its transmission for axial incidence

4   Introduction of an Excitation Source

The 1D cavity is formed on one side a perfect plan E (ground plane of the antenna) and the other side of the Bragg mirror. The cavity has a thickness $\lambda / 2$ and the Bragg mirror is composed of 3 layers of relative dielectric permittivity $\varepsilon_r = 2.6$ and a thickness $\lambda / 4$. The dielectric layers are separated by layers of air, also thick $\lambda / 4$ is the wavelength for which the antenna operates. Here this corresponds to a frequency of 12GHz (figure 2).

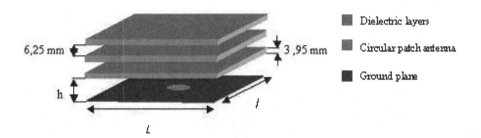

Fig. 2. Antenna and 1D-EBG

However, the antenna having finite dimensions, the resonant frequency of the cavity depends on the transverse dimensions of the EBG material. The calculation of the latter can be approximated by the formula [13]:

$$f_0 = \frac{c}{2\pi} \sqrt{\left(\frac{n\pi}{l}\right)^2 + \left(\frac{m\pi}{L}\right)^2 + \left(\frac{p\pi}{h}\right)^2} \tag{4}$$

Where
n,m,p = indices of the cavity mode.
L,l,h =cavity dimensions.
This cavity has the following dimensions: $l= L= 100$ mm, $h= 12.73$ mm and should work on the mode 111.

5   Results and Discussion

Using the commercial code Ansoft's *HFSS* (High Frequency Structure Simulator), a bi-periodic structure considered infinite in the lateral directions has been simulated at normal incidence [14]. The version used is version 10.1 HFSS is a software package for electromagnetic modeling and analysis of passive, three dimensional structures. It presents a comprehensive and meticulous description of the process of modeling a circular patch antenna with 1D-EBG structure in HFSS. Plots of S-parameter values will be calculated and compared with simulation; square patch antenna with 1D-EBG structure, which is performed in reference [5].

5.1   Reflection Coefficient

The same design procedure, which was used for square patch with 1D-EBG in [5], is used in circular patch with 1D-EBG. The square and circular patch antenna use the same substrate (ε_r = 2.33, h = 1.57 mm) and a power source coaxial.

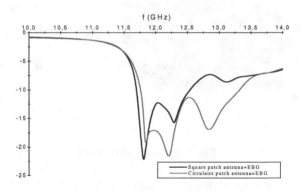

Fig. 3. Simulated reflection coefficient (in dB)

The figure 3 shows the graph of reflection coefficient both structures: square patch antenna+1D-EBG and circular patch antenna+1D-EBG. From the reflection coefficient curve it is clear that the circular patch antenna+1D-EBG have less reflection -17.73dB and operating frequency at 11.92 GHz compared with square patch antenna+1D-EBG has the minimum value is obtained at 11.8GHz and the minimum value obtained is -24dB, we confirm that this study structure is able to use in X-band applications. The antenna shows a wide band behavior between 11.92 GHz and 12.2 GHz.

5.2   2D-Directivity

Two figures below represent the directivity of the two structures in two different planes (Phi = 0 ° and phi = 90 °).

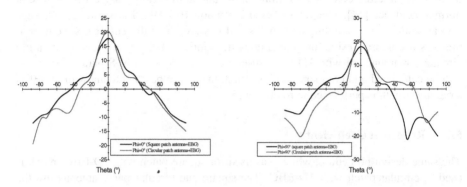

Fig. 4. Simulated directivity (in dB)

The maximum directivity gain obtained from the graph is 21.2 dB for circular patch antenna with 1D-EBG structure. Note that with the directivity EBG becomes narrower. Consequently, the maximum directive gain increases by about 18 dB to 21dB, a 3dB increase therefore. We notice the appearance of side lobes, but they are small enough.

5.3   Radiation Pattern

The figure 5 shows the radiation pattern of the two structures. It is clear from the graph that the radiation is not distributed but directed along a single direction. The Half-Power BeamWidth (HPBW) in the E-plane is 58deg and 66deg in the H-plane. Directional radiation patterns make this structure a good candidate for the antennas used for applications of X-band.

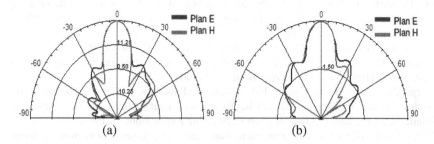

(a)   (b)

Fig. 5. The radiation pattern at 12GHz for:
a) Circular patch+1D-EBG ; b) Square patch+1D-EBG

Table 1 shows the obtained simulated results. As shown in the table, the results obtained from square patch with 1D-EBG are very close to those obtained from circular patch with 1D-EBG.

Table 1. Comparison table between square patch+EBG and circular patch+EBG

	Square patch+1D-EBG	Circular patch+1D-EBG
Optimal frequency	11.8 GHz	11.92 GHz
Reflection coefficient	-24 dB	-17.73 dB
Maximal directivity	18.4 dB	21.2 dB
E-Plane HPBW	62deg	58deg
H-Plane HPBW	38deg	66deg

6   Conclusion

In this paper, circular patch antenna with 1D-EBG has been studied and compared with square patch. From the simulation results, we can see that the directivity gain can be improved by changement of the excitation type (shape of the patch antenna) and using circular patch antenna with 1D-EBG, we could obtain a more directional radiation pattern than that obtained using square patch antenna with 1D-EBG. Moreover, we proved the ability of using circular patch antenna with 1D-EBG with same performance of square patch antenna with 1D-EBG approximately.

References

1. Keshtkar, A., Dastkhosh, A.R.: Circular Microstrip Patch Array Antenna for C-Band Altimeter System. International Journal of Antennas and Propagation (2008)
2. Anubhuti, K., Puran, G., Rajesh, N., Teena, R.: Optimization Of Dual Band Microstrip Antenna Using Ie3d Simulator for C-Band. International Journal of Current Research 3(11)
3. Qu, D., Shafai, L., Foroozesh, A.: Improving microstrip patch antenna performance using EBG substrates. IEEE Proceedings Microwave and Antennas Propagation 153(6) (2006)
4. Fallah-Rad, M., et al.: Enhanced Performance of a microstrip patch antenna using a high impedance EBG structure. IEE Proc. Microw., AP-149(3), 141–146 (2002)
5. Steyaert, D.: Nouvelles structures à bande interdite photonique pour applications antennaires. Master Work, University Bordeaux1 (2006)
6. Durga Prasad, T., Satya Kumar, K.V., Khwaja Muinuddin, M.D., Kanthamma, C.B., Santosh Kumar, V.: Comparisons of Circular and Rectangular Microstrip Patch Antennas. International Journal of Communication Engineering Applications-IJCEA (2011)
7. Mohamed, K., Rahim, A.: Electromagnetic band gap (EBG) structure in microwave device design. Master Work, University Malaysia (2008)
8. Young, M.: The Techincal Writers Handbook. University Science, Mill Valley (1989)
9. Duncombe, J.U.: Infrared navigation—Part I: An assessment of feasibility (Periodical style). IEEE Trans. Electron Devices ED-11, 34–39 (1959)
10. Chen, S., Mulgrew, B., Grant, P.M.: A clustering technique for digital communications channel equalization using radial basis function networks. IEEE Trans. Neural Networks 4, 570–578 (1993)
11. Lucky, R.W.: Automatic equalization for digital communication. Bell Syst. Tech. J. 44(4), 547–588 (1965)
12. Chantalat, R.: Optimisation d'un réflecteur spatial a couverture céllulaire par l'utilisation d'une antenne BIE multisources. Phd thesis (2003)
13. Bingulac, S.P.: On the compatibility of adaptive controllers (Published Conference Proceedings style). In: Proc. 4th Annu. Allerton Conf. Circuits and Systems Theory, New York, pp. 8–16 (1994)
14. Kante, B., Ourir, A., Nawaz Burokur, S., Gadot, F., Lustrac, A.: Metamaterials for optical and radio communications. C. R. Physique 9, 31–40 (2008)

Modeling of Sigma-Delta ADC with High Resolution Decimation Filter

G.N. Sowmya[1], K.S. Vasundara Patel[2], and Rajani Rao[3]

[1] BMSCE, Bangalore
gnsowmya407@gmail.com
[2] Dept of E & C, BMSCE, Bangalore
vasundara.rs@gmail.com
[3] Analog and mixed signal IP Development, LSI India R & D Private Limited, Bangalore

Abstract. This paper presents modeling of Sigma-Delta ADC in time domain and frequency domain. Sigma-Delta converters offer high resolution, high integration, and low cost, making them a good ADC choice for applications such as process control and weighing. Analog block of Sigma-Delta ADC consist of integrator, comparator & feedback loop. Analog block provides one bit stream output, which needs to be decimated by digital filter. The digital part consists of filtering and decimation. Proposed technique uses weighted average method for decimation filter to increase the resolution. To understand the various concepts of Sigma -Delta ADC such as noise shaping, over sampling and digital decimation filtering it is required to build frequency domain model, this makes the analysis simpler. Performance is measured in terms of SNR of decimation filter. Synthesizable Register Transfer Level (RTL) code is written for the decimation filter to verify its performance.

Keywords: Over sampling, Noise shaping, Decimation filter.

1   Introduction

The sigma delta conversion technique has been in existence for many years, but recent technological advances now make the devices practical and their use is becoming widespread [1]. In communication system applications, pipelined ADCs and sigma-delta ADCs attract more research efforts. However, the former should be extended to high resolution and the latter to higher bandwidth. The key feature of these converters is that they are the only low cost conversion method which provides both high dynamic range and flexibility in converting low bandwidth input signals.

1.1   Architecture of Sigma-Delta ADC

The basic block diagram of a first order Sigma-Delta ADC is as shown in figure 1. It is comprised of a 1-bit ADC (typically known as a comparator) driven by the output of an integrator that is fed with an input signal summed with the output of a 1-bit DAC fed from the ADC output. Adding a digital low pass filter (LPF) and a decimator to the digital output will create a Sigma-Delta ADC [2].

V.V. Das and P.M. El-Kafrawy (Eds.): SPIT 2012, LNICST 117, pp. 95–100, 2014.
© Institute for Computer Sciences, Social Informatics and Telecommunications Engineering 2014

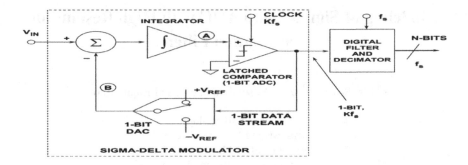

Fig. 1. Block diagram of Sigma-Delta ADC

Sigma-Delta ADC is oversampling ADC. This oversampling results in the two effects. 1) Impact on anti-aliasing filters. 2) Impact on quantization noise.

2   Frequency Domain Modeling

2.1   Modeling of Modulator

In the frequency domain model, the basic approach is to model the transfer functions and hence the frequency responses of the modulator and decimation filter. Over Sampling Ratio is the Ratio of Sampling Frequency to Nyquist Frequency. For example, arbitrarily choosing the OSR as 100 and the Input Frequency as 100 Hz, the Nyquist Frequency is 200 Hz. The OSR of 100 implies the Sampling Frequency is 20000 Hz. Quantization Noise Spectrum is Flat from D.C to Sampling frequency of 20000 Hz (White Noise)and the total Noise Power= $\Delta^2/12$ (Obtained by assuming that the quantization error is uniformly distributed between $-\Delta/2$ to $+\Delta/2$). Where Δ= step size = $1/(2^n-1)$. (Assuming Full Scale output voltage of 1V), Choosing n=1 bit, Δ=1, resulting Noise Power = 0.0833. Uniformly spread this power from 0 to 20K Hz, We obtain the amplitude of the noise spectrum as 0.002041.

The modeling of the modulator mainly depends on its noise transfer function. The desired Noise Transfer function is s/(s+a), where 'a' is half of Sampling Frequency (Fs/2=10000).

Block diagram simplification results in the noise transfer function as 1/(1+I(s)). Where, I(s) is the transfer function of the integrator. The integrator transfer function will be a/s = (10000/s). Signal transfer function is given by I(s)/(1+I(s)) where I(s) is the integrator transfer function , Substituting the integrator transfer function obtained, we get the signal transfer function as a/(s+a). Multiplying the Signal and Noise with the Signal and Noise Transfer Functions respectively, we obtain the Signal and noise output from the Modulator as shown in figure 2.

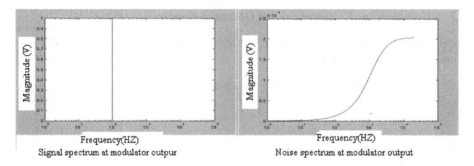

Signal spectrum at modulator output   Noise spectrum at modulator output

Fig. 2. Signal and Noise spectrum at the Modulator Output

Noise spectrum at modulator output shows that noise added to the input signal is moved to the higher frequencies making the band of interest having lesser noise, this technique is called noise shaping it can be changed by modifying the noise transfer function. This noise shaping results in increased SNR compared to other ADC's.

2.2   Modeling of Decimation Filter

Filtering noise which could be aliased back into the baseband is the primary purpose of the digital filtering stage. Its secondary purpose is to take the 1-bit data stream that has a high sample rate and transform it into a high resolution data stream at a lower sample rate. This process is known as decimation. Essentially, decimation is both an averaging filter function and a rate reduction function performed simultaneously. The output of the modulator is a coarse quantization of the analog input. However, the modulator is oversampled at a rate that K times higher than the Nyquist rate. High resolution is achieved by averaging over K data points to interpolate between the coarse quantization levels of the modulator. The process of averaging is equivalent to lowpass filtering in the frequency domain. With the high frequency components of the quantization noise removed, the output sampling rate can be reduced to the Nyquist rate without aliasing noise into the baseband. The Decimation Filters impulse response is either a rectangular or triangular function. Therefore, its Frequency response is a Sinc or Sinc^2 function respectively .The Bandwidth of these filters are selected in such a way that the input signal is well inside the pass-band of these filters. The Signal and Noise Output Spectrum from the Modulator are multiplied by the frequency response of the decimation filter to obtain the final Signal and Noise Outputs. Since the Signals are already in the frequency domain, just squaring and adding the amplitude gives the power of each signal. The Power of the Signal and noise is calculated and the SNR is evaluated as the 10*log10 (signal power / noise power).

2.3   Comparison of Theoretical and Obtained Results

We plot the Ideal SNR and the Obtained SNR vs. the OSR for both the first order and second order decimation filters.

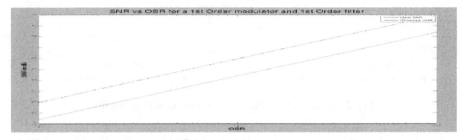

Fig. 3. SNR vs. OSR for a first order decimation filter

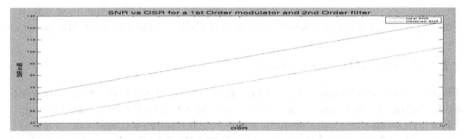

Fig. 4. SNR vs. OSR for a second order decimation filter

In all cases, we observe that there is an offset between the ideal and the obtained SNR. This is because of the attenuation caused to the input signal by the decimation filter which we had not considered in our derivation of the Ideal SNR equation.

3   Time Domain Modeling

A sinusoidal input of 10Hz and sampling frequency of 80 KHz is chosen. Therefore the OSR is 4000. Modulator is modeled as shown in figure 1, The integrator is an ideal integrator whose output is the present input plus the previous output. The comparator is a simple threshold device which outputs a high value if its input is positive and a low value otherwise. The DAC outputs a value of Vref if its input is high and a value of −Vref otherwise [4]. The time domain output of the modulator is shown in figure 5 .We observe that the time domain output has more ones when the input has a high magnitude and the output has more zeros when the magnitude of the input is low also, when the input voltage is close to midscale, we see an equal number of ones and zeros [5].

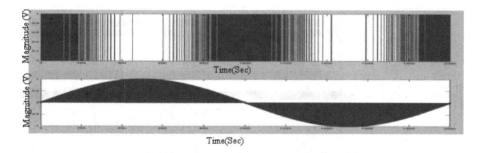

Fig. 5. Time domain output of the modulator

3.1   Time Response of First and Second Order Decimation Filter

The first order filter has a rectangular impulse response, i.e, its output is an average of the previous N inputs where N is the number of taps of the filter. This is decided by the decimation rate. Usually the value of N is chosen in such a way that the output rate is twice or four times the Nyquist rate. The rectangular impulse response results in a Sinc frequency response [5]. The bandwidth of this filter is 40Hz. The bit stream obtained from the modulator is filtered using the first order filter. The second order filter has a triangular impulse response, i.e. its output is a weighted average of the previous N inputs where N is the number of taps of the filter. The triangular impulse response results in a $Sinc^2$ frequency response [5]. The bandwidth of this filter is 80Hz. This is as expected because the second order filter can be visualized and implemented as a cascade of two first order filters.

4   Simulation Results

Time domain model is built in Cadence Virtuoso, switched capacitor integrator is used to model the modulator. Input sine wave of 10Hz frequency and OSR of 4000 is chosen, resulting in 80KHz of Fs, and decimation rate of 1000 is selected. Decimation filter is implemented in Verilog-A model [4]. Input signal, integrator output, filter clock, modulator output and decimation filter outputs are shown in figure 6.

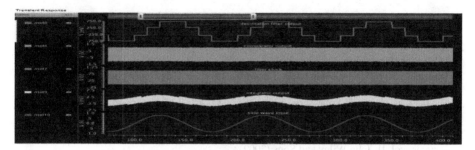

Fig. 6. Output of the modulator and filter

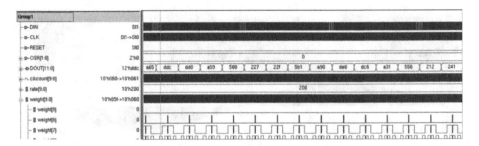

Fig. 7. ADC output with resolution of 12 bits

In Figure 7, first waveform corresponds to the input of the filter (DIN) or the output of the comparator, second waveform is the clock, third waveform is reset signal which is held at logic zero and fourth waveform is 2-bits programmable OSR, fifth waveform represents the 12-bit digital output corresponding to the analog input and other signals are the intermediate signals which helps in debugging.

5   Conclusion

We initially built models of the Sigma-Delta ADC in the frequency domain. We compared the SNR results that we obtain from the frequency domain model with the ideal SNR that we get from the equations that we have derived for various orders of decimation filters and observed that the obtained values were in good agreement with the theoretical values. We also built a time domain model of the Sigma-Delta ADC in Matlab as well as in Cadence Virtuoso schematic editor. Based on the SNR results that we obtained from the frequency and time domain models, we developed a synthesizable Register Transfer Level (RTL) code in Verilog HDL for the optimum decimation filter and verified its performance. Second order filter with first order modulator gives better performance than first order filter with first order modulator with 12 bits of resolution.

References

1. Kester, W.: ADC Architectures III: Sigma-Delta ADC Basics, MT-022-Tutorial. Analog Devices Inc. (2009)
2. Aziz, P.M., Sorensen, H.V., Van Der Spiegel, J.: An overview of sigma-delta converters. IEEE Signal Processing Magazine 13
3. Wideband Sigma-Delta Modulators, Licentiate Thesis in Electronics and Computer Systems Stockholm, Sweden (2010)
4. Analog behavioral Modeling with the Verilog-a Modeling by Dan FitzPatrick Apteq Design Systems, Inc. and Ira Miller, Motorola
5. Jacob Baker, R.: CMOS Mixed Signal Circuit Design. IEEE press series on Microelectronic systems, vol. II. John Wiley and Sons (2002)

A Novel Method for Left Ventricle Volume Measurement on Short Axis MRI Images Based on Deformable Superellipses

Mostafa Ghelich Oghli[1,2], Alireza Fallahi[3], Vahab Dehlaqi[2],
Mohammad Pooyan[4], and Nazanin Abdollahi[4]

[1] Students Research Committee,
Kermanshah University of Medical Sciences, Kermanshah, Iran
[2] Kermanshah University of Medical Sciences, Kermanshah, Iran
[3] Department of Biomedical Engineering, Hamedan University of Technology, Hamedan, Iran
[4] Department of Biomedical Engineering, Shahed University, Tehran, Iran

Abstract. Diagnosis and treatment follow-up of cardiac diseases can rely on numerous cardiac imaging modalities. Among these modalities Cardiac Magnetic Resonance (CMR) has become a reference examination for cardiac morphology, function and perfusion in humans. It is the current reference standard for the assessment of both left and right ventricular volumes and mass. There are numerous automatic and semi-automatic methods for cardiac cavities segmentation and volume measurement but the problem is still open. In this paper a novel semi automatic method is proposed based on parametric model, superellipse, for segmentation and measurement the volume of the left ventricle on short axis MRI images. For fitting superellipse on MR images, a set of data points has been needed as a partial data. These data points are been provided by user and this fact put our method in the category of semi-automatic methods.

Keywords: Left ventricle, Volume measurement, Short axis cardiac MR, Superellipse, Levenberg Marquardt algorithm.

1 Introduction

In recent years Magnetic Resonance Imaging (MRI) has become a reference standard examination for cardiac morphology, function and perfusion in humans [1]. Accurate segmentation of the Left Ventricle (LV) endo- and epicardium boundaries and determination of the volume of ventricular chambers at different phases of the cardiac cycle in 2D cardiac Magnetic Resonance sequences is needed for assessment of ventricular function. The segmentation of these images provides clinically useful indicators of heart function, such as End-systolic volume (ESV), End-diastolic volume (EDV), the ejection fraction (EF) ratio and Myocardial mass.

The segmentation and volume measurement of cardiac chambers is currently performed manually in clinical routine. This long and tedious task, prone to intra- and inter-expert variability, requires about 20 min per ventricle by an expert clinician. The great need for automated methods has led to the development of a wide variety of

V.V. Das and P.M. El-Kafrawy (Eds.): SPIT 2012, LNICST 117, pp. 101–106, 2014.
© Institute for Computer Sciences, Social Informatics and Telecommunications Engineering 2014

segmentation methods [2], for example thresholding [3], pixel classification [4, 5], deformable models and model based segmentation. In left ventricle volume measurement area several works have been performed in literature. Ranganath [6] performed an automatic contour extraction of left ventricular contours from cardiac MRI studies. These algorithms were based on active contour models incorporating contour propagation. Goshtasby et al. [7] applied a two-stage algorithm for extraction of the ventricular chambers in flow-enhanced MR images. They approximate location and size of endocardialy surfaces by intensity thresholding and reposition points on the approximated surfaces to nearest local gradient maxima. Then they fit a cylinder into the point set. A comprehensive review of segmentation methods in short axis cardiac MR images can be found in [1]. In this paper, a parametric superellipse model is used, for fitting on left ventricle in short axis cardiac MRI images. Superellipses are a flexible representation that naturally generalizes ellipses. They can model a large variety of natural shapes, including ellipse, rectangles, parallelograms, and pinched diamonds, by changing a small number of parameters [8, 9]. Superellipses were first formulated by Gardiner [10]. Several approaches have been suggested to determine the parameters of superellipses and approximately all of them need data points for fitting superellipse on them. In the next step using Levenberg-Marquardt algorithm [11] (LMA) for parameter estimation superellipse has been fitted on data points. The final step is the estimation of left ventricle volume which is done by means of generating a superellipsoid from fitted superellipses on each slice.

2   Superellipse Fitting

Superellipses are a flexible representation that can model a large variety of natural shapes, including ellipse, rectangles, diamonds, and pinched diamonds, by changing a small number of parameters. A centered superellipse can be defined in a parametric form by:

$$(\frac{x}{a})^{2/\varepsilon} + (\frac{y}{b})^{2/\varepsilon} = 1 \tag{1}$$

where, squareness parameter $\varepsilon > 0$ specifies the squareness in 2-D plane and (a,b) are the length of semi axes.

Several methods have been proposed for fitting superellipses to the images [12]. An iterative Levenberg-Marquardt algorithm [11] (LMA) is used in this paper for parameter estimation.

Fitting superellipse on a given set of pixel data using least square solution (LMA) achieved by finding the set of model parameters that minimize the sum of the squares of the distances between the model curve and given pixel data. The notion of distance can be interpreted in various ways and Rosin and West [13] investigate several examples. A simple but still effective measure is the algebraic distance given by

$$Q_0(x,y) = \left[\frac{(x-x_c)\cos\theta - (y-y_c)\sin\theta}{a}\right]^{2/\varepsilon} + \left[\frac{(y-y_c)\cos\theta - (x-x_c)\sin\theta}{b}\right]^{2/\varepsilon} - 1 \tag{2}$$

One of the main problems with the algebraic distance is that it results in different distance estimates for different parts of superellipse curves depending on the local curvature of the curve. This is because the conventional algebraic distance measure treats pixels as individual data points and relations between pixels are not exploited. In this paper we propose a modification procedure using adaptive data point selection and parameter λ for more effective convergence of LMA algorithm.

2.1   Fitting Procedure

Like other numeric minimization algorithms, the Levenberg–Marquardt algorithm is an iterative procedure. To start a minimization, the user has to provide an initial guess for the parameter vector, β [11]. In many cases, an uninformed standard guess like β = (1, 1, ... , 1) will work fine; in other cases, the algorithm converges only if the initial guess is close to the final solution.

So our fitting procedure consists of 3 steps:

1. Preparing initial values for Levenberg Marquardt algorithm namely x_c, y_c, a, b, ε, θ, t. Our parameter vector, therefore should be expressed as β { x_c, y_c, a, b, ε, θ, t}

2. Determining data points. These pixels used as prior knowledge for superellipse fitting.

3. Implementation of Levenberg Marquardt algorithm for finding superellipse parameters.

The initial values are given by user. For our propose an uninformed standard guess like β = (1, 1,..., 1) will work fine. Also data points are given by user. After determining data points the Levenberg Marquardt algorithm starts fitting superellipse to partial data. First of all as a problem definition there are a set of data points of independent and dependent variables, (x_i, y_i), optimize the parameters β of the model curve f(x, β) so that the sum of the squares of the deviations

$$S(\beta) = \sum_{i=1}^{m} \left[y_i - f(x_i, \beta) \right]^2 \tag{3}$$

becomes minimal. Levenberg Marquardt algorithm as mentioned is an iterative procedure and needs initial values for parameter vector β.

Fig. 1. (a) Original CMR image (b) Determined initial data point on image

After preparing theses initial values by user algorithm starts its iteration. In each iteration step, the parameter vector, β, is replaced by a new estimate, β + δ. To determine δ, the functions $f(x_i, \beta + \delta)$ are added by $J_i \delta$, Where

$$J_i = \frac{\partial f(x_i, \beta)}{\partial \beta} \tag{4}$$

is the gradient (row-vector in this case) of f respect to β. At a minimum of the sum of squares, called S, the gradient of S with respect to δ is 0. Differentiating the squares in the definition of S, using the above first-order approximation of $f(x_i, \beta + \delta)$, and setting the result leads to:

$$(J^T J + \lambda I)\delta = J^T [y - f(\beta)] \tag{5}$$

where J is the Jacobean matrix whose i[th] row equals J_i, f and y are vectors with i[th] component $f(x_i, \beta)$ and y_i, respectively, I is the identity matrix, giving as the increment, δ, to the estimated parameter vector, β. And finally the (non-negative) damping factor, λ, is adjusted at each iteration. If reduction of S is rapid, a smaller value can be used, whereas if iteration gives insufficient reduction in the residual, λ can be increased. The result of using this algorithm on short axis cardiac MRI can be seen in Fig. 2.

3   3-D Visualization and Estimation of LV Volume

The final step is the calculation of the left ventricle volume. Therefore the segmented pixels of all images are counted and multiplied by their voxel size.

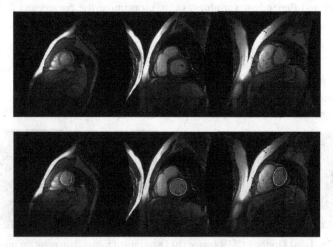

Fig. 2. Result of superellipse fitting on some slices of short axis cardiac MRI images of various patients. Original images (top row) and superellipse fitting result (bottom row).

Fig. 3. 3-D visualization of LV generated from superellipse fitted on short axis plane

The averaged volume is multiplied by the voxel size pixel_spacing_x * pixel_spacing_y * slice_gap and added to the other slices for the final volume. The volume generated for this approach can be seen in Fig. 3.

4   Experimental Results

End-diastolic and end-systolic volumes are clinically important parameters in cardiac ventricular function assessment. So, some of our results in this area are provided here.

Table 1 shows all of the provided information of the image data sets. Columns"EDV1" and"ESV1" contain the results of the parametric volume estimation while columns"EDV2" and"ESV2" contain the older results of the parametric model from the actual patient examination. Our method is tested in 33 image datasets. Our results show better fitting compared to ellipse fitting methods for segmenting left ventricle. This is because of the nature of superellipses that cover a wider range of shapes and consequently our results is closer to the left ventricle borders. As a quantitative comparison, Computational cost reduced in our proposed method, for example 1.3 times faster than [14].

We used Similarity and Specifity index for evaluate our method validation and obtained 88.3% and 85.6% for them.

Table 1. Patients datasets with volume estimation results from the superellipse model

P.Num	EDV1[ml]	ESV1[ml]	EDV2[ml]	ESV2[ml]
1	88.4	24.6	85.1	23
2	69.1	20.2	72.4	22
3	83.2	24.6	88	26.6
4	81.3	10.8	79.9	12.2
5	74.2	27	72	27.7

5   Conclusion

In this paper, a semi- automatic method is proposed for segmentation and measuring the volume of left ventricle. Superellipse models are used for fitting on left ventricle in the short axis cardiac MR images, volume measurement of left ventricle and making a 3-D model of it. Superellipse fitting methods need partial data. These partial data are been gotten from user and this fact put our method in the category of semi-automatic methods. Future works can focus on generation of partial data automatically on the basis of cardiac short axis MR image features.

References

1. Petitjean, C., Dacher, J.N.: A review of segmentation methods in short axis cardiac MR images. Medical Image Analysis 15, 169–184 (2011)
2. Frangi, A.F, Niessen, W.J., Viergever, M.A.: Three-dimensional modeling for functional analysis of cardiac images: a review. IEEE Trans. Med. Imaging 20 (2001)
3. Goshtasby, A., Turner, D.: Segmentation of cardiac cine MR images for extraction of right and left ventricular chambers. IEEE Trans. Med. Imaging 14(1), 56–64
4. Lynch, M., Ghita, O., Whelan, P.: Automatic segmentation of the left ventricle cavity andmyocardium in MRI data. Comput. Biol. Med. 36(4), 389–407 (2006)
5. Kurkure, U., Pednekar, A., Muthupillai, R., Flamm, S., Kakadiaris, I.A.: Localization and segmentation of left ventricle in cardiac cine-MR images. IEEE Trans. Biomed. Eng. 56(5), 1360–1370 (2009)
6. Ranganath, S.: Contour Extraction from Cardiac MRI Studies Using Snakes. IEEE Transactions on Medical Image Processing 14(2), 328–338 (1995)
7. Goshtasby, A., Turner, A.D.: Segmentation of Cardiac Cine MR Images for Extraction of Right and Left Ventricular Chambers. IEEE Transactions on Medical Image Processing 14(1), 56–64 (1995)
8. Barr, A.H.: Superquadrics and angle-preserving transforms. IEEE Comput. Graphic. Applicat. CGA–1, 11–23 (1981)
9. Pentland, P.: Perceptual organization and the representation of natural form. Artif. Intell. 28, 293–331 (1986)
10. Gardiner, M.: The superellipse: a curve that lies between the ellipse and the rectangle. Sci. 4m. 21, 222–234 (1965)
11. Levenberg, K.: A Method for the Solution of Certain Non-Linear Problems in Least Squares. The Quarterly of Applied Mathematics 2, 164–168 (1944)
12. Rosin, P.L.: Fitting superellipses. IEEE Trans. Pattern Anal. Machine Intell. 22, 726–732 (2000)
13. Rosin, P., West, G.: Curve segmentation and representation by superellipses. Proc. IEE: Vision Image Signal Process. 142, 280–288 (1995)
14. Urschler, M., Mayer, H., Bolter, R., Leberl, F.: The livewire approach for the segmentation of left ventricle electron-beam CT images. In: 26th Workshop of the Austrian Association for Pattern Recognition (AGM/AAPR) (2002)

Cooperation Gain in Incremental LMS Adaptive Networks with Noisy Links

Azam Khalili[1], Wael M. Bazzi[2], and Amir Rastegarnia[1]

[1] Department of Electrical Engineering, Malayer University
Malayer, 65719-95863, Iran
{a_rastegar,a.khalili}@ieee.org
[2] Electrical and Computer Engineering Department, American University in Dubai
P.O. Box 28282, Dubai, United Arab Emirates
wbazzi@aud.edu

Abstract. In this paper, we study the influence of noisy links on the effectiveness of cooperation in incremental LMS adaptive network (ILMS). The analysis reveals the important fact that under noisy communication, cooperation among nodes may not necessarily result in better performance. More precisely, we first define the concept of cooperation gain and compute it for the ILMS algorithm with ideal and noisy links. We show that the ILMS algorithm with ideal links outperforms the non-cooperative scheme for all values of step-size (cooperation gain is always bigger than 1). On the other hand, in the presence of noisy links, cooperation gain is not always bigger than 1 and based on the channel and data statistics, for some values of step-size, non-cooperative scheme outperforms the ILMS algorithm. We presented simulation results to clarify the discussions.

Keywords: adaptive networks, cooperation gain, incremental, step-size.

1 Introduction

An adaptive network is a collection of spatially distributed nodes that interact with each other, and function as a single adaptive entity that is able to respond to data in real-time and also track variations in their statistical properties [1-3]. Based on the mode of cooperation between nodes, adaptive networks can be roughly classified into incremental [1-6], diffusion [6-11], and hierarchical [12], [13] algorithms. In incremental based adaptive networks, a Hamiltonian cycle is established through the nodes and each node cooperates only with one adjacent node to exploit the spatial dimension, whilst performing local computations in the time dimension [3]. This approach reduces communications among nodes and improves the network autonomy as compared to a centralized solution [1-3]. In the diffusion based adaptive networks, on the other hand, nodes communicate with all of their neighbors, and no cyclic path is required. The incremental adaptive networks in [1-6] assume ideal links between nodes. However, as we have shown in [14-18], the performance of incremental adaptive network changes considerably in the presence of noisy links. In fact, we show that

V.V. Das and P.M. El-Kafrawy (Eds.): SPIT 2012, LNICST 117, pp. 107–114, 2014.

- noisy links lead to a larger residual MSD, as expected.
- reducing the adaptation step size may actually increase the residual MSD.

In this work, we present other interesting results about the performance of incremental adaptive networks with noisy links. To this aim, we first define the concept of *cooperation gain* for incremental adaptive networks. Then, we calculate the cooperation gain for incremental adaptive networks with ideal links and noisy links. We observe that, when links are ideal, incremental adaptive networks always have a better steady-state performance than non-cooperative scheme, while in the presence of noisy links, depending on data and channel statistics, non-cooperative scheme may have better performance. We also present simulation results to support the derived expressions.

Notation: Bold uppercase letters denote matrices, whereas bold lowercase letters stand for vectors. Symbol * is used for both complex conjugation for scalars and Hermitian transpose for matrices. $\|\mathbf{x}\|_{\Sigma}^2 = \mathbf{x}^* \Sigma \mathbf{x}$ denotes weighted norm for a column vector $\mathbf{x}$. $\mathbf{I}_M$ is $M \times M$ identity matrix and 1_N is $N \times 1$ vector with unit entries.

2   Incremental LMS Adaptive Network

Let's denote by $\mathcal{N} = \{1, ..., N\}$ a set of nodes that communicate according to a given network topology. At time i, each node k has access to scalar measurement $d_k(i)$ and $1 \times M$ regression vector u_k that are related via

$$d_k(i) = \mathbf{u}_{k,i} \mathbf{w}^o + v_k(i) \tag{1}$$

where $M \times 1$ vector $\mathbf{w}^o \in R^M$ is an unknown parameter and $v_k(i)$ is the observation noise term with variance $\sigma_{v,k}^2$. The objective of the network is to estimate $\mathbf{w}^o$ from measurements collected at N nodes. The collected data at all nodes are

$$\mathbf{U} = \begin{bmatrix} \mathbf{u}_1 & \mathbf{u}_2 & \cdots & \mathbf{u}_N \end{bmatrix}^T (N \times M), \quad \mathbf{d} = \begin{bmatrix} d_1 & d_2 & \cdots & d_N \end{bmatrix}^T (N \times 1) \tag{2}$$

It must be noted that $\mathbf{w}^o$ is the solution of the following optimization problem

$$\arg \min_w J(\mathbf{w}) \text{ where } J(\mathbf{w}) = E\{\|\mathbf{d} - \mathbf{U}\mathbf{w}\|^2\} \tag{3}$$

The optimal solution of (3), is given by normal equations [1]

$$\mathbf{w}^o = \mathbf{R}_u^{-1} \mathbf{R}_{du} \tag{4}$$

where

$$\mathbf{R}_{du} = E\{\mathbf{U}^* \mathbf{d}\}, \text{ and } \mathbf{R}_u = E\{\mathbf{U}^* \mathbf{U}\} \tag{5}$$

In order to use (4), each node must have access to the global statistical information $\{\mathbf{R}_u, \mathbf{R}_{du}\}$ which in many applications is not available. To address this issue, the incremental LMS adaptive network is proposed in [3]. The update equation in the ILMS algorithm is given by

$$\hat{\mathbf{w}}_k^{(i)} = \hat{\mathbf{w}}_{r,k}^{(i)} + \mu_k \mathbf{u}_{k,i}^* (d_k(i) - \mathbf{u}_{k,i} \hat{\mathbf{w}}_{r,k}^{(i)}) \tag{6}$$

where $\hat{\mathbf{w}}_k^{(i)}$ denotes the local estimate of $\mathbf{w}^o$ at node k at time i, μ_k is the step size parameter and $\hat{\mathbf{w}}_{r,k}^{(i)}$ is the received local estimate which is given by

$$\hat{\mathbf{w}}_{r,k}^{(i)} = \begin{cases} \hat{\mathbf{w}}_{k-1}^{(i)} & \text{ideal links} \\ \hat{\mathbf{w}}_{k-1}^{(i)} + \mathbf{q}_{k,i} & \text{noisy links} \end{cases} \tag{7}$$

where $\mathbf{q}_{k,i} \in R^{M\times 1}$, is the (time-realization) of channel the noise term between sensor k and $k-1$ which is assumed to have zero mean and covariance matrix $\mathbf{Q}_k = E\{\mathbf{q}_k \mathbf{q}_k^*\}$. Replacing (7) in (6), the update equation of ILMS algorithm with the noisy links changes to

$$\hat{\mathbf{w}}_k^{(i)} = \hat{\mathbf{w}}_{k-1}^{(i)} + \mathbf{q}_{k,i} + \mu_k \mathbf{u}_{k,i}^* (d_k(i) - \mathbf{u}_{k,i}(\hat{\mathbf{w}}_{k-1}^{(i)} + \mathbf{q}_{k,i})) \tag{8}$$

As we have shown in [14, 15], noisy links lead to a larger residual MSE, and also, reducing the adaptation step size may actually increase the residual MSE.

2.1   Steady-State Performance

A good measure of the adaptive network performance is the MSD which for each node k is defined as follows

$$\eta_k = E\{\|\tilde{\mathbf{w}}_{k-1}^{(\infty)}\|_{\mathbf{I}}^2\} \tag{9}$$

where

$$\tilde{\mathbf{w}}_{k-1}^{(i)} = \mathbf{w}^o - \hat{\mathbf{w}}_{k-1}^{(i)} \tag{10}$$

In [14, 15], the mean-square performance of ILMS adaptive network with noisy links has been investigated using the space-time energy conservation argument that was initially proposed in [2]. The analysis relies on the following assumptions data
(A.1) The regression data $\mathbf{u}_{k,i}$ are temporally and spatially independent and identically distributed (i.i.d.) circular white Gaussian random variables with zero mean and diagonal covariance matrix $\lambda \mathbf{I}_M$.
(A.2) $\mathbf{u}_{k,i}$ and $v_k(j)$ are independent of each other for all i and j.

In [14, 15], a complex closed-form expression for MSD has been derived. However, if we consider the following assumption

$$\mu_k = \mu, \ \mathbf{R}_{u,k} = \lambda \mathbf{I}, \ \mathbf{Q}_k = \sigma_{c,k}^2 \mathbf{I}$$

and also assuming small μ, we can approximate η_k as

$$\eta_k^{\text{inc,noisy}} = \frac{M}{2\mu\lambda N} \sum_{k=1}^{N} \left(\mu^2 \sigma_{v,k}^2 \lambda + \sigma_{c,k}^2(1 - 2\mu\lambda)\right) \tag{11}$$

Obviously, the steady-state MSD for an ILMS adaptive network with ideal links can be extracted from (11) for $\sigma_{c,k}^2 = 0$ as

$$\eta_k^{\text{inc,ideal}} = \frac{M\mu}{2N} \sum_{k=1}^{N} \sigma_{v,k}^2 \tag{12}$$

Note that (12) reveals an equalization effect on the MSD throughout the network, i.e. for $k, \ell \in \mathcal{N}$, we have $\eta_k = \eta_\ell$; thus, the average MSD is given as

$$\bar{\eta}^{\text{inc,noisy}} = \frac{1}{N} \sum_{k=1}^{N} \eta_k^{\text{inc,noisy}} = \frac{M}{2\mu\lambda N} \sum_{k=1}^{N} \left(\mu^2 \sigma_{v,k}^2 \lambda + \sigma_{c,k}^2 (1 - 2\mu\lambda) \right) \tag{13}$$

Similarly, the average MSD over all nodes for the ILMS with ideal links becomes

$$\bar{\eta}^{\text{inc,ideal}} = \frac{1}{N} \sum_{k=1}^{N} \eta_k^{\text{inc,ideal}} = \frac{M\mu}{2N} \sum_{k=1}^{N} \sigma_{v,k}^2 \tag{14}$$

2.2   Non-cooperation Scheme

It is noticeable that each node in the network can individually estimate $\mathbf{w}^o$ using its own data $\{d_k, \mathbf{u}_k\}$ and its previous time local estimate $\hat{\mathbf{w}}_{\text{nc},k}^{(i-1)}$ via

$$\hat{\mathbf{w}}_{\text{nc},k}^{(i)} = \hat{\mathbf{w}}_{\text{nc},k}^{(i-1)} + \mu_k \mathbf{u}_{k,i}^* (d_k(i) - \mathbf{u}_{k,i} \hat{\mathbf{w}}_{\text{nc},k}^{(i-1)}) \tag{15}$$

The steady-state MSD for non-cooperative scheme is given by [19]

$$\eta_k^{\text{nc}} = \frac{M\mu\sigma_{v,k}^2}{2} \tag{16}$$

where in this case (non-cooperative scheme), the steady-state MSD is given by

$$\eta_k^{\text{nc}} = \lim_{i \to \infty} E\{\|\tilde{\mathbf{w}}_k^{(i)}\|_I^2\} \tag{17}$$

The average MSD over all nodes of network is given as

$$\bar{\eta}^{\text{nc}} = \frac{M\mu \sum_{k=1}^{N} \sigma_{v,k}^2}{2N} \tag{18}$$

3   Cooperation Gain

In this section we compare the steady-state MSD performance of the ILMS algorithm (6) with a non-cooperative scheme (15). It must be noted that to compare the MSD of non-cooperative scheme with incremental LMS algorithm, we need to replace μ with μN in (18). This is because the incremental algorithm uses N iterations for every measurement time. So we have

$$\bar{\eta}^{\text{nc}} = \frac{M\mu \left(\sum_{k=1}^{N} \sigma_{v,k}^2 \right)}{2} \tag{19}$$

Now, to define the cooperation gain for incremental LMS algorithm, consider a network composed of $N \geq 2$ nodes with a space–time data $\{\mathbf{d}, \mathbf{U}\}$ satisfying the model (1) and the assumptions (A1)-(A3). Let's denote by $\bar{\eta}^{\text{nc}}$, $\bar{\eta}^{\text{inc,ideal}}$ and $\bar{\eta}^{\text{inc,noisy}}$, the average steady-state MSD provided by a non-cooperative scheme, the ILMS algorithm with ideal links and the ILMS algorithm with noisy links respectively. Thus, we can define the cooperation gain for ILMS algorithm with ideal links as

$$\mathcal{G}^{\text{inc,ideal}} = \frac{\overline{\eta}^{\text{nc}}}{\overline{\eta}^{\text{inc,ideal}}} \tag{20}$$

Replacing (19) and (14) in (20) we obtain

$$\mathcal{G}^{\text{inc,ideal}} = N \tag{21}$$

We can conclude from (21) that for all values of μ, the ILMS adaptive network with ideal links has better MSD performance than a non-cooperative scheme, or in formal terms

$$\mathcal{G}^{\text{inc,ideal}} > 1 \tag{22}$$

In addition, the cooperation gain is proportional to the number of nodes N and increasing the number of nodes increases the cooperation gain $\mathcal{G}^{\text{inc,ideal}}$. Similarly, the cooperation gain for the ILMS algorithm with noisy links can be defined as

$$\mathcal{G}^{\text{inc,noisy}} = \frac{\overline{\eta}^{\text{nc}}}{\overline{\eta}^{\text{inc,noisy}}} \tag{23}$$

Replacing (19) and (13) in (23) we obtain

$$\mathcal{G}^{\text{inc,noisy}} = \frac{\mu^2 \lambda N \sum\limits_{k=1}^{N} \sigma_{v,k}^2}{\mu^2 \lambda \sum\limits_{k=1}^{N} \sigma_{v,k}^2 + (1-2\mu\lambda) \sum\limits_{k=1}^{N} \sigma_{c,k}^2} \tag{24}$$

We can conclude from (24) that in the presence of noisy links, the cooperation gain is not always bigger than 1. We have

$$0 < \mathcal{G}^{\text{inc,noisy}} < N \tag{25}$$

The above equation indicates that for some values of data and channel statistics we may have $\mathcal{G}^{\text{inc,noisy}} < 1$. In fact, the required condition for the ILMS algorithm to outperform the non-cooperative scheme is

$$\mathcal{G}^{\text{inc,noisy}} > 1 \tag{26}$$

or equivalently

$$\mathcal{G}^{\text{inc,noisy}} = \frac{\mu^2 \lambda N \sum\limits_{k=1}^{N} \sigma_{v,k}^2}{\mu^2 \lambda \sum\limits_{k=1}^{N} \sigma_{v,k}^2 + (1-2\mu\lambda) \sum\limits_{k=1}^{N} \sigma_{c,k}^2} > 1 \tag{27}$$

The above equation is a quadratic equation in μ which can be rewritten as

$$a\mu^2 + b\mu + c > 0 \tag{28}$$

where

$$a = (N-1)\lambda \left(\sum\limits_{k=1}^{N} \sigma_{v,k}^2 \right), b = 2\lambda \left(\sum\limits_{k=1}^{N} \sigma_{v,k}^2 \right), c = -\left(\sum\limits_{k=1}^{N} \sigma_{c,k}^2 \right) \tag{29}$$

Now, two different cases are possible:

Case I: $\Delta = b^2 - 4ac < 0$: Since $a > 0$, in this case, for $\forall \mu \in \mathcal{D}$ we have $\mathcal{G}^{\text{inc,noisy}} > 1$ so cooperation yields better steady-state performance.

Case II: $\Delta = b^2 - 4ac > 0$: Let x_1 and x_2 be the roots of equation $a\mu^2 + b\mu + c = 0$.

Since $x_1 x_2 = \dfrac{c}{a} < 0$, roots are of opposite sign. If we assume $x_1 < 0$ and $x_2 > 0$, the inequality (26) holds when

$$x_2 < \mu < \sup\{\mathcal{D}\} \tag{30}$$

Therefore, the above discussion reveals that under noisy communication, cooperation among nodes may not necessarily result in better performance.

4   Simulation Results

We consider a distributed network with $N = 20$ nodes, and choose $M = 4$, $\mathbf{w}^o = 1_M / \sqrt{M}$, $\sigma_{v,k}^2 = 10^{-1}$, and $\sigma_{c,k}^2 = 10^{-4}$. Moreover, we assume that the regressors data arise from independent Gaussian, where $\mathbf{R}_{u,k} = \mathbf{I}$. Fig. 2 shows $\bar{\eta}^{nc}$, $\bar{\eta}^{inc,ideal}$ and $\bar{\eta}^{inc,noisy}$ as a function of step size parameter μ. As we can see, both $\bar{\eta}^{nc}$ and $\bar{\eta}^{inc,ideal}$ are monotonically increasing function of μ and $\bar{\eta}^{inc,ideal} > \bar{\eta}^{nc}$ for all μ. Moreover, for all μ, the difference between $\bar{\eta}^{nc}$ and $\bar{\eta}^{inc,ideal}$ is constant, so that the cooperation gain is constant $\mathcal{G}^{inc,ideal} = N = 20$ (see Fig. 1).

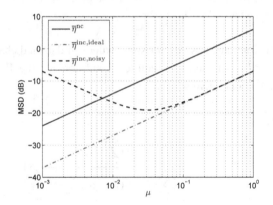

Fig. 1. $\bar{\eta}^{nc}$, $\bar{\eta}^{inc,ideal}$ and $\bar{\eta}^{inc,noisy}$ as a function of step size parameter μ

On the other hand, in noisy links case, the steady-state MSD ($\bar{\eta}^{inc,noisy}$) is not a monotonically increasing function of step size (see from Fig. 2). Specifically, for some values of μ, the non-cooperative scheme provides better performance $\mathcal{G}^{inc,noisy} < 1$; while for some values of μ the ILMS algorithm has better performance ($\mathcal{G}^{inc,noisy} > 1$). Fig. 2 also shows $\bar{\eta}^{inc,noisy}$ in terms of μ.

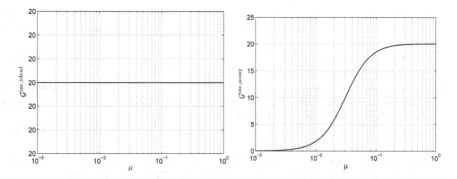

Fig. 2. $\bar{\eta}^{\text{inc,ideal}}$ versus μ (left) and $\bar{\eta}^{\text{inc,noisy}}$ versus μ (right)

5   Conclusion

In this paper, we considered the performance of incremental LMS adaptive networks in the presence of noisy links. We first defined the concept of cooperation gain for incremental adaptive networks. Then we showed that when the communication links are ideal, the ILMS algorithm has better performance than the non-cooperative scheme for every step size value, or equivalently cooperation gain is always bigger than 1. On the other hand, in the presence of noisy links, cooperation gain is not a constant function of μ and depending on data and channel statistics, non-cooperative scheme may have better performance. Finally we presented simulation results to support the derived expressions.

References

1. Lopes, C.G., Sayed, A.H.: Incremental adaptive strategies over distributed networks. IEEE Transactions on Signal Processing 55(8), 4064–4077 (2007)
2. Sayed, A.H., Lopes, C.G.: Distributed recursive least-squares strategies over adaptive networks. In: Proc. Asilomar Conference on Signals, Systems and Computers, pp. 233–237 (2006)
3. Li, L., Chambers, J.A., Lopes, C.G., Sayed, A.H.: Distributed estimation over an adaptive incremental network based on the affine projection algorithm. IEEE Transactions on Signal Processing 58(1), 151–164 (2010)
4. Ram, S.S., Nedic, A., Veeravalli, V.V.: Stochastic incremental gradient descent for estimation in sensor networks. In: Proc. Asilomar Conference on Signals, Systems and Computers, pp. 582–586 (2007)
5. Lopes, C.G., Sayed, A.H.: Randomized incremental protocols over adaptive networks. In: Proc. IEEE ICASSP, Dallas, TX, pp. 3514–3517 (2010)
6. Cattivelli, F., Sayed, A.H.: Analysis of spatial and incremental LMS processing for distributed estimation. IEEE Transactions on Signal Processing 59(4), 1465–1480 (2011)
7. Lopes, C.G., Sayed, A.H.: Diffusion least-mean squares over adaptive networks: Formulation and performance analysis. IEEE Trans. on Signal Processing 56(7), 3122–3136 (2008)

8. Cattivelli, F.S., Lopes, C.G., Sayed, A.H.: Diffusion recursive least-squares for distributed estimation over adaptive networks. IEEE Trans. on Signal Processing 56(5), 1865–1877 (2008)

9. Cattivelli, F.S., Sayed, A.H.: Diffusion LMS strategies for distributed estimation. IEEE Transactions on Signal Processing 58(3), 1035–1048 (2010)

10. Stankovic, S.S., Stankovic, M.S., Stipanovic, D.M.: Decentralized parameter estimation by consensus based stochastic approximation. In: Proc. IEEE Conference on Decision and Control, New Orleans, pp. 1535–1540 (2007)

11. Shin, Y.-J., Sayed, A.H., Shen, X.: Adaptive models for gene networks. PLoS ONE 7(2), e31657 (2012), doi:10.1371/journal.pone.0031657

12. Cattivelli, F.S., Sayed, A.H.: Multilevel diffusion adaptive networks. In: Proc. IEEE Int. Conf. Acoustics, Speech, Signal Processing (ICASSP), Taipei, Taiwan (2009)

13. Schizas, I.D., Mateos, G., Giannakis, G.B.: Distributed LMS for consensus-based in-network adaptive processing. IEEE Transactions on Signal Processing 57(6), 2365–2382 (2009)

14. Khalili, A., Tinati, M.A., Rastegarnia, A.: Performance analysis of distributed incremental LMS algorithm with noisy links. Inter. Journal of distributed sensor networks 2011, 1–10 (2011)

15. Khalili, A., Tinati, M.A., Rastegarnia, A.: Steady-state analysis of incremental LMS adaptive networks with noisy links. IEEE Trans. Signal Processing 59(5), 2416–2421 (2012)

16. Khalili, A., Tinati, M.A., Rastegarnia, A.: Analysis of incremental RLS adaptive networks with noisy links. IEICE Electron. Express 8(9), 623–628 (2011)

17. Khalili, A., Tinati, M.A., Rastegarnia, A., Chambers, J.A.: Steady-state analysis of diffusion LMS adaptive networks with noisy links. IEEE Trans. Signal Processing 60(2), 974–979 (2012)

18. Khalili, A., Tinati, M.A., Rastegarnia, A., Chambers, J.A.: Transient analysis of diffusion least-mean squares adaptive networks with noisy channels. Wiley Int. Journal of Adaptive Control and Signal Processing 26(2), 171–180 (2012)

19. Sayed, A.H.: Fundamentals of Adaptive Filtering. John Wiley and Sons, New York (2003)

Effect of Finite Wordlength on the Performance of an Adaptive Network

Wael M. Bazzi[1], Amir Rastegarnia[2], and Azam Khalili[2]

[1] Electrical and Computer Engineering Department, American University in Dubai
P.O. Box 28282, Dubai, United Arab Emirates
wbazzi@aud.edu
[2] Department of Electrical Engineering, Malayer University
Malayer, 65719-95863, Iran
{a_rastegar,a.khalili}@ieee.org

Abstract. In this paper we consider the performance of incremental least mean square (ILMS) adaptive network when it is implemented in finite-precision arithmetic. We show that unlike the infinite-precision case, the steady-state curve, described in terms of mean square deviation (MSD) is not always a monotonic increasing function of step-size parameter. More precisely, when the quantization level is small, reducing the step-size may increase the steady-state MSD.

Keywords: adaptive networks, distributed estimation, least mean-square (LMS), quantization.

1   Introduction

An adaptive network is a collection of nodes that interact with each other, and function as a single adaptive entity that is able to respond to data in real-time and also track variations in their statistical properties. [1]. Although adaptive networks were initially proposed in the literature to perform decentralized information processing and inference tasks, they are also well-suited to model complex and self-organized behavior encountered in biological systems, such as fish joining together in schools and birds flying in formation [2-4].

Depending on the manner by which the nodes communicate with each other, they may be referred to as incremental algorithms [5-9] or diffusion algorithms [10-13]. Incremental strategies rely on the use of a cyclic path through the network. In general, determining a cyclic path that covers all nodes is an NP-hard problem. The given algorithms in [10–13] use different adaptive filter in their structure, such as LMS, recursive least-squares (RLS), and affine projection. In comparison, in adaptive diffusion implementations, information is processed locally at the nodes and then diffused in real-time across the network and no cyclic path is required.

In the original incremental LMS (ILMS) adaptive network [5], it is assumed that the infinite-precision weights (local estimates) are exchanged among the nodes through ideal links. More precisely, in [5] some theoretical relations which explain the steady-state performance of ILMS algorithm (in terms of mean-square deviation (MSD), excess mean-square error (EMSE), and mean-square error (MSE)) are derived. In [14, 15] we have studied the performance of ILMS estimation algorithm when it is implemented in finite-precision arithmetic. The importance of such a study arises from the fact that the performance of adaptive networks (like ILMS) can vary significantly when they are implemented in finite-precision arithmetic.

In this paper, our objective is to go beyond these earlier works in [14, 15] to show that the steady-state behavior of quantized ILMS adaptive network is different form its unquantized version. More precisely, unlike the infinite-precision case, the MSD curve is not a monotonically increasing function of step-size parameter. We use the derived results in [14, 15] to explain the mentioned result.

Throughout the paper, we adopt boldface letters for random quantities and normal font for nonrandom (deterministic) quantities. The * symbol is used for both complex conjugations for scalars and Hermitian transpose for matrices.

2   Incremental LMS Algorithm

Consider a network composed of N nodes which are used to estimate an unknown vector $w^o \in R^M$ from measurements collected at N nodes in a network. Each node k has access to time-realizations $\{d_k(i), u_{k,i}\}$ of zero-mean spatial data $\{d_k, u_k\}$ where each d_k is a scalar measurement and each u_k is a $1 \times M$ row regression vector. In [2] the ILMS adaptive network has been proposed to estimate w^o. The update equation in ILMS is given by

$$\psi_{k,i} = \psi_{k-1,i} - \mu u_{k,i}^* \left(e_k(i) \right) \tag{1}$$

Where $e_k(i) = d_k(i) - u_{k,i}\psi_{k-1,i}$ and μ is the step-size. In (1) the $M \times 1$ vector $\psi_{k,i}$ denotes the local estimate of w^o at node k at time i. Due to incremental cooperation, the calculated estimates are sequentially circulated from node to node (see Fig. 1).

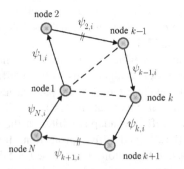

Fig. 1. A schematic of ILMS adaptive network

3   Quantized Incremental LMS, (Q-ILMS)

The ILMS algorithm can be implemented in finite-precision at every node k as shown in Fig. 2. In the finite-precision case the update equation (1) changes to [7, 8]

$$\psi_{k,i}^q = \psi_{k-1,i}^q + \mu u_{k,i}^* e_k^q(i) - p_{k,i} \tag{2}$$

where e_k^q and $\psi_{k,i}^q$ are the quantized values of e_k and $\psi_{k,i}$ respectively. Moreover, $p_{k,i}$ stands for the effect of quantization errors in evaluation of $\psi_{k,i}^q$. Its covariance matrix is given by [7]

$$R_{p,k} = E\{p_{k,i}p_{k,i}^*\} = 2\sigma_r^2 I_M + \mu^2 \sigma_r^2 E\{\mid e_k^q(i) \mid^2\} \tag{3}$$

In (3) σ_r^2 is the variance of quantization error which is given by

$$\sigma_r^2 = \frac{1}{12}\frac{L_r^2}{2^{n_r}} \quad \sigma_r^2 = \frac{1}{12}\frac{L_r^2}{2^{n_r}} \tag{4}$$

where n_r and L_r, denote the number of bits and the saturation level of quantization.

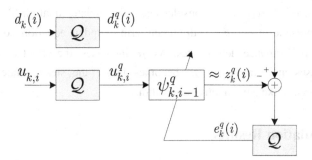

Fig. 2. A block diagram representation of quantized implementation of ILMS algorithm at node k

The steady-state performance of adaptive networks can be expressed in terms of MSD at every node k which is defined as

$$\eta_k = E\{\lVert w^o - \psi_{k-1,\infty} \rVert^2\} \tag{5}$$

As we have shown in [7], for Q-ILMS with Gaussian data, the MSD at every node k can be approximated as

$$\eta_k \approx (\mu_1^2 \sigma_{\bar{v},1}^2 \lambda_1^T + b_1^T + \cdots + \mu_N^2 \sigma_{\bar{v},N}^2 \lambda_k^T + b_N^T)\Omega^{-1}c \tag{6}$$

where $\sigma_{\bar{v},k}^2$ variance of modified noise variable defined in [7]. The other symbols are Λ_k is a diagonal matrix with the eigenvalues of $R_{u,k}$, Γ_k is a diagonal matrix with the eigenvalues of $R_{p,k}$, $\lambda_k = \mathrm{diag}\{\Lambda_k\}$ (a $M \times 1$ vector), $b_k = \mathrm{diag}\{\Gamma_k\}$ (a $M \times 1$ vector), $c = \mathrm{diag}\{I_M\}$ (a $M \times 1$ vector), and also

$$\Omega = 2(\mu_1\Lambda_1 + \mu_2\Lambda_2 + \cdots \mu_N\Lambda_N) \tag{7}$$

To show the non-monotonic dependence of the MSD with respect to the step-size in finite-precision case we assume that for all nodes we have $R_{u,k} = \lambda I_M$, $\mu_k = \mu$, $\sigma_{\bar{v},k}^2 = \sigma_{\bar{v}}^2$ and $b_k = \gamma\mathrm{diag}\{I_M\}$. Using these assumptions we have

$$\eta_k = \frac{M(\mu^2\sigma_{\bar{v}}^2 + \gamma)}{2\mu} \tag{8}$$

which clearly is not a monotonic increasing function of μ. We can also easily see that as the number of bits (i.e. n_r) increases, we have $\sigma_r^2 \to 0$ and $(b_k) \to 0$. As a result, η_k approaches the MSD of a ILMS adaptive networks which is a monotonic increasing function of μ.

To explain this behavior we consider again the update equation (2). For small μ, the channel noise term say $p_{k,i}$ is dominant term in update equation, so as $\mu \to 0$, the steady state performance deteriorates. As μ increases, the effect of channel noise term decreases and finally as μ becomes larger the steady state performance deteriorates again like any adaptive algorithm.

4   Simulation Results

In this section we present the simulation results to clarify the discussions. To this aim, we consider a network with $N = 15$ nodes with independent Gaussian regressors where their eigenvalue spread is 1. We assume that unknown vector $w^o = [1\,1\,1\,1]^T$ relates to the $\{d_k(i), u_{k,i}\}$ via $d_k(i) = u_{k,i}w^o + v_k(i)$ where $v_k(i)$ is white noise term with variance $\sigma_{v,k}^2 \in (0, 10^{-1})$. To implement the Q-ILMS, we set $L_r = 1$. The steady-state curves are generated by running the network learning process for 2000 iterations. The MSD curve is obtained by averaging the last 200 samples. Each curve is obtained by averaging over 100 independent experiments.

Fig. 3 shows the global MSD (which is defined as $1/N\sum_{k=1}^{N}\eta_k$) for different values of μ and n_r (including sign bit). As it is clear from Fig. 3, there the steady-state curve is not a monotonic increasing function of step-size. Moreover, for sufficiently large number of bits, the MSD curve becomes a monotonic increasing function of μ.

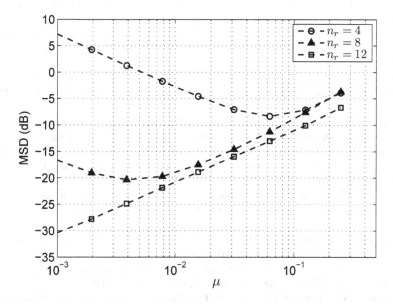

Fig. 3. The steady-state MSD (in dB) curve as a function of μ and for different number of bits n_r

5   Conclusions

In this paper, we considered the steady-state evaluation of the finite-precision DILMS algorithm. Using the results derived in [7] and [8] it was shown that unlike the infinite-precision case, in the quantized case the steady-state MSD curve is not always a monotonic increasing function of step-size parameter. Specifically, when the quantization level is small, reducing the step-size may increase the steady-state MSD. This behavior of adaptive networks has also been observed when the links between the nodes in the network are noisy (see [9, 10]).

References

1. Sayed, A.H., Cattivelli, F.: Distributed adaptive learning mechanisms. In: Haykin, S., Ray Liu, K.J. (eds.) Handbook on Array Processing and Sensor Networks, pp. 695–722. Wiley (2009)
2. Tu, S.Y., Sayed, A.H.: Mobile adaptive networks. IEEE J. Selected Topics on Signal Processing 5(4), 649–664 (2011)
3. Chen, J., Sayed, A.H.: Bio-inspired cooperative optimization with application to bacteria motility. In: Proc. ICASSP, Prague, Czech Republic, pp. 5788–5791 (2011)
4. Li, J., Sayed, A.H.: Modeling bee swarming behavior through diffusion adaptation with asymmetric information sharing. EURASIP Journal on Advances in Signal Processing 18 (2012), doi:10.1186/1687-6180-2012-18

5. Lopes, C.G., Sayed, A.H.: Incremental adaptive strategies over distributed networks. IEEE Trans. on Signal Process. 55(8), 4064–4077 (2007)
6. Ram, S.S., Nedic, A., Veeravalli, V.V.: Stochastic incremental gradient descent for estimation in sensor networks. In: Proc. Asilomar Conf. Signals, Systems, Computers, Pacific Grove, CA, pp. 582–586 (2007)
7. Sayed, A.H., Lopes, C.G.: Distributed recursive least-squares strategies over adaptive networks. In: Proc. Asilomar Conf. Signals, Systems, Computers, Monterey, CA, pp. 233–237 (2006)
8. Li, L., Chambers, J.A.: A new incremental affine projection based adaptive learning scheme for distributed networks. Signal Process 88(10), 2599–2603 (2008)
9. Lopes, C.G., Sayed, A.H.: Randomized incremental protocols over adaptive networks. In: Proc. IEEE Int. Conf. Acoustics, Speech, Signal Processing (ICASSP), Dallas, TX, pp. 3514–3517 (2010)
10. Lopes, C.G., Sayed, A.H.: Diffusion least-mean squares over adaptive networks: Formulation and performance analysis. IEEE Trans. Signal Process. 56(7), 3122–3136 (2008)
11. Cattivelli, F.S., Sayed, A.H.: Diffusion LMS strategies for distributed estimation. IEEE Trans. Signal Process. 58(3), 1035–1048 (2010)
12. Cattivelli, F.S., Sayed, A.H.: Diffusion strategies for distributed Kalman filtering and smoothing. IEEE Trans. Autom. Control 55(9), 2069–2084 (2010)
13. Cattivelli, F.S., Lopes, C.G., Sayed, A.H.: Diffusion recursive least-squares for distributed estimation over adaptive networks. IEEE Trans. Signal Process. 56(5), 1865–1877 (2008)
14. Rastegarnia, A., Tinati, M.A., Khalili, A.: Performance analysis of quantized incremental LMS algorithm for distributed adaptive estimation. Signal Process 90(8), 2621–2627 (2010)
15. Rastegarnia, A., Tinati, M.A., Khalili, A.: Steady-state analysis of quantized distributed incremental LMS algorithm without Gaussian restriction. Signal, Image and Video Process (to appear)
16. Khalili, A., Tinati, M.A., Rastegarnia, A.: Steady-state analysis of incremental LMS adaptive networks with noisy links. IEEE Trans. Signal Processing 56(5), 2416–2421 (2011)
17. Khalili, A., Tinati, M.A., Rastegarnia, A., Chambers, J.A.: Steady-state analysis of diffusion LMS adaptive networks with noisy links. IEEE Trans. Signal Processing 60(2), 974–979 (2012)

Dynamic Neuro-genetic Weights Connection Strategy for Isolated Spoken Malay Speech Recognition System

Noraini Seman, Zainab Abu Bakar, and Nordin Abu Bakar

Faculty of Computer and Mathematical Sciences,
Universiti Teknologi MARA (UiTM), 40450 Shah Alam,
Selangor, Malaysia
{aini,zainab,nordin}@tmsk.uitm.edu.my

Abstract. This paper presents the fusion of artificial intelligence (AI) learning algorithms that combined genetic algorithms (GA) and neural network (NN) methods. These both methods were used to find the optimum weights for the hidden and output layers of feed-forward artificial neural network (ANN) model. Both algorithms are the separate modules and we proposed dynamic connection strategy for combining both algorithms to improve the recognition performance for isolated spoken Malay speech recognition. There are two different GA techniques used in this research, one is standard GA and slightly different technique from standard GA also has been proposed. Thus, from the results, it was observed that the performance of proposed GA algorithm while combined with NN shows better than standard GA and NN models alone. Integrating the GA with feed-forward network can improve mean square error (MSE) performance and with good connection strategy by this two stage training scheme, the recognition rate can be increased up to 99%.

Keywords: Artificial Neural Network, Conjugate Gradient, Genetic Algorithm, Global Optima, Feed-forward Network.

1 Introduction

Speech is the most natural way of communication for humans. The aim of speech recognition is to create machines that are capable of receiving speech from humans (or some spoken commands) and taking action upon this spoken information [1]. Although it was once thought to be a straightforward problem, many decades of research has revealed the fact that speech recognition is a rather difficult task to achieve, with several dimensions of difficulty due to the non-stationary nature of speech, the vocabulary size, speaker dependency issues, etc. [1]. However, there have been quite remarkable advances and many successful applications in speech recognition field, especially with the advances in computing technology beginning in the 1980s.

In recent years, there has been an increasing interest in classification approach to improvements the recognition of speech sounds. Various approaches have been made up to develop the speech recognizer or classifier and over the years there are three

V.V. Das and P.M. El-Kafrawy (Eds.): SPIT 2012, LNICST 117, pp. 121–130, 2014.

speech recognition approaches that have been developed. Dynamic time warping (DTW) is the oldest approach and is an algorithm for measuring similarity between two sequences which may vary in time or speed [2][3]. However, this technology has been displaced by the more accurate Hidden Markov Model (HMM) that has become the primary tool for speech recognition since the 1970s. Hidden Markov Model (HMM) is a statistical model in which the system being modeled is assumed to be a Markov process with unknown parameters. This algorithm is often used due to its simplicity and feasibility of use.

However in late 1980s, artificial intelligent (AI) based approaches are considered for training the system to recognize speech using an artificial neural network (ANN) algorithms. This technology is capable of solving much more complicated recognition tasks, and can handle low quality, noisy data, and speaker independence. Researchers have started to consider the ANN as an alternative to the HMM approach in speech recognition due to two broad reasons: speech recognition can basically be viewed as a pattern classification problem, and ANN can perform complex classification tasks [4]. Given sufficient input-output data, ANN is able to approximate any continuous function to arbitrary accuracy.

However, the main obstacles that faced by NN model is a longer learning time when the data set becomes greater. NN learning is highly important and is undergoing intense research in both biological and artificial networks. A learning algorithm is the heart of the NN based system. Error Back-Propagation (EBP) [5] is the most cited learning algorithm and yet powerful method to train ANN model [6]. However, there are several drawbacks in the EBP learning algorithms; where the main basic defect is the convergence of EBP algorithms which are generally slow since it is based on *gradient descent* minimization method. Gradient search techniques tend to get trapped at local minima.

Recently, many researchers tried to overcome this problem by using the stochastic algorithm, such as Genetic Algorithms (GA) [7], since they are less sensitive to local minima. Genetic Algorithm (GA) based learning provides an alternative way to learn for the ANN, which involves controlling the learning complexity by adjusting the number of weights of the ANN. However, GA is generally slow compared to the fastest versions of gradient-based algorithms due to its nature to find a global solution in the search space. Thus, to have better time to converge, it is a good idea to combine the global search GA method with matrix solution second order gradient based learning methods known as Conjugate Gradient (CG) method to find the optimal values for the weights in two-layer Feed-Forward NN architecture. Therefore, we proposed fusion techniques of artificial intelligence (AI) algorithm which combines GA in the first layer and CG in the second layer to achieve optimum weights for FF network. Our algorithm aims to combine the capacity of GA and CG in avoiding local minima and the fast execution of the NN learning algorithm.

In this work, the GA-ANN model is used for validation recognition performances of isolated spoken Malay utterances and evolution in network connection weights using GA will be highlighted. Malay language is a branch of the Austronesian (Malayo-Polynesian) language family, spoken as a native language by more than 33,000,000 persons distributed over the Malay Peninsula, Sumatra, Borneo, and numerous smaller islands of the area and widely used in Malaysia and Indonesia as a second language [8]. The direction of this work is composed into several sections, where Section 2, will explain the Malay speech materials. The details of the methods and implementation of the methods will be described in Section 3. Section 4 describes the results and discussions on the experimental of the training and validation approaches. Lastly, in Section 5, the paper is ended with conclusions.

2   Speech Collection

All experiments are conducted on the whole *hansard* document of Malaysian House of Parliament that consists of spontaneous and formal speeches. *Hansard* document is the daily record of the words spoken in the hearings of parliamentary committees. *Hansard* is not a verbatim (word for word) record of parliamentary business but is a useful record that enables interested people to check what members and senators have said and what witnesses have told parliamentary committees. The document comprises of live video and audio recorded that consists of disturbance and interruption of speakers, and contain noisy environment from different kind of speakers (Malay, Chinese and Indian). The reason of choosing this kind of data is due to its natural and spontaneous speaking styles during each session.

The most frequently words used during eight hours of one day Parliament session are determined. After some analysis, the quantitative information shows that only 50 words that most commonly used by the speakers with more than 25 repetitions. The selection of 50 words are the root words that formed by joining one or two syllables structures (CV/VC – consonant or vowel structure) that can be pronounced exactly as it is written and can control the distribution of the Malay language vocalic segments. However, the vocabulary used in this study consisted of seven words as given in Table 1, due to different selection according to their groups of syllable structure with maximum 25 repetitions and spoken by 20 speakers. Thus, the speech data set consists of 3500 utterances of isolated Malay spoken words. For the experiments, all the audio files were re-sampled at a sampling rate of 16 kHz, where the frame size is 256 kbps. All the signals data will be converted into a form that is suitable for further computer processing and analysis.

Table 1. Selected Malay words as speech target sounds

Words	Structures	Occurrences
ADA (*have*)	V + CV	3037
BOLEH (*can*)	CV + CVC	5684
DENGAN (*with*)	CV + CCVC	7433
IALAH (*is*)	VV + CVC	4652
SAYA (*i*)	CV + CV	6763
UNTUK (*for*)	CV + CVC	4101
YANG (*that*)	CVCC	4718

3   Methods and Implementation

The general idea towards this work is to generate a speech recognizer for isolated spoken Malay utterances by implementing genetic algorithm (GA) with Artificial Neural Network (ANN) to determine the suitable network architecture and to improve the recognition performance in an offline mode. The overall process of this model is described as a block diagram as shown in Fig. 1 below.

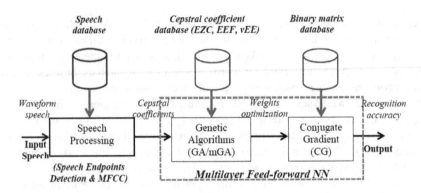

Fig. 1. Block diagram of the isolated spoken Malay speech recognition system

All the speech inputs will go through the first block of speech processing techniques that involved spectral analysis, speech boundary or endpoint detection methods, time axis normalization, feature extraction to form vector input signals for further analysis and recognition purposes. The pre-processing block designed in speech recognition aims towards reducing the complexity of the problem before the next stage start to work with the data.

Classification is the next step to identify input speeches based on the feature parameters. A two-layer feed-forward neural network with one hidden layer and one output layer was used in this work. Only one hidden layer was utilized as it had proved that an ANN with one hidden layer was sufficient in performing process mapping arbitrarily [9]. The approach combines genetic algorithm (GA) with matrix solution methods to achieve optimum weights for hidden and output layers. The proposed method is to apply genetic algorithm (GA) in the first layer and conjugate gradient (CG) method in the second layer of the FF ANN architecture as depicted in Fig. 2. These two methods are combined together using proposed dynamic connection strategy, where a feedback mechanism exists for both the algorithms.

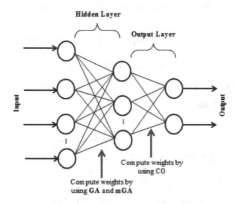

Fig. 2. The two-layer ANN architecture for the proposed weights connection of Neuro-Genetic learning algorithms

The proposed method will be compare with the standard ANN that used error back-propagation (EBP) learning algorithm. In this study, trial and error approach was used to determine the optimum topology of the network. It was found that the optimum topology of the network could be best estimated using a network with 20 hidden neurons. Using this network topology, the training and validation errors were 1.9143×10^{-5} and 1.6126×10^{-4} respectively.

In this work, we proposed two variations of genetic algorithm (GA) that can be applied for weights searching in the first layer of ANN. The first strategy is the primitive or straight GA which is applied to ANN phenotype using a direct encoding scheme and we follow exactly the work done by [10]. This GA methodology uses the standard two point crossover or interpolation as recombination operator and Gaussian noise addition as mutation operator. Meanwhile, as the second strategy, we proposed slight variations of the standard GA that is used for testing and known as mutation Genetic Algorithm (**mGA**), where the only genetic operator to be considered is mutation. The mutation is applied using a variance operator. The stepwise operation for mGA can be described as follows:

Step 1: Uniform distribution technique will be used to initialize all the hidden layer weights of a closed interval range of [-1, +1]. A sample genotype for the lower half gene from the population pool for input (n), hidden units (h), output (m) and number of patterns (p) can be written as in Equation (1).

$$\begin{vmatrix} x_{11}\mu_{11}x_{12}\mu_{12}...x_{1n}\mu_{1n}x_{21}\mu_{21}x_{22}\mu_{22}... \\ x_{2n}\mu_{2n}...x_{h1}\mu_{h1}x_{h2}\mu_{h2}...x_{hn}\mu_{hn} \end{vmatrix} \quad (1)$$

where, range (x) initially is set between the closed interval [-1, +1]. Each values of variance vectors (μ) is initialized by a Gaussian distribution of mean (0) and standard deviation (1).

Step 2: The fitness for the population is calculated based on the phenotype and the target for the ANN.

$$netOutput = f(hid * weight) \tag{2}$$

where, hid is the output matrix from the hidden layer neurons, $weight$ is the weight matrix output neurons and f is the sigmoid function is computed as in Equation (3) and (4).

$$RMSError = \sqrt{\frac{\sum_{i=1}^{n}(netOutput - net)^2}{n * p}} \tag{3}$$

$$popRMSError_i = norm(RMSError_i) \tag{4}$$

Step 3: Each individual population vector ($\mathbf{w}_i$, $\mathbf{\eta}_i$), $i = 1, 2,..., \mu$ creates a single offspring vector ($\mathbf{w}'_i$, $\mathbf{\eta}'_i$) for $j = 1,2,...,n$ as in Equation (5) and (6).

$$\eta'_i(j) = \eta_i(j)\exp(\tau'N(0,1) + \tau Nj(0,1)) \tag{5}$$

$$w'_i(j) = w_i(j) + \eta'_i(j)Nj(0,1) \tag{6}$$

Step 4: Repeat **step 2**, if the convergence for the mGA is not satisfied.

Meanwhile, the weights for the output layer is computed using the conjugate gradient (CG) method where the output of the hidden layer is computed as sigmoid function [f(.)] for the weighted sum of its input. The CG algorithm is a numerical optimization technique designed to speed up the convergence of the back-propagation algorithm. It is in essence a line search technique along any set of conjugate directions, instead of along the negative gradient direction as is done in the steepest descent approach. The power of the CG algorithm comes from the fact that it avoids the calculation of the Hessian matrix or second order derivatives, yet it still converges to the exact minimum of a quadratic function with n parameters in at most n steps [11]. The conjugate gradient algorithm starts by selecting the initial search direction as the negative of the gradient as in Equation (7) and (8).

$$\underline{p}_0 = -\underline{g}_0 \tag{7}$$

$$\underline{g}_i = \nabla \underline{F}(\underline{x})|_{x=x_k} \tag{8}$$

where $\underline{x}$ is the vector containing the weights and biases and $\underline{F}(\underline{x})$ is the performance function, that is the mean square error (MSE). The search directions ($\underline{p}_i$) are called *conjugate* with respect to a positive definite Hessian matrix if,

$$\underline{p}_i^T \underline{A}_{\underline{p}i} = 0 \quad \text{for } i \neq j$$

(9)

where $\underline{A}$ represents the Hessian matrix [$\nabla^2 \underline{F}(\underline{x})$].

The above condition can be modified to avoid the calculation of the Hessian matrix for practical purposes and is given as in Equation (10).

$$\nabla \underline{g}_i^T \underline{p}_i = 0 \quad \text{for } i \neq j$$

(10)

The new weights and biases are computed by taking a step with respect to the learning rate (α_i) along the search direction that minimizes the error as in Equation (11).

$$\underline{x}_{i+1} = \underline{x}_i + \alpha_i \underline{p}_i$$

(11)

where, the learning rate (α_i) for the current step is given by Equation (12).

$$\underline{p}_{i+1} = -\underline{g}_{i+1} + \beta_{i+1} \underline{p}_i$$

(12)

where the scalar (β_i) which can be viewed as a momentum added to the algorithm (Duda et al. 2001) is given by one of three common choices where we adopted *Fletcher and Reeves* formula for the current implementation.

$$\beta_i = \frac{\underline{g}_{i+1}^T \underline{g}_{i+1}}{\underline{g}_i^T \underline{g}_i}$$

(13)

The algorithm iterates along successive conjugate directions until it converges to the minimum, or a predefined error criterion is achieved. As is obvious from the above steps, the conjugate gradient algorithm requires batch mode training, where weight and bias updates are applied after the whole training set is passed through the network, since the gradient is computed as an average over the whole training set [6]. In this work, since the network architecture is a two-layer feed-forward ANN, the input nodes in the first layer will begin with the range compression for the applied input (based on pre-specified range limits) so that it is in the open interval (0,1) and transmit the result to all the nodes in the second layer, which is the hidden layer. The hidden nodes perform a weighted sum on its input and then pass through the sigmoidal activation function before sending the result to the next layer, which is the output layer. The output layers also perform the same weighted sum operation on its input and pass through the sigmoidal activation function to produce the final result. The vital and challenging task is to find suitable rules of joining two different techniques for the given ANN architecture. The combination of the GA and the CG method provides much possibilities of joining the two different methods [10].

We proposed the dynamic connection strategy for combining these two methods, where the CG method is called after one generation run for GA/mGA method. The best fitness population is halved and the upper half is saved as the weights for output layers. Then, the GA/mGA is run for the remaining generation and the flowchart of the process is illustrated as depicted in Fig. 3.

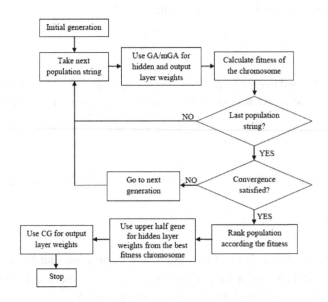

Fig. 3. The proposed dynamic weights connection strategy process diagram

4   Results and Discussion

A total of 3500 data were generated using these model inputs for modeling purposes. The data were equally divided into training and testing set. The network was obtained after undergoing a series of training using two different algorithms. In order to improve network generalization ability, early stopping techniques was applied to CG training. In this technique, validation error was monitored during the training process. When the validation error increases for a specified number of iterations, the training was stopped to prevent over fitting. For weights evolved using GA, the number of generation was used to stop the iteration.

The word recognition results obtained with the average classification rate and 95% confidence interval for the training and testing sets of all the methods used in the study is depicted in Table 2. There are 50 experiments were done to choose perfect Hidden Neurons Number (HNN) for the models. Here we specified the network configuration with the best HNN is (50-20) of multilayer feed-forward network structure.

Table 2. Confidence interval for training and testing sets with different methods

OVERALL CLASSIFICATION RATE			WORDS	DATA BELONGING TO:											
EBP	GA+CG	VGA+CG		ADA			BOLEH			DENGAN			IALAH		
93.17%	97.94%	99.17%		EBP	GA+CG	VGA+CG	EBP	GA+CG	VGA+CG	EBP	GA+CG	VGA+CG	EBP	GA+CG	VGA+CG
DATA IDENTIFIED AS:			ADA	95.88333	99.05417	99.72083	0.279167	0.045833	0.008333	3.875	1.053833	0.158333	0.25833	0.033335	0.004167
			BOLEH	1.345833	0.3375	0.075	95.46917	96.80833	99.56417	2.4625	1.279167	0.5875	1.295833	0.739333	0.304167
			DENGAN	1.9125	0.479167	0.1625	0.845833	0.283333	0.1375	89.475	96.67083	98.43333	3.670833	1.0875	0.591667
			IALAH	0.016667	0.004167	0	0.7	0.204167	0.045833	1.683333	0.625	0.208333	88.10417	96.61667	98.41667
			SAYA	0	0	0	0.908333	0.354167	0.058333	0.575	0.066667	0.008333	2.5	0.75	0.454167
			UNTUK	0.145833	0.05	0.125	1.7525	0.304167	0.095833	1.170833	0.158333	0.0375	1.33333	0.3125	0.129167
			YANG	0.695833	0.075	0.029167	0.025	0	0	0.758333	0.168667	0.066667	1.0375	0.266667	0.1

OVERALL CLASSIFICATION RATE			WORDS	DATA BELONGING TO:								
EBP	GA+CG	VGA+CG		SAYA			UNTUK			YANG		
93.17%	97.94%	99.17%		EBP	GA+CG	VGA+CG	EBP	GA+CG	VGA+CG	EBP	GA+CG	VGA+CG
DATA IDENTIFIED AS:			ADA	0.275	0.029167	0.004167	0.004167	0	0	0.579167	0.066667	0.016667
			BOLEH	2.033333	0.6875	0.245833	1.658333	0.55	0.183333	0.05	0.008333	0
			DENGAN	0.258333	0.033333	0.029167	0.075	0	0.004167	0.15	0.033333	0.0125
			IALAH	3.458333	1.55	0.725	3.325	0.875	0.308333	0.133333	0.0625	0.045833
			SAYA	89.10833	96.17917	98.525	0.591667	0.108333	0.0125	0.058333	0.0125	0
			UNTUK	3.658333	1.175	0.416667	94.20833	98.44167	99.4875	0.1	0	0
			YANG	1.208333	0.245833	0.054167	0.1375	0.025	0.004167	98.92917	99.81667	99.925

The maximum number of epochs for network training was set to 1,000 after observing that convergence was reached within the range. From the result, it shows that the best network trained using the coalition of different AI algorithms. Here, the proposed algorithm using mutation Genetic Algorithm (mGA) and Conjugate Gradient (CG) yielded 99.17% of overall classification rate. The proposed method outperformed other two training networks where 97.94% obtained from fusion of standard GA and CG, meanwhile standard ANN using EBP algorithm yielded 93.17% is the lowest among other two algorithms. Although the difference in overall classification performances between standard GA and CG (GA+CG) and the mGA with CG (mGA+CG) may seem small, the difference between the two algorithms becomes more significant when the individual confusions matrices and 95% confidence interval plots are examined.

The degradation in recognition is very noticeable on all the vocabulary words except from word "ADA" and "YANG". The spreads in confidence intervals of the words "BOLEH" and "UNTUK" obtained with the GA+CG algorithm are 16.25% and 18.55% respectively. Whereas the spreads for the same words obtained with the mGA+CG method are 5.6% and 3.7% respectively. Therefore, the mGA+CG leads to more accurate and reliable learning algorithm to trained the FF network for this word recognition study than the standard GA+CG algorithm does.

Since the calculation started with random initial weights, each run produced different results even though the network architecture was maintained. Thus, in order to obtain an optimal solution, repeated runs were practiced and only the best result was recorded. This can be done because the convergence time of CG training method was really fast.

Owing to this fact, GA combined with CG has some given advantages. Moreover, the performances in the validation sets were considered better than standard ANN using EBP algorithm and this proved that this scheme was adequate with a sufficient accuracy.

5   Conclusions

Based on the results obtained in this study, ANN is an efficient and effective empirical modeling tool for estimating the speech process variable by using other easily available process measurements. The use of multilayer feed-forward network with delay values in model input variables is sufficient to give estimation to any arbitrary accuracy. Even though the conventional EBP method is widely used, but the GA is more preferable as the optimal solution searching is population based that using gradient information. Integrating the GA with CG as second order gradient based learning method can improve MSE performance and by this two stage training scheme, the recognition rate can be increasing up to 85%. However, speech recognition rate still has room for improvement, where much effort is needed to improve GA method for speeding up the learning process in ANN model.

References

1. Deller, J.R., Proakis, J.G., Hansen, J.H.L.: Discrete-Time Processing of Speech Signal. Macmillan, New York (1993)
2. Itakura, F.: Minimum prediction residual principle applied to speech recognition. IEEE Transactions on Acoustic, Speech and Signal Processing 1975 23(1), 67–72 (1975)
3. Sakoe, H., Chiba, S.: Dynamic programming algorithm optimization for spoken word recognition. IEEE Transactions on Acoustic, Speech and Signal Processing 26(1), 43–49 (1978)
4. Panayiota, P., Costa, N., Costantinos, S.P.: Classification capacity of a modular neural network implementing neurally inspired architecture and training rules. IEEE Transactions on Neural Networks 15(3), 597–612 (2004)
5. Rumelhart, D.E., Hinton, G.E., Williams, R.J.: Learning internal representation by error propagation. In: Parallel Distributed Processing, Exploring the Macro Structure of Cognition. MIT Press, Cambridge (1986)
6. Duda, R.O., Hart, P.E., Stork, D.G.: Pattern Classification, 2nd edn. Wiley-Interscience, New York (2001)
7. Goldberg, D.E.: Genetic Algorithm in Search, Optimization and Machine Learning. Addison-Wesley, Reading (1989)
8. Britannica, Encyclopedia Britannica Online (2007), http://www.britannica.com/eb/article-9050292
9. Hornik, K.J., Stinchcombe, D., White, H.: Multilayer Feedforward Networks are Universal Approximators. Neural Networks 2(5), 359–366 (1989)
10. Ghosh, R., Yearwood, J., Ghosh, M., Bagirov, A.: Hybridization of neural learning algorithms using evolutionary and discrete gradient approaches. Computer Sciernce Journal 1(3), 387–394 (2005)
11. Hagan, M.T., Demuth, H.B., Beale, M.H.: Neural Network Design. University of Colorado, Campus Publishing Service (1996)

Multi Objective Linear Array Synthesis Using Differential Evolution and Modified Invasive Weed Optimization Techniques

G. LalithaManohar[1], A.T. Praveen Kumar[2], and K.R. Subhashini[2]

[1] Electronic Department, AMA University, Bahrain
lalitha.amaiu@gmail.com
[2] Dept. of Electrical Engg, NIT, Rourkela-769008, India
{pk.vizag,subppy}@gmail.com

Abstract. A radiation pattern synthesis methods based on the ecological inspired equations is proposed for linear antenna arrays. The amplitude weights of the elements are optimized by heuristic evolutionary tools like Differential Evolution (DE) and Invasive weed optimization to maintain a multi objective specified pattern. The characteristics of the two algorithms are explored by experimenting on a multi task fitness function .The simulation study claims that the DE is arguably a powerful tool in terms of computational time. This paper provides a comprehensive coverage and comparative study of the two above said algorithms, focusing on the pattern synthesis.

Keywords: Pattern synthesis, Antenna arrays, Differential Evolution, Multi-Objective fitness function, Invasive weed optimization.

1 Introduction

The synthesis of equispaced linear array patterns with a shaped beam has been considered by some authors in the specialized literature [1]. There are many applications where the antenna pattern is required to be shaped to achieve a desired effect. In this paper a technique for the synthesis of shaped beam antenna pattern of a linear array is described .The fields radiated from a linear array are a superposition of the fields radiated by each element in the presence of other elements. Each element has an excitation parameter and this can be individually adjusted so that the excitation can be as desired. The excitation of each element will be complex, with amplitude and phase. Antenna array synthesis essentially involves determination of the amplitude and phase of the elements that will produce a desired radiation pattern. The synthesis of an antenna array with a specific radiation pattern, limited by several constraints is a nonlinear optimization problem. Evolutionary search method provides an efficient way to choose the design parameters. Although this method has been successfully applied in many areas such as Digital communication [2], signal processing [3], it is not well known to the electromagnetic community. It is the goal of this paper to introduce Evolutionary techniques to the electromagnetic community and demonstrate its great potential in electromagnetic optimizations.

V.V. Das and P.M. El-Kafrawy (Eds.): SPIT 2012, LNICST 117, pp. 131–136, 2014.

Antenna array optimization has received a great attention in the electromagnetic community. Unlike deterministic algorithms, one does not need expert knowledge of antenna's physics to achieve optimal result. In Section 2 proposed algorithms DE and IWO for training the Linear antenna array is described. Section 3 is dedicated for discussion and experimental results.

2   Overview of DE and IWO

IWO is a population-based algorithm that replicates the colonizing behaviour of weeds. The algorithm for IWO may be summarized as follows:

- A finite number of weeds are initialized randomly spread over the entire D-dimensional search space. This initial population of each generation will be termed as $X = \{x_1, x_2, x_3 \ldots x_m\}$
- Each member of the population X is allowed to produce seeds within a specified region centered at its own position. The number of seeds produced by X_i, $i \in \{1,2\ldots\ldots,m\}$ depends on its relative fitness in the population with respect to the best and worst fitness. The number of seeds produced by any weed varies linearly from $seed_{min}$ to $seed_{max}$ with $seed_{min}$ for the worst member and $seed_{max}$ for the best member in the population.
- The generated seeds are being randomly distributed over the D- dimensional search space by normally distributed random numbers with mean equal to zero; but varying variance. This step ensures that the produced seeds will be generated around the parent weed, leading to a local search around each plant. However, the standard deviation (SD) of the random function is made to decrease over the iterations. If sd_{max} and sd_{min} be the maximum and minimum standard deviation and if pow be a real no. , then the standard deviation for a particular iteration may be given as in equation

$$sd_{ITER} = \left(\frac{iter_{max}-iter}{iter_{max}}\right)^{pow} (sd_{max} - sd_{min}) + sd_{min} \tag{1}$$

- Some modifications are incorporated in the classical IWO algorithm to enhance the performance. IWO with the suggested modifications performs much better than the classical IWO; the modified standard deviation for a particular iteration may be given as in equation

$$sd_{ITER} = \left(\frac{iter_{max}-iter}{iter_{max}}\right)^{pow} |cos(iter)| \ (sd_{max} - sd_{min}) + sd_{min} \tag{2}$$

- Fig.1 illustrates the decrement of sd with iterations for classical IWO and the modified IWO.
- The |cos(iter)| term adds an enveloped as well as periodical variation in sd, which helps in exploring the better solutions quickly and prevents the new solutions from discarding an optimal solution when the sd is relatively large. This facilitates quicker detection of optimal solutions and better results as compared to the classical IWO.

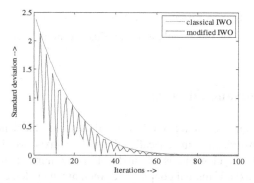

Fig. 1. Comparison of the variations of standard deviation (sd) with iterations for the classical and modified IWO

A differential evolution algorithm (DEA) is an evolutionary computation method that was originally introduced by Storn and Price in 1995. DE uses a population P of size Np, composed of floating point encoded individuals that evolve over G generations to reach an optimal solution. Each individual Xi is a vector that contains as many parameters as the problem decision variables D.

$$P^{(G)} = [X_i^{(G)}, \ldots\ldots\ldots X_{N_p}^{(G)}]$$

$$X_i^{(G)} = [X_{1,i}^{(G)}, \ldots\ldots\ldots X_{D,i}^{(G)}]^T, \ i = 1, \ldots, N_p \tag{3}$$

The optimization process in differential evolution is carried out with three basic operations viz, mutation, crossover and selection. This algorithm starts by creating an initial population of $N\,p$ vectors. Random values are assigned to each decision parameter in every vector according to

$$X_{j,i}^{(0)} = X_j^{min} + \eta_j * (X_j^{max} - X_j^{min}) \tag{4}$$

Where $j = 1, \ldots\ldots\ldots, D$; X_j^{min} and X_j^{max} are the lower and upper bounds of the jth decision parameter and η_j is a uniformly distributed random number with in [0, 1]. The mutation operator creates mutant vectors (X_i') by perturbing a randomly selected vector (X_a) with the difference of two other randomly selected vectors $(X_b$ and $X_c)$,

$$X_i^{'(G)} = X_a^{(G)} + F * (X_b^{(G)} - X_c^{(G)}), \ i = 1, \ldots\ldots\ldots\ldots, N_p \tag{5}$$

Where X_a, X_b and X_c are randomly chosen vectors $\in \{1, \ldots\ldots\ldots\ldots, N_p\}$ and $a \neq b \neq c \neq i$. The scaling constant (F) is an algorithm control parameter used to control the perturbation size in the mutation operator and improve algorithm convergence. The crossover operation generates trial vectors (X_i'') by mixing the parameters of the mutant vectors with the target vectors (X_i) according to a selected probability distribution. Crossover constant C_R is an algorithm parameter that controls the diversity of the population and aids the algorithm to escape from local optima.

3   Simulation and Discussion

A linear array of an even number of identical isotropic elements (such as vertical monopoles), is positioned symmetrically along the x-axis, as shown in Fig.1. The separation between the elements is "d" and "M" is the number of elements placed at each side of the y-axis. If mutual coupling between antenna elements is neglected, and assuming that the amplitude of excitations is symmetrical about the y-axis, the radiation pattern (AF) for the described structure can be written as

$$AF = \sum_{n=1}^{N} e^{j(n-1)(kd\cos\theta + \beta)} \tag{6}$$

This can be written as $AF = \sum_{n=1}^{N} e^{j(n-1)\psi}$ where $\psi = kd\cos\theta + \beta$, I= [I$_1$, I2,....,I$_M$], I$_n$'s are the excitation coefficients of the array elements, k=2π/λ is the phase constant, and θ the angle of incidence of a plane wave. The objective function is formulated as an optimization task that takes care of the side lobe level, desired pattern, and null width. The objective function is designed to have the of the weighted summation of different constraints given by

$$f_{SL} = \alpha * |MLL|_{mean} + \beta * |MSLL - DSLL|_{mean} +$$
$$\gamma * |MNL - DNL|_{mean} + \eta * |AF_0(\theta) - AF_d(\theta)|_{mean}$$

MSLL=Measured side lobe level; DSLL=Desired side lobe level; MNL=Measured Null level; DNL=Desired Null level; MLL=Main lobe level. The desired pattern is considered to have the following specifications Beam width: 10^0; Null points: [45^0 135^0]; Null Width: 2^0; Side Lobe Level: 20dB Main Beam=90^0 ; Null Side Lobe Level:-40dB.The parametric setup of the two algorithms is given in the Table.1. The weight coefficients of the fitness function given in the Equation are set as [α =0.55, β=0.2, γ=0.1, η=0.15].

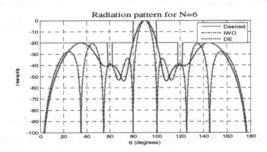

Fig. 2. Normalized radiation pattern of ULA for 6 elements

The pattern in the Fig.2 shows that DE has performed well in detecting the nulls and maintaining the side lobe level -20dB. IWO out performed DE in terms of half power beam width and main lobe level. The experiment is repeated increasing the number of array elements. Graphical and statistical comparisons of the two algorithms are carried out.

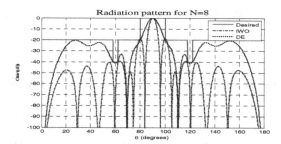

Fig. 3. Normalized radiation pattern for 8 elements

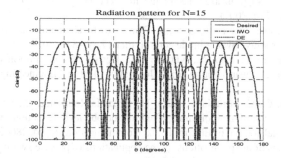

Fig. 4. Normalized radiation pattern for 15 elements

The results reveals that DE performs equally well with respect to IWO. The computational time of DE (2.8 min) is very less when compared to IWO (5.3min). More over IWO requires a huge parametric set up in comparison with DE. The simulated results reveal the fact that IWO can be applicable for a thin beam formation. But DE outperforms IWO in detecting the Null locations and in terms of computation time. As the number of array elements increases IWO suffers more computational burden.

4   Conclusion

In this paper the synthesis of a uniform linear array is done using two evolutionary techniques DE and IWO. The design problem has been recast as an optimization task which amounts for various constraints. As evident from the simulation results DE performs at par with IWO in satisfying the desired objectives at a less computational time. The simulation is done using MATLAB 7.0. The DE can be an attractive tool for different array synthesis. DE Algorithm optimizes the amplitude weights of the

Linear Array to drive down the Side lobe levels and to satisfy the Desired Null levels. Differential Evolution (DE) algorithm is a new heuristic approach mainly having three advantages; finding the true global minimum regardless of the initial parameter values, fast convergence, and using few control parameters. From the simulation results, it was observed that the convergence speed of DE is significantly better than genetic algorithms. Therefore, DE algorithm seems to be a promising approach for engineering optimization problems.

References

1. Balanis, C.A.: Antenna Theory Analysis and Design, 3rd edn. John Willey&Sons. Inc., New York (2007)
2. Uzkov, A.I.: An approach to the problem for optimum directive antenna design. C. R. Acad. Sci. USSR 35, 33 (1946); Rattan, M., Patterh, M.S., Sohi, B.S.: Antenna array Optimization using Evolutionary Approaches. Apeiron 15(1), 78–93 (2008)
3. Weng, W.C., Yang, F., Elsherbeni, A.Z.: Linear Antenna Array synthesis using Taguchi's Method: A novel Optimization Technique in Electromagnetics. IEEE Trans. Antennas Propag. 55, 723–730 (2007)
4. Guney, K., Durmus, A., Basbug, S.: A Plant growth simulation algorithm for pattern nulling of Linear arrays by amplitude control. Pier 17, 69–84 (2007)
5. Shihab, M., Najjar, Y., Dib, N., Khodier, M.: Design of non uniform circular antenna arrays using particle swarm optimization. Journal of Electrical Engineering 59(4), 216–220 (2008)
6. Rocha-Alicano, C., Covarrubias-Rosales, D., Brizuela-Rodriguez, C., Panduro-Mendoza, M.: Differential evolution algorithm applied to sidelobe level reduction on a planar array. AEU International Journal of Electronic and Communications 61(5), 286–290 (2007)
7. Poli, R.: Analysis of the publications on the applications of particle swarm optimization. J. Artificial Evol. Appl. Article ID 685175, 10 pages (2008)
8. Khodier, M., Christodoulou, C.: Linear array geometry synthesis with minimum sidelobelevel and null control using particle swarm optimization. IEEE Trans. Antennas Propagat. 53(8), 2674–2679 (2005)
9. Khodier, M., Al-Aqeel, M.: Linear and circular array optimization: A study using particle swarm intelligence. Progress in Electromagnetics Research, PIER 15, 347–373 (2009)
10. Singh, U., Kumar, H., Kamal, T.S.: Linear array synthesis using biogeography based optimization. Progress in Electromagnetics Research M 11, 25–36 (2010)
11. Mikki, S.M., Kishk, A.A.: Particle Swarm Optimizaton: A Physics-Based Approach. Morgan & Claypool (2008)
12. Vaskelainen, L.I.: Iterative least-squares synthesis methods for conformalarray antennas with optimized polarization and frequency properties. IEEE Trans. Antennas Propag. 45(7), 1179–1185 (1997)
13. Dohmen, C., Odendaal, J.W., Joubert, J.: Synthesis of conformalarrays with optimized polarization. IEEE Trans. Antennas Propag. 55(10), 2922–2925 (2007)
14. Li, J.Y., Li, L.W., Ooi, B.L., Kooi, P.S., Leong, M.S.: On accuracy of addition theorem for scalar Green's function used in FMM. Microw. Optical Technol. Lett. 31(6), 439–442 (2001)

Evaluation of CIE-XYZ System for Face Recognition Using Kernel-PCA

Hala M. Ebied

Scientific Computing Department, Faculty of Computer and Information Sciences,
Ain Shams University, Cairo, Egypt
hala_mousher@hotmail.com

Abstract. paper evaluates the performance of face recognition with different CIE color spaces. The XYZ and L*a*b* color spaces are compared with the gray image (luminance information Y). The face recognition system consists of a feature extraction step and a classification step. The Kernel-PCA is used to construct the feature space. Kernel-PCA is a nonlinear form of Principal Component Analysis (PCA). The k-nearest neighbor classifier with cosine measure is used in the classification step. Experiments using FEI color database with 200 subjects, show that the b* color component can improve the recognition rate.

Keywords: face recognition, CIE-XYZ color space, kernel-PCA.

1   Introduction

Face recognition from images is a sub-area of the general object recognition problem. Most face recognition methods have been developed using gray scale still images. Over the last several years, Color information provides important information in face recognition. Recent research has evinced that color cues contribute in recognizing faces, especially when shape cues of the images are degraded [1]. Various color spaces have been developed by the researchers for face recognition [2, 3].

Feature extraction is important step in the to perform face recognition process in real time. One needs to reduce the huge amounts of pixels in the raw face image to save time for the decision step. Feature extraction refers to transforming face space into a feature space. The most popular method to achieve this target is through applying the Eigenfaces algorithm [4]. The Eigenfaces algorithm is a classical statistical method using the linear Karhumen-Loeve transformation (KLT) (also known as Principal component analysis (PCA)). In contrast to linear PCA, Schölkopf et al. [5] extended principal component analysis to a nonlinear form based on kernel methods.

In this paper, the XYZ and L*a*b* color spaces are compared with the gray image (luminance information Y). The kernel-PCA has been applied on each color component independently. The remainder of this paper is organized as follows. The next section provides related works about color face recognition. In Section 3 the

V.V. Das and P.M. El-Kafrawy (Eds.): SPIT 2012, LNICST 117, pp. 137–143, 2014.

research describes the CIE-XYZ color space. Section 4 explains the Kernel-PCA and classification rule. Section 5 discusses the results. The paper concludes in section 6.

2   Related Works

Recent research provides that color may provide useful information for face recognition. Choi et al. [1] studied how color features affect the recognition performance with respect to changes in face resolution. The effectiveness of color on low-resolution faces has been tested on eigenfaces, fisherfaces, and Bayesian. The results show that color features decrease the recognition error rate by at least an order of magnitude over intensity-driven features when low-resolution faces (25×25 pixels or less) are applied to three face recognition methods.

In [6], the color local Gabor wavelets (CLGWs) and color local binary pattern (CLBP) were proposed for face recognition. The results show that the proposed color local texture features are able to provide excellent recognition rates for face images taken under severe variation in illumination, as well as for small- (low-) resolution face images. Wang et al. [7] has been presented RGB matrix-representation model to describe the color face image.   The color-Eigenfaces are computed for feature extraction using 2DPCA. Nearest neighborhood classification approach is adopted to identify the color face samples. Experimental results on CVL and CMU PIE color face database has been shown a good performance of the proposed color face recognition approach.

Shih and Liu [2] assessed comparatively the performance of content-based face image retrieval in different color spaces using the standard algorithm Principal Component Analysis (PCA). Experimental results using FERET database have been shown that some color configurations, such as R in the RGB color space and V in the HSV color space, help improve face retrieval performance. Liu and Liu [3] presented a robust face recognition method using novel hybrid color space, the RCrQ color space. Wang et al. [8] presented the tensor discriminant color space (TDCS) model which optimizes one color space transformation matrix and two discriminant projection matrices simultaneously. Experimental results on the AR and Georgia Tech color face database have been systematically performed.

3   CIE-XYZ Color Space

Commission International de l'Eclairage (CIE) considered the tri-stimulus values for red, green, and blue to be undesirable for creating a standardized color model [9]. The reformulated tri-stimulus values were indicated as XYZ. The CIE-XYZ system is at the root of all colorimetry. It is defined such that all visible colors can be defined using only positive values, and, the Y value is luminance. The transformation from the RGB color space to the XYZ color space is as follows [10].

$$\begin{bmatrix} X \\ Y \\ Z \end{bmatrix} = \begin{bmatrix} 0.607 & 0.174 & 0.201 \\ 0.299 & 0.587 & 0.114 \\ 0.000 & 0.066 & 1.117 \end{bmatrix} \begin{bmatrix} R \\ G \\ B \end{bmatrix} \qquad (1)$$

CIE adopted two different uniform diagrams, CIELuv and CIELab. The Yxy, Yuv, L*u*v*, L*a*b*, and L*ch color spaces are a transformation of CIE- XYZ. The CIE-L*a*b* is a color space that describes all colors visible to the human eye [9]. It was created to serve as a device independent model to be used as a reference. The L*a*b* color space is separated into lightness (L*) and color information (a*, b*). L* scales from 0 to 100. The a* and b* axes have no specific numerical limits. Positive a* is red and negative is green. Positive b* is yellow and negative is blue. The L*a*b* color space is defined based on XYZ tri-stimulus as follows:

$$L^* = \begin{cases} 116(\frac{Y}{Y_0})^{1/3} - 16 & if \ \frac{Y}{Y_0} > 0.008856 \\ 903.3(Y/Y_0) & otherwise \end{cases} \qquad (2)$$

$$a^* = 500 \left[f\left(\frac{X}{X_0}\right) - f\left(\frac{Y}{Y_0}\right) \right], \ b^* = 200 \left[f\left(\frac{Y}{Y_0}\right) - f\left(\frac{Z}{Z_0}\right) \right] \qquad (3)$$

where $f(U) = U^{1/3}$ if U > 0.008856 and f(U) = 7.787U+(16/116) otherwise, and X_0, Y_0, and Z_0 are the tri-stimulus values of the reference illuminant (light source.

4   Kernel PCA and Nearest Neighbor Classifier

Schölkopf et al. [5] have developed a nonlinear PCA called Kernel-PCA. The kernel-PCA is not interested in principal components in input space, but rather in principal components of variables which are nonlinearly related to the input variables [11]. They compute PCA in another dot product feature space F, which is related to the input space RMN by a possibly nonlinear map, $\varphi:R^{MN}{\rightarrow}F$.

The $\{\varphi(x_i)\}$, $i = 1, 2, ..., n$, denote the images of center input vectors x_i included in the feature space [12]. It is assumed that preprocessing has been done to satisfy the zero mean condition of all feature vectors over the training sample, i.e. $1/n \sum_{i=1}^{n} \varphi(x_i)$. Kernel function is the inner product term and denote as the scalar, $k(x,x_i) = \varphi^T(x_i) \varphi(x)$, $i = 1, 2, ..., n$. Compute the $k(x_i, x_j)$ as the ij-th element of the n-by-n matrix K, $K = \{k(x_i, x_j)\} = \{\varphi^T(x_i) \varphi(x_j)\}_{i, j} = 1, 2, ..., n$ (4)

The covariance matrix in **F** is $R = \frac{1}{n}\sum_{i=1}^{n} \varphi(x_i)\varphi^T(x_i)$ (5)

One now solves the *eigenvalue problem* $RV = \lambda V$ (6)

where λ is an eigenvalue of R and V is the associate eigenvector. Then

$$K\alpha = n\lambda\alpha \qquad (7)$$

where λ is an eigenvalue of K and α is the associate eigenvector. For the purpose of principal component extraction one needs to compute projections onto the eigenvectors $V=[v_1, v_2, \ldots, v_n]$ in F. Let x be a test point, with an image $\varphi(x)$ in F, then

$$y_q = v_q^T \varphi(x) = \sum_{j=1}^{n} \alpha_{q,j} \varphi^T(x_j)\varphi(x) \tag{8}$$

In brief, the following steps were necessary to compute the principal components: first, compute the dot product matrix K defined by eq (4); second, compute its eigenvectors (eq. (7)) and normalize them in F; third, compute projections of a test point onto the eigenvectors by eq. (8).

In our work, the Gaussian kernel functions are used. The Gaussian kernel, also called Radial basis kernel is $k(x, y) = \exp\left(-\frac{\|x-y\|^2}{2\sigma^2}\right)$, where the width σ, common to all the kernels, is specified a priori by the user.

The k-nearest neighbor classifier (k-NN) is used in our experiments to classify objects by finding the closest k neighbors in the feature space [13]. The k-NN rule classifies finds the k neighbors of the query point z with the minimum distances between z and all prototype feature points $\{z_{ci}, 1 \leq c \leq C, 1 \leq i \leq n_c\}$. Different parameters are used with k-NN, such as value of k nearest neighbors and distance model. In our work, the Euclidean norm distance $d(z, z_{ci}) = \|z - z_{ci}\|$ is used at the place of distance model. Besides, the cosine similarity measure $cos(z, z_{ci}) = (z^T z_{ci})/(\|z\| . \|z_{ci}\|)$ is used at the place of distance model. We choose k = 1 to find the class of the closest query point.

5   Experiments

In our experiments, eight images for 200 subjects from the FEI database are used with a total of 1600 images. The FEI face database is a Brazilian face database that contains a set of face images taken at the Artificial Intelligence Laboratory of FEI in São Bernardo do Campo, São Paulo, Brazil[1]. We cropped the face region of each face image and resized to a resolution of 55×77 pixels. Fig. 1 shows some samples of one person used in our experiments.

In the Kernel-PCA feature extraction method, we choose the Gaussian function as the Kernel function. The performance of the Gaussian kernel function is affected by its width σ. We choose the width σ equal 3000 [14]. The performance of the kernel-PCA is affected by varying the number of principal components that projected from the PCA. For the experiments, we choose 200 principal components [14]. For each color space used in this paper, we define three individual color component images. Before apply the kernel-PCA, each color component image is normalized to zero mean and unit variance.

In the 1-nearest neighbor classifier, we compare between two distance models, the Euclidean distance and cosine measure, to find out the true class of the test patterns. Two different sets are randomly selected for training, starting from 1 training image per person until 7 training images per person. The remaining set (unseen during

---

[1] This database is publicly available on
http://www.fei.edu.br/~cet/facedatabase.html

training) is used for testing; so every experiment is repeated two times. The correct recognition rate is considered to evaluate the performance of different color spaces.

The first set of experiments was performed to determine the impact of changed the distance model in the 1-nearest neighbor classifier. Fig. 2 shows the performance of Euclidean distance and cosine measure on the gray image (luminance Y component). The correct recognition rates expressed as functions of the number of training samples per person. One can observe from fig. 2 that the cosine measure outperforms the Euclidean distance. Therefore, the cosine measure is used in the remaining experiments.

Fig. 1. Some sample images of one person of the FEI database

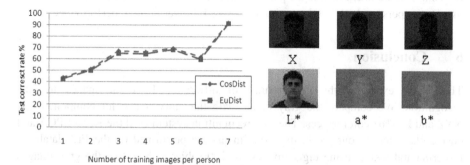

Fig. 2. Performance of *Kernel*-PCA with Euclidean distance and cosine measure on the gray image

Fig. 3. Illustration of X, Y and Z components of XYZ color space, and L*, a*, and b* of L*a*b* color space

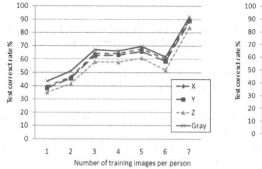

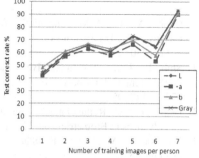

Fig. 4. Performance of Kernel-PCA with X, Y, and Z color components independently, and the gray image

Fig. 5. Performance of Kernel-PCA with L*, a*, and b* color components independently, and the gray image

The second set of experiments was performed to compare between the color spaces XYZ, and L*a*b* on the performance of the face recognition. The results are compared with the gray image (luminance information Y). The kernel-PCA has been applied to each color component independently. Fig. 3 illustrates the three color components corresponding to the XYZ and L*a*b* color spaces.

Fig. 4 and Fig. 5 show the performance of the XYZ color space and L*a*b* color space, respectively. For the XYZ color space, the performance with Z component declined the recognition rate. The gray image (luminance Y component) is more effective than the use of one individual XYZ color components. With 7 images per person during the training phase, the average test correct recognition rate by gray image (luminance Y component) is 92%, 186 images correctly of the 200 test faces (93 %) in the first experiment and 182 images correctly of the 200 test faces (91 %) in the second repeat experiment. For the L*a*b* color space, one can observe from Fig. 5 that the b* color component perform better than L* and a* color components by using few numbers of images per person. Fig. 5 shows that with few numbers of images per person, the L* and gray image have a little variation in performance.

6   Conclusion

This paper evaluates the performance of different CIE color spaces in face recognition. We compare the gray image with the individual color components of XYZ and L*a*b* color spaces. The face recognition system used the Kernel-PCA and cosine classifier. In our work, the experiments are performed on the FEI database. Experimental results using eight images for 200 subjects show that the gray images performed a recognition rate of 92%. The b* from the L*a*b* color space outperforms all the used color components.

References

1. Choi, J.Y., Ro, Y.M., Plataniotis, K.N.: Color Face Recognition for Degraded Face Images. IEEE Transactions on Systems, Man, and Cybernetics—part B: Cybernetics 39(5), 1217–1230 (2009)
2. Shih, P., Liu, C.: Comparative Assessment of Content-Based Face Image Retrieval in Different Color Spaces. Int. J. Pattern Recognition and Artificial Intelligence 19(7), 873–893 (2005)
3. Liu, Z., Liu, C.: Robust Face Recognition Using Color. In: 3rd IAPR/IEEE Int. Conference on Advances in Biometrics, pp. 122–131 (2009)
4. Pentland, T., Moghadam, B., Starner, T.: View based and modular eigenspaces for face recognition. In: IEEE Conference on Computer Vision and Pattern Recognition, pp. 84–91 (1994)
5. Schölkopf, B., Smola, A., Müller, K.R.: Nonlinear Component Analysis as a Kernel Eigenvalue Problem. J. Neural Computing 10(5), 1299–1319 (1998)
6. Choi, J.Y., Ro, Y.M., Plataniotis, K.N.: Color Local Texture Features for Color Face Recognition. IEEE Transactions on Image Processing 21(3), 1366–1380 (2012)

7. Wang, C., Yin, B., Bai, X., Sun, Y.: Color Face Recognition Based on 2DPCA. In: 19th International Conference on. J. Pattern Recognition (ICPR 2008), pp. 1–4 (2008)
8. Wang, S., Yang, J., Zhang, N., Zhou, C.: Tensor Discriminant Color Space for Face Recognition. IEEE Transactions on Image Processing (2011), doi: 10.1109/TIP.2011.2121084
9. Choi, J.Y., Ro, Y.M., Plataniotis, K.N.: A comparative study of preprocessing mismatch effects in color image based face recognition. J. Pattern Recognition (2010), doi:10.1016/j.patcog.2010.08.020
10. Weeks, A.R.: Fundamentals of electronic image processing. SPIE Optical Engineering Press. IEEE Press, Washington, USA (1996)
11. Jarillo, G., Pedrycz, W., Reformat, M.: Aggregation of classifiers based on image transformations in biometric face recognition. J. Machine Vision and Applications 19, 125–140 (2008)
12. QingShan, L., Rui, H., HanQing, L., SongDe, M.: Kernel-Based Nonlinear Discriminant Analysis for Face Recognition. J. Comput. Sci. & Technol. 18(6), 788–795 (2003)
13. Orozco-Alzate, M., Castellanos-Domínguez, C.G.: Comparison of the nearest feature classifiers for face recognition. Machine Vision and Applications Journal 17, 279–285 (2006)
14. Ebied, H.M.: Feature Extraction using PCA and Kernel-PCA for Face Recognitio. In: 8th International Conference on INFOrmatics and Systems (INFOS 2012), pp. 74–80 (2012)

Derivation of New Expression of SNIR for Multi Code Multi Carrier CDMA Systems

Lamia Touria Aboura and Ali Djebbari

Telecommunications and Digital Signal Processing Laboratory. Djillali Liabes
University, Sidi Bel-Abbes, Algeria
l.aboura@yahoo.fr

Abstract. This paper analyze a new process of transmission combining multiple
access technique, CDMA, to multi code and multi carrier techniques, denoted
as Multi Code Multi Carrier CDMA or MC-MC-CDMA. This method, very
advantageous, seems to be very attractive for fourth generation (4G) wireless
system. Its potential is then shown in the present paper, by analyzing and
comparing the performance of the system with those of Multi Code CDMA and
MC-CDMA systems. Results indicate that this system outperforms both the two
other systems.

Keywords: CDMA, Multi Code Multi Carrier CDMA, SNIR, interferences.

1 Introduction

The progress in wireless communication entails a demand for higher data rates and
good spectral efficiency. Future generation systems will have to accommodate with
these requirements. So, a new system denoted MC-MC-CDMA have been suggested
based on the combination of MC-CDMA and Multi Code CDMA. There has been
came research in trying to combine the advantages of both systems to get a more
powerful system; MC-CDMA is attracted because of its higher capacity and its
powerful method of combating channel fading [1],[2],[3],[4] and using Multi Code-
CDMA can provide multi-rate services [5],[6],[7].

The MC-MC-CDMA were introduced by [8]. In these systems a high data rate
stream is split into a number of parallel low rate streams and then the low rate streams
are spread by different sequences and added together. The resulting data is then split
into a number of parallel low rate streams and each sub stream modulates a different
subcarrier before transmission. In [9], an M-ary symbol selects one of M code
sequences for transmission. Each chip of the code sequence is copied onto P branches
and for the user-specific sequence it is then multiplied with the corresponding branch
i.e. the pth chip of the user-specific sequence is multiplied with the pth branch of the
copier. Each of these branches then modulates one of the P orthogonal subcarriers and
the results are summed.

V.V. Das and P.M. El-Kafrawy (Eds.): SPIT 2012, LNICST 117, pp. 144–153, 2014.
© Institute for Computer Sciences, Social Informatics and Telecommunications Engineering 2014

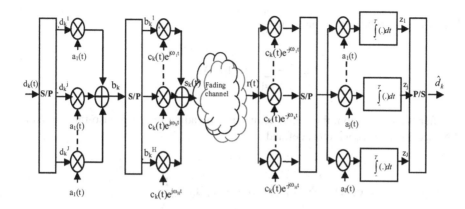

Fig. 1. Transmitter/Receiver system model for MC-MC-CDMA

In this article, the analytical framework of MC-MC-CDMA system described in [8] is employed when we derived the expression of Signal-to-Noise plus Interferences ratio (SNIR) to evaluate the performance of the system. The results show that our system is very effective to eliminate, simultaneously, the effects of multipath interference, multi-carrier, multi-user and the interference between symbols.

2   System Model

The transmitter and receiver are shown in Fig. 1. At the transmitter side, the data bit stream of the kth user $d_k(t) = d_k^I(t) - jd_k^Q(t)$, where $d_k^I(t)$ and $d_k^Q(t)$ are the inphase and quadrature component, respectively, is serial-to-parallel (S/P) converted into J substreams which is coded by an orthogonal signal $a_j(t)$. The resulting signal $b_k(t)$, called superstream, is S/P converted again, spread by $c_k(t)$ and modulated with H orthogonal carriers. The bit stream, with duration T is given by [8]

$$d_k(t) = \sum_i d_k^i \, \Pi_{\frac{T}{HJ}} \, (t - i\frac{T}{HJ}). \tag{1}$$

where d_k^i is ith value of the kth bit stream.

The code set a_j for the jth substream is given by

$$a_j(t) = \sum_{i=0}^{N_a-1} a_j^i \Pi_{T_a} (t - iT_a), \; T_a = \frac{T}{H.N_a}. \tag{2}$$

where T_a is the chip duration of the code, N_a is its length and a_j^i is the ith value of the code $a_j \in \{\pm 1\}$.

The superstream $b_k(t)$ with duration $\dfrac{T}{H}$ is

$$b_k(t) = \sum_{j=1}^{J} a_j(t)d_{kj}(t). \tag{3}$$

After S/P conversion, the superstreams are spreading by the pseuso-random Noise (PN) sequence, $c_k(t)$, which is defined

$$c_k(t) = \sum_{i=0}^{N_c-1} c_k^i \, \Pi_{T_c}(t - iT_c), \; T_c = \frac{T}{N_c}. \tag{4}$$

c_k^i is the ith bit value of the PN code and N_c is its length. Notice that the spreading code on all the subcarriers is the same for one particular user.

The transmitting signal of the kth user can be expressed as

$$s_k(t) = \sum_{h=1}^{H} \sqrt{2P_k} \, \mathrm{Re}[b_k(t)c_k(t)e^{j\omega_h t}]. \tag{5}$$

where P_k is the power of user k distributed among the carriers; if we assume perfect power control, then all users have the same power $P_1 = P_2 = \ldots = P_k = P$. ω_h is the angular carrier frequency.

The channel is considered as conventional multipath channel with equivalent transfer function, $h(t)$ given by

$$h(t) = \sum_{l=0}^{L-1} A_{kl} \, e^{j\phi_{kl}} \delta(t - \tau_{kl}) \ . \tag{6}$$

where L is the number of propagation path ; A_{kl} is the path gain of lth path of the kth user; τ_{kl} is the path time delay uniformly distributed over [0, T] ; Φ_{kl} is the l phase uniformly distributed over [0, 2π]. It is assumed that the channel path gain A_{kl} has a Nakagami distribution.

The received signal, $r(t)$, for all K users is given by

$$r(t) = \sqrt{2P} \sum_{k=1}^{K} \sum_{h=1}^{H} \sum_{j=1}^{J} \sum_{l=1}^{L} \left\{ A_{kl} a_j(t - \tau_{kl}) c_k(t - \tau_{kl}) \times \mathrm{Re}[d_{kjh}(t - \tau_{kl})e^{j(\omega_h(t-\tau_{kl})+\phi_{kl})}] \right\}$$
$$+ n(t). \tag{7}$$

where d_{kjh} is the data symbol of jth substream of hth superstream and $n(t)$ is the additive white gaussien noise (AWGN).

At the receiver part, the received signal is first demodulated by locally generated carrier, despread by the PN sequence and then P/S converted; his output is then despread again by each orthogonal code for multicode component in order to recover substream before correlation. Finally, the substreams are recovered from the correlated data.

For convenience and yet no loss of generality, we assume that the signal for the first user, first carrier, first orthogonal code via the first path is considered as the reference. The signal received [8] can be written as

$$r(t) = \sqrt{2P}\{A_{11}a_1(t)c_1(t)\times[d^I_{111}(t)\cos(\omega_1 t) + d^Q_{111}\sin(\omega_1(t)] + \sum_{l=2}^{L} A_{11}a_1(t-\tau_{11})c_1(t-\tau_{11})$$

$$\times[d^I_{111}(t-\tau_{11})\cos(\omega_1(t-\tau_{11})+\phi_{11}) + d^Q_{111}(t-\tau_{11})\sin(\omega_1(t-\tau_{11})+\phi_{11})]$$

$$+ \sum_{j=2}^{J}\sum_{l=1}^{L} A_{11}a_j(t-\tau_{11})c_1(t-\tau_{11})[d^I_{1jl}(t-\tau_{11})\cos(\omega_1(t-\tau_{11})+\phi_{11})$$

$$+ d^Q_{1jl}(t-\tau_{11})\sin(\omega_1(t-\tau_{11})+\phi_{11})] + \sum_{h=2}^{H}\sum_{j=1}^{J}\sum_{l=1}^{L} A_{11}a_j(t-\tau_{11})c_1(t-\tau_{11})$$

$$\times[d^I_{1jh}(t-\tau_{11})\cos(\omega_h(t-\tau_{11})+\phi_{11}) + d^Q_{1jh}(t-\tau_{11})\sin(\omega_h(t-\tau_{11})+\phi_{11})]$$

$$+ \sum_{k=2}^{K}\sum_{h=1}^{H}\sum_{j=1}^{J}\sum_{l=1}^{L} A_{kl}a_j(t-\tau_{kl})c_k(t-\tau_{kl})[d^I_{kjh}(t-\tau_{kl})\cos(\omega_h(t-\tau_{kl})+\phi_{kl})$$

$$\tag{8}$$

$$+ d^Q_{kh}(t-\tau_{kl})\sin(\omega_h(t-\tau_{kl})+\phi_{kl})]\}$$

$$+ n(t).$$

Thus, r(t) can be written according six components as follows

$$r(t)=r_{DS}(t)+ r_{MPI}(t)+ r_{ISSI}(t)+ r_{ICI}(t)+ r_{MUI}(t)+n(t). \tag{9}$$

Where $r_{DS}(t)$ is the desired signal, corresponding $k=h=j=l=1$;
$r_{MPI}(t)$ is the MultiPath Interferences caused by the propagation of the desired signal, $k=h=j=1$; via all path except the first path.
$r_{ISSI}(t)$ is the Inter SubStream Interferences caused by other substream except the first substream, $j=1$.
$r_{ICI}(t)$ is the Inter Carriers Interferences caused by all other carriers other than the desired, $h=1$ for the first user.
$r_{MUI}(t)$ is the MultiUser Interferences, caused by all other users except the first user, $k=1$.
Assuming synchronous detection ($\tau_{11}= \phi_{11}= 0$); the output for the correlator for $k=h=j=l=1$ is given by

$$z_1(t)= \int_0^T r(t)a_1(t)c_1(t)[\cos(\omega_1 t)- j\sin(\omega_1 t)]\, dt \tag{10}$$

By substiting (8) to (10), we obtained

$$z_{DS}(t)= \sqrt{\frac{P}{2}}T A_{11}[d^I_{111}(t)- jd^Q_{111}(t)] \tag{11}$$

$$z_{MPI}(t)=\sqrt{\frac{P}{2}}\sum_{l=2}^{L}A_{11}\int_{0}^{T}a_1(t-\tau_{11})a_1(t)c_1(t-\tau_{11})c_1(t)\times\{d_{111}^{I}(t-\tau_{11})$$

$$\cos(\theta_{11})+d_{111}^{Q}(t-\tau_{11})\sin(\theta_{11})+jd_{111}^{I}(t-\tau_{11})\sin(\theta_{11})-jd_{111}^{Q}(t-\tau_{11})\cos(\theta_{11})\}dt. \tag{12}$$

$$z_{ISSI}(t)=\sqrt{\frac{P}{2}}\sum_{j=2}^{J}\sum_{l=1}^{L}A_{11}\int_{0}^{T}a_j(t-\tau_{11})a_1(t)c_1(t-\tau_{11})c_1(t)$$

$$\times\{d_{111}^{I}(t-\tau_{11})\cos(\theta_{11})+d_{111}^{Q}(t-\tau_{11})\sin(\theta_{11})+jd_{111}^{I}(t-\tau_{11})\sin(\theta_{11})-jd_{111}^{Q}(t-\tau_{11})\cos(\theta_{11})\}dt. \tag{13}$$

$$z_{ICI}(t)=\sqrt{\frac{P}{2}}\sum_{h=2}^{H}\sum_{j=1}^{J}\sum_{l=1}^{L}A_{11}\int_{0}^{T}a_j(t-\tau_{11})a_1(t)c_1(t-\tau_{11})c_1(t)$$

$$\times\{\cos(\theta_{11})[d_{1jh}^{I}(t-\tau_{11})\cos(\omega_h-\omega_l)t+d_{1jh}^{Q}(t-\tau_{11})\sin(\omega_h-\omega_l)t]$$

$$+\sin(\theta_{11})[d_{1jh}^{Q}(t-\tau_{11})\cos(\omega_h-\omega_l)t-d_{1jh}^{I}(t-\tau_{11})\sin(\omega_h-\omega_l)t]$$

$$+j\cos(\theta_{11})[d_{1jh}^{Q}(t-\tau_{11})\cos(\omega_h-\omega_l)t-d_{1jh}^{I}(t-\tau_{11})\sin(\omega_h-\omega_l)t]$$

$$+j\sin(\theta_{11})[d_{1jh}^{I}(t-\tau_{11})\cos(\omega_h-\omega_l)t+d_{1jh}^{Q}(t-\tau_{11})\sin(\omega_h-\omega_l)t]\}dt. \tag{14}$$

$$z_{MUI}(t)=\sqrt{\frac{P}{2}}\sum_{k=2}^{K}\sum_{h=1}^{H}\sum_{j=1}^{J}\sum_{l=1}^{L}A_{kl}\int_{0}^{T}a_j(t-\tau_{kl})a_1(t)c_k(t-\tau_{kl})c_1(t)$$

$$\times\{\cos(\theta_{kl})[d_{kjh}^{I}(t-\tau_{kl})\cos(\omega_h-\omega_l)t+d_{kjh}^{Q}(t-\tau_{kl})\sin(\omega_h-\omega_l)t]$$

$$+\sin(\theta_{kl})[d_{kjh}^{Q}(t-\tau_{kl})\cos(\omega_h-\omega_l)t-d_{kjh}^{I}(t-\tau_{kl})\sin(\omega_h-\omega_l)t]$$

$$+j\cos(\theta_{kl})[d_{kjh}^{Q}(t-\tau_{kl})\cos(\omega_h-\omega_l)t-d_{kjh}^{I}(t-\tau_{kl})\sin(\omega_h-\omega_l)t]$$

$$+j\sin(\theta_{kl})[d_{kjh}^{I}(t-\tau_{kl})\cos(\omega_h-\omega_l)t+d_{kjh}^{Q}(t-\tau_{kl})\sin(\omega_h-\omega_l)t]\}dt. \tag{15}$$

$$z_n(t)=\int_{0}^{T}n(t)a_1(t)c_1(t)[\cos(\omega_1 t)-j\sin(\omega_1 t)]dt. \tag{16}$$

To simplify the expressions (12) to (16), we assume BPSK modulation and we define the functions

$$G_{jv,hu}^{k}(xy)=\sum_{l=0}^{L}A_{kl}g^{y}(\theta_{kl})R_{jv,hu}^{x}(\tau_{kl})$$

$$\hat{G}_{jv,hu}^{k}(xy)=\sum_{l=0}^{L}A_{kl}g^{y}(\theta_{kl})\hat{R}_{jv,hu}^{x}(\tau_{kl}) \tag{17}$$

$R_{jv,hu}^{x}(\tau_{kl})$ and $\hat{R}_{jv,hu}^{x}(\tau_{kl})$ are correlation function where j, v are the jth and vth multicode, and h, u are the hth and uth frequency, respectively.

x can be sinus or cosinus function of correlation function ; y can be sinus or cosinus function of function g having phase θ_{kl}.

The interferences component can be rewritten as

$$z_{MPI}(t)=\sqrt{\frac{P}{2}}[G_{11,11}'^{1}(cc)+\hat{G}_{11,11}'^{1}(cc)] \tag{18}$$

G' and $\hat{G}'$ are same expressions with G and $\hat{G}$ but with path from 2 to L.

$$z_{ISSI}(t) = \sqrt{\frac{P}{2}} \sum_{j=2}^{J} [G_{j1,11}^1(cc) + \hat{G}_{j1,11}^1(cc)] \tag{19}$$

$$z_{ICI}(t) = \sqrt{\frac{P}{2}} \sum_{h=2}^{H} \sum_{j=1}^{J} [G_{j1,h1}^1(cc) + \hat{G}_{j1,h1}^1(cc)] - \sqrt{\frac{P}{2}} \sum_{h=2}^{H} \sum_{j=1}^{J} [G_{j1,h1}^1(ss) + \hat{G}_{j1,h1}^1(ss)] \tag{20}$$

$$z_{MUI}(t) = \sqrt{\frac{P}{2}} \sum_{k=2}^{K} \sum_{h=1}^{H} \sum_{j=1}^{J} [G_{j1,h1}^k(cc) + \hat{G}_{j1,h1}^k(cc)] - \sqrt{\frac{P}{2}} \sum_{k=2}^{K} \sum_{h=1}^{H} \sum_{j=1}^{J} [G_{j1,h1}^k(ss) + \hat{G}_{j1,h1}^k(ss)]$$

$$\tag{21}$$

3   Performance Analysis

To evaluate the performance of the system, we calculate the Signal-to-Noise plus Interferences ratio (SNIR), which is the ratio of signal power to noise plus interference variance; thus, we need to find variance of all the interferences and noise terms, then we assume that all terms are zero means, statistically independent random variables.

The signal power is

$$S = (z_{DS})^2 = \frac{P}{2}(A_{11})^2 T^2. \tag{22}$$

The noise variance is

$$\sigma_n^2 = E[z_n^2] = \frac{N_0 T}{4}. \tag{23}$$

For the other variance, we have

$$\sigma_{MPI}^2 = \frac{P}{2} E[\{G'^1_{11,11}(cc) + \hat{G}'^1_{11,11}(cc)\}^2] \tag{24}$$

$$\sigma_{MPI}^2 = \frac{P}{2} \left[\frac{N_1 T_C^2}{3} \right] \sum_{l=2}^{L} var A_{ll}.$$

Where N_1 is the number of chip per bit of input data $d_k(t)$ before the first S/P conversion ; thus : $N_1 = \frac{N_a}{J} = \frac{N_c}{JH}$ and $T = N_c T_c = JHN_1 T_c$, The *MPI* variance becomes

$$\sigma_{MPI}^2 = \frac{P}{2}\left[\frac{T^2}{3JHN_c}\right]\sum_{l=2}^{L} \text{var}\, A_{ll}.$$

For *ISSI* variance, we have J-1 substream, then

$$\sigma_{ISSI}^2 = \frac{P}{2}(J-1)\frac{T^2}{3JHN_c}\sum_{l=1}^{L} \text{var}\, A_{ll}. \tag{25}$$

The *ICI* variance is equal to

$$\sigma_{ICI}^2 = \frac{JPT^2}{2}\sum_{h=2}^{H}\frac{F^c(h)-F^s(h)}{4\pi^2 J^2(h-1)^2 N_1}\sum_{l=1}^{L} \text{var}\, A_{ll}. \tag{26}$$

With

$$F^c(h) = N_c\left\{\frac{1}{N_c}-\frac{1}{2N_c}\cos4\pi\frac{J(h-1)}{T}gT_c +\frac{1}{\pi J(h-1)}\sin2\pi\frac{J(h-1)}{T}gT_c\cos2\pi\frac{J(h-1)}{T}(g+1)T_c\right.$$

$$-\frac{1}{2\pi J(h-1)}\sin2\pi\frac{J(h-1)}{T}gT_c\cos2\pi\frac{J(h-1)}{T}gT_c +\frac{1}{N_c}-\frac{1}{2N_c}\cos4\pi\frac{J(h-1)}{T}(g+1)T_c$$

$$+\frac{1}{2\pi J(h-1)}\sin2\pi\frac{J(h-1)}{T}(g+1)T_c\cos2\pi\frac{J(h-1)}{T}(g+1)T_c$$

$$\left.-\frac{1}{\pi J(h-1)}\sin2\pi\frac{J(h-1)}{T}(g+1)T_c\cos2\pi\frac{J(h-1)}{T}gT_c\right\}. \tag{27}$$

$$F^s(h) = N_c\left\{\frac{1}{N_c}+\frac{1}{2N_c}\cos4\pi\frac{J(h-1)}{T}gT_c +\frac{1}{4\pi J(h-1)}\sin4\pi\frac{J(h-1)}{T}(g+1)T_c\right.$$

$$-\frac{1}{\pi J(h-1)}\sin2\pi\frac{J(h-1)}{T}(g+1)T_c\cos2\pi\frac{J(h-1)}{T}gT_c +\frac{1}{2\pi J(h-1)}\sin2\pi\frac{J(h-1)}{T}gT_c\cos2\pi\frac{J(h-1)}{T}gT_c$$

$$+\frac{1}{N_c}+\frac{1}{2N_c}\cos4\pi\frac{J(h-1)}{T}(g+1)T_c -\frac{1}{\pi J(h-1)}\cos2\pi\frac{J(h-1)}{T}(g+1)T_c\sin2\pi\frac{J(h-1)}{T}(g+1)T_c$$

$$\left.+\frac{1}{\pi J(h-1)}\cos2\pi\frac{J(h-1)}{T}(g+1)T_c\sin2\pi\frac{J(h-1)}{T}gT_c\right\}. \tag{28}$$

The variance of multi user is given by

$$\sigma_{MUI}^2 = \frac{PT^2}{2}J(K-1)\left\{\frac{T^2}{3JHN_c}+\sum_{h=1}^{H}\frac{F^c(h)-F^s(h)}{4\pi^2 J^2(h-1)^2 N_1}\right\}\times\sum_{l=1}^{L} \text{var}\, A_{kl} \tag{29}$$

The variances of interferences depend of variance of the gain A_{kl}; Assuming $var[A_{11}] = \Omega$ and $\sum_{l=1}^{L} var\, A_{kl} = \Omega Q(L, \delta)$, with $Q(L, \delta) = \dfrac{1 - e^{-L\delta}}{1 - e^{-\delta}}$.

Therefore, the totally variance can written as

$$\sigma_T^2 = \frac{PT^2}{2}\left\{ \frac{1}{3JHN_c}\Omega(Q(L, \delta) - 1) + \frac{J-1}{3JHN_c}\Omega Q(L, \delta) + \left\{ \sum_{h=2}^{H} \frac{J[F^c(h) - F^s(h)]}{4\pi^2 J^2(h-1)^2 N_1} \right\}\Omega Q(L, \delta) \right.$$

$$\left. + \left\{ \frac{J(K-1)}{3JHN_c} + \sum_{h=1}^{H} \frac{J(K-1)[F^c(h) - F^s(h)]}{4\pi^2 J^2(h-1)^2 N_1} \right\} \times \Omega Q(L, \delta) + \frac{1}{2\dfrac{E_b}{N_0}} \right\}$$

(30)

where $E_b = PT$.

Finally, the SNIR is

$$\gamma = \frac{\dfrac{p}{2}{A_{11}}^2 T^2}{\sigma_T^2}$$

(31)

4   Result of Simulation

Having derived the output SNIR, the performance of the system is presented in this section. We used parameters listed in table1.

Table 1. Simulation parameters

Parameter	Value
Nakagami parameter	m=1
Number of user	K=20
Number of multipath	L=3
Number of substreams	J=8
Number of carriers	H=8
Local mean power	Ω=10dB
Multipath decay factor	δ=5x10^{-7}

Fig. 2 illustrates SNIR performance for BPSK and QPSK modulation schema, versus the Signal-to-noise ratio. It is seen that the BPSK performance better than the QPSK, but QPSK can transmit two more information than BPSK.

Fig. 3 shows SNIR performance as a function of the SNR for several values of number of users K for BPSK and QPSK modulations; It is clear from those two figures that, as many users are transmitting signal simultaneously, the SNIR decreases; this appears clearly in Figure 4; Hence, the higher the number of users, the higher the multiuser interference caused by the unwanted user and consequently the performance become worse.

A plot of the SNIR performance of the different system MC-MC-CDMA, MC-CDMA and MultiCode CDMA is shown in Figure 5; the figure clearly shows that the MC-MC-CDMA system has the highest SNIR performance of all the systems compared. Indeed, our system eliminates, simultaneously, the effects of multipath interference, multi-carrier, multi-user and the interference between symbols.

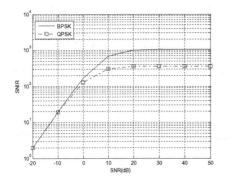

Fig. 2. SNIR for BPSK and QPSK modulations

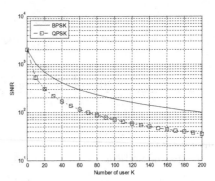

Fig. 3. Effect of number of users, K, on the SNIR, SNR=10dB

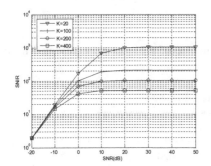

Fig. 4. Effect of number of users, K, in the SNIR

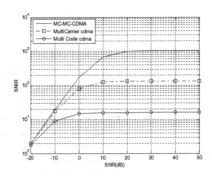

Fig. 5. SNIR performance for different CDMA based systems

5   Conclusion

On the basis of principle of multi-carrier CDMA and multi code CDMA technology, a novel MC-MC-CDMA schema is developed in this paper. We have analyzed the performance of this system in term of SNIR; It was shown that MC-MC-CDMA outperforms the MC-CDMA and Multi code-CDMA systems. Our system is very effective in reducing the interferences, and improving the quality of the wireless link.

References

1. Hara, S., Prasad, R.: Overview of Multicarrier CDMA. IEEE Commun. 35(12), 126–133 (1997)
2. Sourour, E., Nakagawa, M.: Performance of orthogonal multicarrier CDMA in a multipath fading channel. IEEE Trans. Commun. 44, 356–367 (1996)
3. Park, J.H., Kim, J.E., Choi, S.Y., Cho, N.S., Hong, D.S.: "Performance of MCCDMA systems in non-independent Rayleigh fading. In: IEEE Int. Commun. Conf., Vancouver, BC Canada, vol. 1, pp. 6–10 (1999)
4. Ryu, K.W., Park, J.O., Park, Y.W.: Performance of multicarrier CS/CDMA in frequency-selective Rayleigh fading channels. In: 2003 Spring IEEE 57th Semiannual Vehicular Technology Conf., vol. 2, pp. 1258–1262 (2003)
5. Kim, I.M., Shin, B.C., Kim, Y.J., Kim, J.K., Han, I.: Throughput improvement scheme in multicode CDMA. Electronics Letters 34, 963–964 (1998)
6. Hsiung, D.W., Chang, J.F.: Performance of multicode CDMA in a multipath fading channel. IEEE Commun. 147, 365–370 (2000)
7. Raju, G.V.S., Charoensakwiroj, J.: Orthogonal codes performance in multicode CDMA. In: 2003 IEEE Int. Conf. on Systems, Man and Cybernetics, vol. 2, pp. 1928–1931 (2003)
8. Lee, J.W.: Performance analysis of Multi-code Multi Carrier CDMA communication system. Master Degree Thesis, Univ. Akron, Akron, OH (2004)
9. Kim, T., Kim, J., Andrews, J.G., Rappaport, T.S.: Multi-code Multi-Carrier CDMA: Performance Analysis. In: IEEE Int. Conf., vol. 2, pp. 973–977 (2004)

A Requirements Analysis Approach for Web Engineering

Shailey Chawla[1] and Sangeeta Srivastava[2]

[1] Department of Computer Science, University of Delhi, Delhi - 110007, India
[2] Department of Computer Science, Bhaskaracharya College, Sec-2, Dwarka, Delhi, India
{shaileychawla,sangeeta.srivastava}@gmail.com

Abstract. We propose to improve the Web engineering methods by incorporating the concepts of Goals, Aspects and Scenarios. As a result of their dynamic nature, perceptive interface features, large and heterogeneous audience, and navigational access to information Web based applications are engineered differently from other Information System. Our approach works closely with the Web specific functional and non-functional Requirements and delivers models with lesser conflicts, better choice amongst alternatives and handles crosscutting concerns for modeling personalization and non-functional requirements. We have enhanced and extended User Requirements Notation to meet the Web specific needs. We also propose a systematic approach for automatically constructing the Web specific GRL diagrams.

Keywords: Web Engineering, Goals, Aspects, Scenarios, User Requirements Notation, Requirements.

1   Introduction

Web applications are engineered differently as they involve multiple stakeholders, and the size and purpose of the applications are also varied [1]. These unique characteristics of Web applications have led to evolution of Web Engineering approaches that explicitly focus on web oriented analysis and design of Web applications. These approaches have focused on issues like navigation, presentation etc. that are important for Web application development. However, they fail to capture other issues like adaptability, softgoals etc that meet the real goals and expectations of the stakeholders. As a result even though the web application looks assuring and attractive yet it might not be able to cater to individual user needs, goals and expectations. These lacunae lead to increased costs and maintenance problems in the project. Web applications need all the more attention here because of heterogeneous customers, dynamic behavior and vast reach in contrast to the traditional applications, where the users are known and their expectations can be easily captured.

In recent times, Goal oriented Requirements Engineering [2][3] has become very popular for analyzing the requirements in depth and capturing the stakeholders needs and goals from the software application. According to Lamsweerde , Goal-oriented

V.V. Das and P.M. El-Kafrawy (Eds.): SPIT 2012, LNICST 117, pp. 154–159, 2014.

requirements engineering (GORE) is concerned with the use of goals for eliciting, elaborating, structuring, specifying, analyzing, negotiating, documenting, and modifying requirements[3]. It has been also established that stakeholders pay more attention to goal models compared to the UML models because they can relate to the concepts more closely. Some work has been done by researchers [4][5][6][7] on web engineering approaches taking into account the Goal driven analysis, but many concepts of goal driven analysis like design rationale, conflict resolution, goal prioritization have been surpassed and not taken in totality. Analysis on Goals in web engineering is discussed in [8]. In parallel to Goal and Scenario based approaches mainly [9], there has been lot of active work going on in Aspect oriented Software Development[10]. Aspect orientation separates all features of a program and modularizes all of them.

2   Background and Motivation

Various Web Engineering approaches have been discussed in detail in [11][12]. A detailed work on Goal based Web Engineering has been done predominantly in [12] and [14][15]. Both these approaches have enhanced web engineering by incorporating Goal driven analysis using i*[13] approach. The work done in above approaches is application of GORE in Web application development and then transformation to a web design approach.. Our approach also integrate goals and scenarios, we go further and extend the User Requirements Notation[9] for modeling requirements in developing Web applications. User Requirements notation is currently the only standard that handles goals and scenarios together. We also incorporate an extension of URN i.e. AoURN[19] (Aspect oriented URN), for analyzing the crosscutting concerns in Web requirements domain like the Personalization concern and Non-functional Requirements concern. In the next step we map these user requirements using Goal requirements language (GRL) into GRL diagrams that primarily deals with ambiguous requirements and goals. GRL notation is based on i* approach[13] for handling stakeholder's intentions and NFR framework[16] for evaluating and analyzing the goals. UCM stands for Use case Maps that depict the walkthroughs or the scenarios for different use cases and goals. Our approach helps the requirements engineer to elicit and analyze the goals and requirements with the stakeholders. Also it automatically creates the requirements analysis diagrams, specific for comprehensive analysis of Web application. We also study the softgoals in detail for any conflicts in concern interaction graphs. The overall outline has been explained in [17] see Fig.1. We have worked here with the non-functional requirements such that they are integral to the system and they affect the system at every step and area. Web Functional requirements have been classified by many web engineering approaches [18], keeping that constant we had also extended the classification for non-functional requirements in[17].

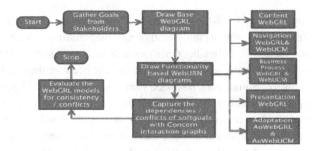

Fig. 1. Requirements Engineering methodology for Web application development

3   The Requirements Analysis Approach for Web Applications

Our approach will help the requirements engineer for elicitation of the goals from the stakeholders and also do the systematic analysis of the same. The approach will consist of a series of algorithms, in the first step a Level 0 WebGRL diagram would be drawn where Web specific goals and softgoals would be defined and sub goals found. The next level of diagrams would be the detailed analysis of each kind of functional requirements like navigation, content, personalization etc. For each of these, information would be taken from the base WebGRL diagram and further elicitation would be done from the stakeholders by the requirements engineer. For constructing Base WebGRL diagram, we have extended the basic GRL notation[9] for according to our web requirements classification symbolized different requirements. From the following set only one can be a chosen for a particular node.
enum GRLNode={Goal, Softgoal, task, resource}

There would be links connecting the nodes, that can be represented as the Link set with four members, the link ID which is the unique identification number, Linktype, to and from which are the pointers to the nodes. The Linktype is represented as <<enumeration>> because only one type can be chosen. The decomposition link can be either AND or OR. The contribution link would also have contribution weights shown in the set below.

Link={ ID, Linktype, to, from }
enum Linktype={{Decomposition,DecompositionLink}, ,{Contribution,Contribution_weight}, {correlation,contribution_weight}, means-end, dependency }
enum DecompositionLink={And,Or}
enum Contribution_weight={make,help,some+,unknown,some-,hurt,break }

The primary input to the algorithm are the goals that are described in the following set.

Goal={ID, Name, incoming_link, outgoing_link, Ftype}

The ID would be the unique identification number for the Goal, it may be automatically generated for each new entry of goal. The Name would be entered by the Requirements Engineer, the incoming and outgoing links mentioned here represent any kind of Linktype mentioned in the above paragraph, initially set to NULL. The Ftype signifies the type of Functional Goals, described in the next paragraph. The sub goals mentioned by the requirements engineer have to be put into the relevant web functional category as shown in the following set Ftype.

enum Ftype = {Content, Navigation, Business Process, Presentation, Personalization}.

The superset Stype indicates the set of different softgoal categories. At the Base WebGRL diagram level, all the non-functional requirements except the non-functional requirements specific to the functional requirements will be specified. The non-functional requirements specific to the product, organization, Actor's expectations, Legal, Environmental, Project specific non-functional requirements / constraints have to be identified at this level. The sets defining them are shown below.

Stype={Product_stype, Org_stype, Actor_stype, Legal_stype, Env_stype, Project_stype}
product_stype = {Usability, Conformance, Security, Efficiency}
Org_Stype = {Organizational objectives }
Actor_Stype={User friendliness, Empathetic, Understandability}
Legal_Stype={conformance to standards, legal issues}
Env_Stype={compatibility, sustainability}
Project_stype={Resource Constraints, Cost, Human Proficiency}

The softgoals mentioned above are specified along with the softgoals relevance, that will further help in prioritizing, conflict resolution and choice of alternatives. For each of the sets shown above, would have a corresponding set describing its details. For a specific Web application, the attributes of the softgoals can also be cited. One softgoal can have 0 to many attributes. Softgoal relevance can be zero if the softgoal is not relevant, one or more if the softgoal is relevant.

Softgoal= {ID, Name, Attribute, incoming_link, outgoing_link, Soft_relevance}
Soft_relevance={Indispensable(5), Very critical(4), Critical(3),Moderate(2), Little(1), not relevant(0) }

The resource or tasks can be represented with the following information:

Resource={ID, Name, incoming_link, outgoing_link}
Task={ID, Name, incoming_link, outgoing_link}

3.1   Algorithm for Construction of Base WebGRL Diagram for a Given Problem

1. Input the primary < Goal>(s) for creation of this web application.
2. For each primary <Goal> plotted in step 1
    a. Input from user if goal can be further decomposed to subgoals
    b. If yes, input the sub<Goal>(s), with its <Ftype>.
    c. Set outgoing link of the primary goal as decomposition link(AND/OR).
3. For each sub <Goal> entered in step 2
    a. Input from user if the goals need further refinement.
    b. If yes, input the subgoals as <Goal> with its <Ftype>
    c. Set the <link> between the parent and the subgoal.
    d. Do the subgoals mentioned here need further refinement, if yes go to   step 'a' else exit from the loop.
4. For each sub-member of the super set <Stype>
    a. enter the soft_relevance for each softgoal.
    b. If soft_relevance > 0
    c. Then Input the attributes for the softgoals, along with the incoming or outgoing links.
    d. Also update the incoming / outgoing links of corresponding goals.
    e. Do the attribute need further refinement,if so go to step c.

5. Do any of the softgoals mentioned in step 4 and 5, need further refinement to goals / softgoals.
   a. If yes, input <Goal> or <Softgoal> and update the links.
6. Specify if softgoal/goal need to be operationalized to tasks.
   a. If yes, specify the task, the means_end link, any other relation with other goals, incoming link, outgoing link and represent it with hexagon.
7. If need of resource, mention it with its relation to the hard/softgoals.

4   Online Bookshop Example

We take the example of an online book shop to describe our approach. The following goals and softgoals are gathered in initial meeting with stakeholder:-

Goals a)Primary goal- Sell books, b)Provide information about books, c) Facilitate payments, d) Maintain customer details

Softgoals-a) Increase profit by retaining old customers and attracting new customers, b) Provide secure means of financial transactions, c) Build a user – friendly web application, d) The web application should be easy to maintain.

Base WebGRL diagram for Online Book Shop example is as shown in Figure 2.

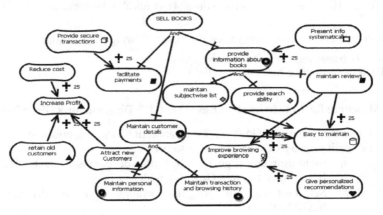

Fig. 2. Base WebGRL diagram for Online Book Shop using enhanced notation from[17]

5   Conclusion and Future Work

In this paper we have presented an approach that improves the Web Requirements Engineering methods by integrating the concepts of Goals, Scenarios and Aspects. The algorithm presented would assist the requirements engineer to clearly elicit and analyse requirements that would reduce the conflicts, minimize maintenance issues and also provide design alternatives. The algorithm here draws the first WebGRL diagram that depicts the application outlook in future. Our future work includes transformation and further refinement from Base WebGRL diagram for each kind of web-specific functional requirement in the second level to do exhaustive study of the system.

References

1. Srivastava, S., Chawla, S.: Multifaceted Classification of Websites for Goal oriented Requirements Engineering. In: Ranka, S., Banerjee, A., Biswas, K.K., Dua, S., Mishra, P., Moona, R., Poon, S.-H., Wang, C.-L. (eds.) IC3 2010. CCIS, vol. 94, pp. 479–485. Springer, Heidelberg (2010)
2. Mylopoulos, C., Yu, E.: From Object-Oriented to Goal-Oriented Requirements Analysis. Communications of the ACM 42(1) (January 1999)
3. van Lamsweerde, A.: GORE: From Research to practice. In: Proc. RE 2004: 12th IEEE International Requirements Engineering Conference, Kyoto (September 2004)
4. Bolchini, D., Paolini, P.: Goal-Driven Requirements Analysis for Hypermedia-intensive Web Applications. Requirements Engineering Journal, 85–103 (2003)
5. Jaap, et al.: e-Service design using i* and e3 value modeling. IEEE Software 23 (2006)
6. Azam et al.: Integrating value based requirements engineering models to WebML using VIP business modeling framework (2007)
7. Garrigós, I., Mazón, J.-N., Trujillo, J.: A Requirement Analysis Approach for Using i* in Web Engineering. In: Gaedke, M., Grossniklaus, M., Díaz, O. (eds.) ICWE 2009. LNCS, vol. 5648, pp. 151–165. Springer, Heidelberg (2009)
8. Srivastava, S., Chawla, S.: Goal Oriented Requirements Engineering for Web Applications: A Comparative Study. Int. J. of Recent Trends in Engineering and Technology 4(2), 96–98 (2010)
9. ITU-T, Recommendation Z.151 (11/08): User Requirements Notation (URN)
10. Filman, R., Friedman, D.: Aspect-Oriented Programming is Quantification and Obliviousness. In: Fillman, E., Clark, A. (eds.) Aspect-Oriented Software Development, pp. 1–7. Addison-Wesley, Boston (2005)
11. Nora, K., Escalona, M.: Requirements Engineering for Web Applications – A Comparative Study. Journal of Web Engineering 2(3), 193–212 (2004)
12. Aguilar, J.A., Garrigós, I., Mazón, J.-N., Trujillo, J.: Web Engineering Approaches for Requirement Analysis - A Systematic Literature Review. In: WEBIST (1), pp. 187–190 (2010)
13. Yu, E.: Towards Modelling and Reasoning Support for Early-Phase Requirements Engineering. In: Proceedings of the 3rd IEEE Int. Symp. on Requirements Engineering (RE 1997), Washington D.C., USA, pp. 226–235 (January 1997)
14. Aguilar, Garrigós, I., Mazón, Trujillo, J.: An MDA Approach for Goal-Oriented Requirement Analysis in Web Engineering. J. Univ. Comp. Sc. 16(17), 2475–2494 (2010)
15. Aguilar, J., Garrigós, I., Mazón: A Goal-Oriented Approach for Optimizing Non-functional Requirements in Web Applications. In: ER Workshops 2011, pp. 14–23 (2011)
16. Chung, L., Nixon, B.A., Yu, E., Mylopoulos, J.: Non-Functional Requirements in Software Engineering. Kluwer Academic Publishers, Dordrecht (2000)
17. Chawla, S., Srivastava, S.: Improving Web Requirements Engineering with Goals, Aspects and Scenarios. In: SCES 2012, March 16-18. IEEE (2012)
18. Chawla, S., Srivastava, S., Bedi, P.: GOREWEB Framework for Goal Oriented Requirements Engineering of Web Applications. In: Aluru, S., Bandyopadhyay, S., Catalyurek, U.V., Dubhashi, D.P., Jones, P.H., Parashar, M., Schmidt, B. (eds.) IC3 2011. CCIS, vol. 168, pp. 229–241. Springer, Heidelberg (2011)
19. Mussbacher, G.: The Aspect-Oriented User Requirements Notation: Aspects, Goals, And Scenarios. In: 10th International Conference on Aspect-Oriented Software Development (AOSD 2011), pp. 59–60. ACM (2011)

Qualitative Analysis Model for Qualifying the Components for Reusability Using Fuzzy Approach

V. Subedha and S. Sridhar

Research Supervisor, Sathyabama University, Chennai, India
subedha@gmail.com, drssridhar@yahoo.com

Abstract. A reusable software component is a component in an executable form where it can be plugged into the environment. In order to reuse the high quality components from an existing environment, finding the measurable characteristics of the reusable software components and their corresponding metrics is an important issue. Although, some characteristics are impossible to measure or predict directly there are still many characteristics that can be used for measuring the reusable software component. We propose a qualitative analysis model to assess the quality of the component and this proposed model is feasible and can achieve high quality reusable components compare with other model in the existing literature. We measure the quality of the components for reuse with functional coverage report, software reuse metrics and minimum extraction time. Using these measures the identified set of components is classified into qualified set and not qualified set for reusability. The qualified set for reusability will give high potential and high quality reusable components which will increase the reuse frequency and reuse utility level. The reusability degree of the component can be obtained with the help of Fuzzy Rules.

Keywords: Software reuse, reusability metrics, quality of reusability, fuzzy logic, component assessment model.

1 Introduction

Software reuse [1] is the process of using the existing software assets. Software assets or components include all software products, schemas, architectures, requirements, proposals, specifications, design, user manuals, plans, interface, data, templates and test suites. The reuse experts pay much attention to extract the component but neglect the quality of the components to be reused. To achieve a significant reuse with components, there should be a well define quality model for evaluating the reusability [2].

If there is more number of components available in the repositories, it is necessary to discover some software reuse metrics to qualify the components based on characteristics of components [3]. Individual software metric cannot measure the overall quality characteristics of the reusable software component. So, in this paper we propose a quality analysis model for assessing the quality of the reusable software components. The fundamental motivation of this proposed model is to achieve high

V.V. Das and P.M. El-Kafrawy (Eds.): SPIT 2012, LNICST 117, pp. 160–167, 2014.

potential benefits of reuse. Three important characteristics of reusability are i) Functional usefulness of the component which is to be reused ii) Time for Extracting the Component from the existing library and iii) Quality of the component

So, we combine the metrics based on the functional coverage report, software reuse metrics and minimum extraction time and we use fuzzy rules for qualifying the component for reusability. The rest of the paper is structured as follows: section 2 briefly describes the existing literature. In section 3, we describe the proposed qualitative analysis model for qualification. Section 4 gives the definitions of measures and metrics. In section 5, the process of qualitative analysis model for the qualification phase using Fuzzy rules. Section 6 presents the evaluation of qualitative analysis model, while section 7 concludes this work.

2   Related Work

Several works has been done in this area. Some of them are as:

In 2005, Richard W. Selby [4], investigated, analyzed, and evaluated software reusability by mining software repositories from a NASA software development environment that actively reuses software. The author achieved an average reuse of 32 percent per project. In 2006, Parvinder S. Sandhu and Hardeep Singh [5] proposed reusability evaluation model for assessing the reusability of software components. The authors proposed Neuro-fuzzy Inference engine can be used to evaluate the reusability. In 2007, Parvinder S. Sandhu Pavel Blecharz and Hardeep Singh [6] proposed Quantitative Investigation of impact of the factors contribution towards measuring the reusability of software components which helps to evaluate the quality of the components. They used Taguchi approach in analyzing the significance of different attributes in deciding the reusability level of a particular component.

In 2008, GUI GUI and Paul D. Scott[7] proposed new measure of coupling and cohesion to assess the reusability of components. They shown that the new measures proposed by them was consistently superior at the time of measuring the component reusability. They used five metrics for coupling and five metrics for cohesion and they were very good predictors for evaluation the reusability of the component.

In 2009, Parvinder S. Sandhu, Harpreet Kaur and Amanpreet Singh [8] proposed reusability evaluation system for object oriented software components. In 2010, Sonia Manhas, Rajeev Vashisht, Parvinder S. Sandhu and Nirvair Neeru [9] proposed reusability evaluation model for assessing reusability of software components. The different neural network approaches are used for the modeling of the reusability data.

In 2011, Fazal-e-Amin, Ahmad Kamil Mahmood and Alan Oxley [10] proposed reusability attribute model for assessing reusability of software components. The proposed model is derived using the GQM approach. In 2012, Ajay Kumar [12] proposed a model for classification of the reusability of software components using support vector machine. In all existing model the static metrics are defined to evaluate the quality of the components for reusability where we propose dynamic metrics to evaluate the quality of the components for reusability.

3   Proposed Qualitative Analysis Model for Qualification

The proposed qualitative analysis model is used to assess the r component quality for high potential benefits and high quality reuse in order to increase the productivity. The specific steps involved in the qualitative analysis model are

1. Identify the characteristics for quality analysis of reusable software components
2. Selection of metrics to measure the identified characteristics and this metrics will serves as a qualifier for quality analysis in the qualification phase
3. Integrate all the metrics and give the priority to the metrics
4. In measurement invocation the assessment was carried out using the qualifiers and the entire set of identified reusable components is classified as qualified set for reuse and not qualified set for reuse.

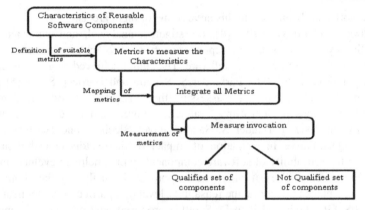

Fig. 1. Qualitative Analysis Model

As shown in the fig. 1. The first step is to discover the characteristics of reusable software components which can be applicable to the environment.

The second step is to select the metrics to measure the characteristics and derive the quality attributes and also this metrics will serve as a qualifier for quality analysis in the qualification phase. This is done by collecting the list of metric and choosing the metrics which is easy, robust and useful for the software component reusability. Once we identified the qualifier in next step, we have to define the computing values of the metrics and integrate them. In the fourth step invoke the measurement and this step classifies the entire identified set as qualified or not qualified for reusability.

4   Measures and Metrics in Qualitative Analysis Model

In software engineering measurement, a metric is a quantitative indicator of a software attribute. A metrics model specifies relationships between metrics and the characteristics being measured by these metrics. In this section a description of the measures and metrics which are used to assess reusability is provided.

4.1   Functional Verification Measure

The first step involved in functional verification of the component in collecting the requirements of the reusability. By using coverage directed test generation for functional verification by genetic algorithm the reuser generates, executes a set of test cases and functional coverage report of the component is collected. We use the statement coverage and branch coverage as metrics for coverage analysis to qualify the candidate component for reusability.

4.2   Reuse Measure

The functional usefulness of the component is measured by reuse frequency which is an indirect measure of the functional usefulness of a component. We measure the functional usefulness as that frequently used system is a good candidate for reuse in context level in similar domain. Hence we choose the metrics reuse frequency as a qualifier for qualifying the components. Reuse frequency of each component can be calculated using the equation (1).

$$\text{Reuse Frequency} = \frac{n(C)}{\frac{1}{n}\sum_{i=1}^{n} n(Si)} \tag{1}$$

where n(C) is total number of reference to the Component, n(Si) is total number of reference for each Standard Components in the existing environment & n is the total number of component in the existing environment.

4.3   Time Measure

The components having the extraction time less than the average extraction time is qualified for reuse. The reason for choosing the extraction time as metrics is to speed up the process of reuse. The extraction time and the optimal path for the extraction are calculated using a scheme called as minimum Extraction Time First.

5   Process of Qualitative Analysis Model Using Fuzzy Rules

Each individual metrics plays an important role to measure the individual characteristic of the reusable components. But these metrics individually cannot provide an overall measurement, so we combine these metrics as the measurement of the reusable software component. In this model we assign different weights to different metrics and it is combining into overall measurement and the fuzzy rules are used to classify the components for reusable or not for reusable.

5.1   Metrics Suite Combination for Higher-Level

The metric data for the component qualification were collected using the different tools and they are combined to higher level to measure the quality. The four set of primitive metrics are combine into one higher-level measurement as follows:

LV_1: Linguistic Values for Statement coverage metric & W_1: Weight for LV_1
LV_2: Linguistic Values for Branch coverage metric & W_2: Weight for LV_2
LV_3: Linguistic Values for Extraction time metric & W_3: Weight for LV_3
LV_4: Linguistic Values for reuse frequency metric & W_4: Weight for LV_4
We combine these four metrics into a quality measurement as formula (2)

$$QM = LV_i \, W_i \quad \text{Where} \quad \sum_{i=1}^{4} wi = 1 \tag{2}$$

5.2   Design of Linguistic Variables for Selected Metrics

Linguistic variables are then assigned to the metrics based on their values. The assignment of the linguistic variable depends on the range of the metrics measurement. We recommend that all linguistic value of each primitive metric shall be normalized between LOW, MEDIUM and HIGH

Linguistic variables for statement coverage: Statement coverage is assigned with two linguistic variables LOW and HIGH based on the coverage report. If the statement coverage is 100% then the linguistic variable is HIGH else it is LOW.

Linguistic variables for Branch coverage: Branch coverage is assigned with three linguistic variables LOW, MEDIUM and HIGH based on the coverage report. If the branch coverage is >90% then the linguistic variable is HIGH else if it is within the range 85% - 90% then it is MEDIUM else it is LOW.

Linguistic variables for Extraction time: The components having the extraction time less than the average extraction time is qualified for reuse from the component repositories. Extraction time is assigned with two linguistic variables as LOW and HIGH. If the extraction time is less than the average extraction time is assigned with linguistic variable HIGH else it is assigned with LOW.

Linguistic variables for reuse frequency: Reuse-Frequency is assigned with two linguistic variables LOW and HIGH as constants in the range of less than 1 and greater than 1.

Linguistic variables for reusability degree: Reusability degree is the output parameter which is use to measure the reusability and assigned with two linguistic variables LOW and HIGH as constants in the range of less than or equal to 0.8 and greater than 0.8.

5.3 Fuzzy Rules for Qualifying the Components

Fuzzy inference is the process of formulating the mapping from a given input to an output using fuzzy logic. The mapping then provides a basis for decision-making. The process of fuzzy inference involves all of the pieces like membership functions, fuzzy logic operators and if-then rules. Consider a fuzzy system having the following rule base.

Rule 1 : if u is A1 and x is B1 and y is C1 and z is D1, then R=w11+w21+w31+w41

Rule 2 : if u is A2 and x is B2 and y is C2 and z is D2, then R=w12+w22+w32+w42.

. . . .

Rule n : if u is An and x is Bn and y is Cn and z is Dn, then R= w1n+w2n+w3n+w4n

Let the membership functions of fuzzy sets Ai, Bi, Ci, Di where i=1, 2, 3.....n be μ_{Ai}, μ_{Bi}, μ_{Ci}, μ_{Di}. Evaluating the rule premises results in (3)

$$R_i = \mu_{Ai}(u) + \mu_{Bi}(x) + \mu_{Ci}(y) + \mu_{Di}(z) \qquad (3)$$

where R_i is the reusability degree of the ith component.

With the help of the fuzzy-rules the knowledge base for calculating the reusability degree of the reusable software components is calculated. As there are totally four inputs, in which three inputs have two membership functions and other input have three membership functions. After all the possible combinations the size of the rule base comes out to be 2*3*2*2=24. Examples rules could be :

If (statement coverage is LOW) and (branch coverage is LOW) and (extraction time is LOW) and (reuse frequency is LOW) then (Reusability Degree is LOW)

If (statement coverage is HIGH) and (branch coverage is HIGH) and (extraction time is HIGH) and (reuse frequency is LOW) then (Reusability Degree is HIGH)

5.4 Weight Value Selection

After collecting the metrics for assessing the reusability degree and assigning the linguistic variable for each metrics, we select the suitable weight values to compute the quality measurement value for assessing the reusability degree. Production rules can be generated to select the weight value.

R11: if LV_1 = LOW then w11   R12: if LV1 = HIGH then w12   R21: if LV_2 = LOW then w21   R22: if LV2 = MEDIUM then w22   R23: if LV2 = HIGH then w23
R31: if LV3 = LOW then w31   R32: if LV3 = HIGH then w32
R41: if LV4 = LOW then w41   R42: if LV4 = HIGH then w42

6 Evaluation of Qualitative Analysis Model

In this section we describe experiments with proposed qualitative analysis model qualifying the components with our own test cases. All necessary information for calculating the quality of the components is given in the following Table 1. Accordingly, Table 2 presents the measurement data for high reuse components and it shows that in general 40 to 50 percent of identified components for possible reuse.

Table 1. Identified Set of components for reusability with all metrics

Component Number	Statement Coverage	Branch Coverage	Extraction Time	Reuse Frequency
1	95%	85%	0.941	0.80
2	100%	95%	0.047	1.70
3	100%	80%	1.023	0.71
4	100%	95%	0.177	0.98
5	100%	90%	0.056	0.41
6	100%	85%	0.320	1.50
7	100%	95%	0.913	1.40
8	100%	95%	0.781	0.30
9	90%	75%	1.001	0.79
10	100%	80%	0.328	1.25

Table 2. Classified Set of components for reuse and not reuse

Component Number	Weight for reusability degree using fuzzy rules	Linguistic variables For Reusability degree	Status of the Component
1	0.36	LOW	Not Qualified
2	1.0	HIGH	Qualified
3	0.43	LOW	Not Qualified
4	0.84	HIGH	Qualified
5	0.80	LOW	Not Qualified
6	0.91	HIGH	Qualified
7	0.85	HIGH	Qualified
8	0.69	LOW	Not Qualified
9	0.16	LOW	Not Qualified
10	0.74	LOW	Not Qualified

The Component reuse percentage for reusability is calculated and shown in the following figure 2.

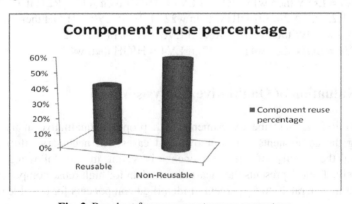

Fig. 2. Bar chart for component reuses percentage

7   Conclusion

One of the main important issue in reusing the software component is to optimize the process of identifying the suitable components for a given requirements. Effective reuse is only possible with effective assessment and classification. In this paper we have presented the stat-of-art of the qualitative analysis model especially in the context of software reuse.

We proposed a new model for quality assessment based on fuzzy rules. The main purpose of this model is to measure the quality of the component in order to realize the reusability of component effectively and to identify the best components in terms of their reusability. We need to expand the number of metrics in order to provide adequate coverage with respect to reusability of a component. We intend to apply this model in a wider variety of applications through several platforms to determine the impact and to design an automated tool for component classification.

References

1. Frakes, W.B., Kang, K.: Software Reuse Research: Status and Future. IEEE Transactions on Software Engineering 31(7), 529–536 (2005)
2. Choi, S.W., Her, J.S., Kim, S.D.: Qos Metrics for Evaluating Services from the Perspective of Service Provides. In: Proceedings of IEEE International Conference on e-business engineering (ICEBE 2007), pp. 622–625 (2007)
3. Singh, S., Thapa, M., Singh, S., Singh, G.: Software Engineering – Survey of Reusability Based on Software Component. International Journal of Computer Applications (0975 – 8887) 8(12), 39–42 (2010)
4. Selby, R.W.: Enabling Reuse-Based Software Development of Large-Scale Systems. IEEE Transaction of Software Engineering 31(6), 495–510 (2005)
5. Sandhu, S., Singh, H.: Automatic Reusability Appraisal of Software Components using Neuro-Fuzzy Approach. International Journal of Information Technology 3(3), 209–214 (2006)
6. Sandhu, P.S., Blecharz, P., Singh, H.: A Taguchi Approach to Investigate Impact of Factors for Reusability of Software Components. World Academy of Science, Engineering and Technology, 135–140 (September 2007)
7. Gui, G., Scott, P.D.: New coupling and cohesion Metrics for Evaluation of Software Component Reusability. In: Proc. ICYCS, pp. 1181–1186 (2008)
8. Sandhu, P.S., Kaur, H., Singh, A.: Modeling of Reusability of Object Oriented Software System. World Academy of Science, Engineering and Technology (30), 162–165 (2009)
9. Manhas, S., Vashisht, R., Sandhu, P.S., Neeru, N.: Reusability Evaluation Model for Procedure Based Software Systems. International Journal of Computer and Electrical Engineering 2(6), 1107–1110 (2010)
10. Fazal-e-Amin, Mahmood, A.K., Oxley, A.: Reusability Assessment of Open Source Components for Software Product Lines. International Journal on New Computer Architectures and Their Applications (IJNCAA) 1(3), 519–533 (2011)
11. Kumar, A.: Measuring Software Reusability using SVM based Classifier Approach. International Journal of Information Technology and Knowledge Management 5(1), 205–209 (2012)

K-Means Segmentation of Alzheimer's Disease in Pet Scan Datasets – An Implementation

A. Meena[1] and K. Raja[2]

[1] Sathyabama University, Chennai, India
[2] Narasu's Sarathy Institute of Technology, Salem, India
kabimeena2@hotmail.com, raja_koth@yahoo.co.in

Abstract. The Positron Emission Tomography (PET) scan image requires expertise in the segmentation where clustering algorithm plays an important role in the automation process. The algorithm optimization is concluded based on the performance, quality and number of clusters extracted. This paper is proposed to study the commonly used K- Means clustering algorithm and to discuss a brief list of toolboxes for reproducing and extending works presented in medical image analysis. This work is compiled using AForge .NET framework in windows environment and MATrix LABoratory (MATLAB 7.0.1).

Keywords: Clustering, K- means, PET scan images, AForge .NET framework, MATLAB, MIPAV.

1 Introduction

Positron Emission Tomography (PET) detects chemical and physiological changes related to functional metabolism [1, 7]. This scan images are more sensitive than other image techniques such CT and MRI because the other imaging techniques only shows the physiology of the body parts.

This paper presents a study on the application of well known K-Means clustering algorithm. This algorithm is used to automate process of segmentation of the tumor affected area based on the datasets classified by its type, size, and number of clusters [2]. The rest of the paper is organized as follows. Section 2 states the related work in this area; section 3 describes the K-Means clustering algorithms, section 4 and section 5 presents the implementation methods. Comparison between AForge .NET framework and MATLAB are made in the concluding section.

2 Related Work

Digital image processing allows an algorithm to avoid problems such as the build-up of noise and signal distortion occuring in analog image processing.

Fulham *et al.* (2002) stated that quantitative positron emission tomography provides the measurements of dynamic physiological and biochemical processes in humans. Ciccarelli *et al.* (2003) and Meder *et al.* (2006) proposed a method to identify sclerosis that disrupts the normal organization or integrity of cerebral white

V.V. Das and P.M. El-Kafrawy (Eds.): SPIT 2012, LNICST 117, pp. 168–172, 2014.

matter and the underlying changes in cartilage structure during osteoarthritis. Functional imaging methods are also being used to evaluate the appropriateness and efficacy of therapies such as Parkinson's disease, depression, schizophrenia, and Alzheimer's disease [5]. Quantum dots (qdots) are fluorescent nano particles of semiconductor material which are specially designed to detect the biochemical markers of cancer (Carts-Powell, 2006). Osama (2008) explained about the comparision of clustering algorithms and its application based on the type of dataset used. In 2009, Stefan *et al.* described the structured patient data for the analysis of the implementation of a clustering algorithm. These authors correlated images of the dementia affected brain with other variables, for instance, demographic information or outcomes of clinical tests [6]. In this paper, clustering is applied to whole PET scans.

3   K-Means Clustering Algorithm

Clustering is used to classify items into identical groups in the process of data mining. It also exploits segmentation which is used for quick bird view for any kind of problem. K-Means is a well known partitioning method. Objects are classified as belonging to one of k groups, k chosen a priori [3]. Cluster membership is determined by calculating the centroid for each group and assigning each object to the group with the closest centroid. This approach minimizes the overall within-cluster dispersion by iterative reallocation of cluster members [4].

Pseudo code for centroid calculation

```
Step1: Initialize / Calculate new centroid
Step2: Calculate the distance between object and every
       centroid
Step3: Object Clustering
Step4: If any object moved from one cluster to the other,
       go to step1 or Stop
```

Pseudo code for image segmentation

```
Step1: Initialize centroids corresponding to required
       number  of clusters
Step2: Calculate original centroid  (Call K- Means)
Step3: Calculate the mask
Step4: Do the segmentation process
```

4   AForge .NET Framework

4.1   Text Conversion

The sample data was collected from Alzheimer's Disease Neuroimaging Initiative (ADNI) [9, 10]. The given input image consisting of various pixels points is then converted to byte stream. The converted byte stream is stored in a jagged array in the form of a text file as datasets.

4.2   Data Preprocessing and Image Retrieval

The dataset in the form of text file is imported into the system then it is converted in the Comma Separated Values (CSV) format. The converted CSV in byte stream is used to initialize the jagged pixel array and the array is transformed to bitmap image. Using jagged array the length of each array pixel can be adjusted. It can use less memory and be faster than two dimensional arrays because of uneven shape.

The image retrieved from the byte stream is shown in the form of the thumbnail view in this part of the system and the system's mode displays the rows and columns. This jagged index is used to reallocating the pixel values to its corresponding centroid values.

4.3   Knowledge Based Cluster Analysis

This part of the system is to select the K- Means clustering algorithm for the given dataset and to segment an image. Randomly the number of cluster is selected as 5. The clustering algorithm is used to automate the process of segmentation here when the clustering is done based on the pixel values. It can be changed to its pixel values so that the image segmentation is made possible in the byte stream.

5   Matlab

The given image image is loaded in to MATLAB. First the number of clusters is assigned. Then the centroid (c) initialization is calculated as follows

$$c = (1:k)*m / (k+1) \tag{1}$$

where the double precision image pixel in single column (m) value and number of centroid (k) is used to calculate the initial centroid value

The calculation of distance (d) between centroid and object is derived from

$$d = abs (o (i) - c) \tag{2}$$

Equation (2) o(i) is known as one dimensional array distance. Using that value, new centroid is calculated in equation 3

$$nc(i) = sum (a.*h(a)) / sum (h(a)) \tag{3}$$

where the value object clustering function (a) and non zero element obtained from object clustering h(a) is used to compute the new centroid (nc) value. The resultant new centroid value is used for masking creation and then the image segmentation.

6   Results on Synthetic Image

Figs. 1 are the segmenting results on a synthetic image using K-Means clustering algorithms in AForge .NET and MATLAB.

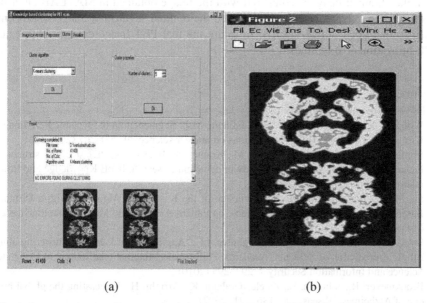

(a)   (b)

Fig. 1. Segmentation results on synthetic image. (a) AForge .NET result. (b) MATLAB result.

The obtained image from MATLAB and .NET framework is analyzed using Medical Image Processing And Visualization (MIPAV) tool. The selection volume of interest is identified and the statistical parameter is listed below. Fig. 2 shows that the co efficient of variance value in .NET framework is lesser than MATLAB environment and it is the proof for less significant distribution in .NET

S. No	Parameter	Result obtained from	
		MATLAB	.NET
1.	Average	86.0916	79.2168
2.	Standard Deviation	92.0758	65.3007
3.	Coefficient of variance	106.951	82.433

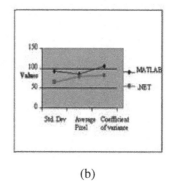

(a)   (b)

Fig. 2. Results obtained from Aforge .NET and MATLAB. (a) Statistical Values. (b) Graph representation.

7   Conclusion and Future Work

This paper deals with the basic K-Means algorithm in different working platform. First the K-Means is tested on AForge.NET framework in windows environment. Then the obtained image is compared with the image obtained in MATLAB environment. AForge .NET environment produced the optimal segmented image when compared to that got from MATLAB. In future the real PET image datasets with exact CPU utilization is to be studied.

References

1. Wong, K.-P., Geng, D., Meikle, S.R., Fulham, M.J.: Segmentation of Dynamic PET Images Using cluster analysis. IEEE Transactions on nuclear science 49, 200–207 (2002)
2. Hapfelmeier, A., Schmidt, J., Muller, M., Kramer, S.: Interpreting PET scans by structured Patient Data: A Data mining case study in dementia Research. IEEE Knowledge and Information Systems, 213–222 (2009)
3. Su, M.C., Chou, C.H.: A Modified Version of the K – Means Algorithm with a Distance Based on Cluster Symmetry. IEEE Trans. on Pattern Analysis and Machine Intelligence 23, 674–680 (2001)
4. Oyelade, O.J., Oladipupo, O.O., Obagbuwa, I.C.: Application of k-Means Clustering algorithm for prediction of Students' Academic Performance. International Journal of Computer Science and Information Security 7, 292–295 (2010)
5. Brookmeyer, R., Johnson, E., Ziegler-Graham, K., Arrighi, H.: Forecasting the global burden of Alzheimer's disease, pp. 186–191 (2007)
6. Pham, D.L., Xu, C., Prince, L.: Current methods in medical images segmentation. Annual review of biomedical engineering 2, 315–337 (2000)
7. Wagber, H.N., Szabo, Z., Buchanan, J.W.: Principles of nuclear medicine. Pensylvania, 564–575 (1995)

Comparative Study between ICI Self Cancellation and Symmetric Symbol Repetition

Fatima Zohra Boumediene, Mohamed Tayebi, and Merahi Bouziani

Laboratory of Telecommunications and Digital Signal Processing
University of Sidi Bel Abbes, 22000, Algeria
{tayebi_med,boumediene_faty}@hotmail.com

Abstract. The frequency shifts created by the imperfections of local oscillators and the Doppler-effect generating inter-carrier interference responsible for the degradation of system performance. Several studies have been developed to reduce this interference. A comparative study of different methods facilitates the choice of the most appropriate algorithm. Our study investigates and compares two algorithms, the ICI Self Cancellation and Symmetric Symbol Repetition. In terms of CIR, it appears that the method of Symmetric Symbol Repetition offers better performance; however, these same performances degrade rapidly when the carrier offset frequency increases. In terms of performance stability, the ICI Self Cancellation is most appropriate.

Keywords: Orthogonal frequency division multiplexing (OFDM), Inter-carriers Interferences (ICI), Carrier to Interferences Ratio (CIR), Carrier Frequency Offset (CFO), ICI Self Cancellation, Symmetric Symbol Repetition (SSR).

1 Introduction

OFDM has been discovered in the sixties by chang (1966) [1], however, is through new technologies that the OFDM has emerged [2]. The OFDM has invaded the world of wireless communications such as Digital Audio Broadcasting (DAB) and Digital Video Broadcasting (DVB), and recently the OFDM has found several applications in the optical domain [3] - [4]. It is well known that OFDM is sensitive to carrier frequency offset. The frequency shift caused by the local oscillators and the Doppler-effect causes a loss of orthogonality and results in the appearance of inter-carrier interference (ICI). To overcome this problem, a number of algorithms have been developed. The first was the algorithm of ICI Self Cancellation [5], then the algorithm called Symmetric Symbol Repetition (SSR) [6] and lastly the method of conjugate transmission [7]. Our work is to make a comparative study between the algorithms mentioned. The outcome of the study leads us to say that the method of ICI Self Cancellation is more appropriate in a radio mobile channel, while the algorithm of SSR gives better performances in fixed links. This document is structured as follows; section 2 examines the OFDM characterized by CFO. Section 3 make a comparative study between two existing algorithms, the ICI Self Cancellation and the Symmetric Symbol Repetition. Section 4 concludes the work.

V.V. Das and P.M. El-Kafrawy (Eds.): SPIT 2012, LNICST 117, pp. 173–177, 2014.

2   OFDM Characterized by CFO

In digital communication, the transmitter and receiver can be either fixed or mobile. In a fixed link, the imperfections of the local oscillators of the transmitter and receiver are constant and therefore the carrier frequency offset is constant, whereas if the transmitter or the receiver moves, the carrier frequency offset is variable .

Due to the frequency difference between transmitter and receiver, the received signal after the bloc of Fast Fourier Transform (FFT) is equal to [5]:

$$Y(k) = X(k)S(0) + \sum_{\substack{m=0 \\ m \neq k}}^{N-1} X(m)\ S(m-k) \tag{1}$$

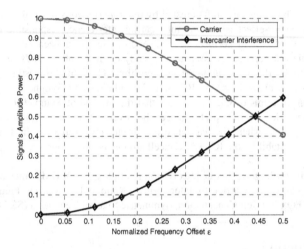

Fig. 1. Signal power and interference power

The complex coefficients are given by the relation [5]:

$$S(m-k) = \frac{sin\pi(m-k+\varepsilon)}{Nsin\frac{\pi}{N}(m-k+\varepsilon)}\ e^{j\pi(1-\frac{1}{N})(m-k+\varepsilon)} \tag{2}$$

Where ε represents the normalized carrier frequency offset. The carrier power is proportional to [8]:

$$|S(0)|^2 = \left|\frac{sin\pi\varepsilon}{Nsin\frac{\pi}{N}\varepsilon}\right|^2 \tag{3}$$

While the interferences power is proportional to [8]:

$$\sum_{\substack{m=0 \\ m \neq k}}^{N-1} |S(m-k)|^2 = \sum_{\substack{m=0 \\ m \neq k}}^{N-1} \left|\frac{sin\pi(m-k+\varepsilon)}{Nsin\frac{\pi}{N}(m-k+\varepsilon)}\right|^2 \tag{4}$$

Figure 1 describes the variation of useful signal power and interference power. We notice easily that when the normalized carrier frequency offset ε increases, the useful signal power deteriorates while the interference power increases.

3   Existing Algorithm

To minimize inter-carrier interference, different algorithms have been developed. Our choice was focused on the ICI self-cancellation and Symmetric Symbol repetition (SSR). The ICI Self Cancellation was proposed by Haggman and Zhao in 1996, and again in 2001[5]. The CIR of OFDM is given by the following equation [5]:

$$CIR_1 = \frac{|S(0)|^2}{\sum_{l=1}^{N-1}|S(l)|^2} \tag{5}$$

The CIR of ICI Cancellation is given by [5]:

$$CIR_2 = \frac{|2S(0) - S(1) - S(-1)|^2}{\sum_{\substack{l=2 \\ l\ even}}^{N-1} |2S(l) - S(l+1) - S(l-1)|^2} \tag{6}$$

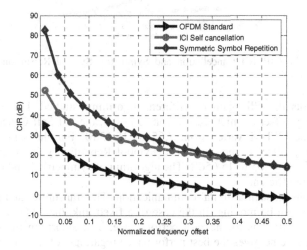

Fig. 2. Comparison between two algorithms

The Symmetric Symbol repetition (SSR) was proposed by Sathanathan [6], in 2000; the obtained CIR is written:

$$CIR_3 = \frac{|2S(0) - S(-1) - S(1)|^2}{\sum_{\substack{l=2 \\ l\ even}}^{N-1} |S(l) + S(N-l) - S(N-l-1) - S(l+1)|^2} \tag{7}$$

Figure 2 plots the different CIR. It clearly shows that both methods improve system performance, but that of symmetric Symbol Repetition is more efficient for small values of normalized carrier frequency offset ε.

To compare the two algorithms, we proposed two criteria for performance comparison; the gain and the stability of the CIR. We will calculate the CIR gain of the ICI Self Cancellation compared to OFDM, it is written as follows:

$$G = 10 * \log_{10}(CIR_2) - 10 * \log_{10}(CIR_1) \tag{8}$$

Similarly, we calculate the gain of CIR of Symmetric Symbol Repetition compared to OFDM:

$$G = 10 * \log_{10}(CIR_3) - 10 * \log_{10}(CIR_1) \tag{9}$$

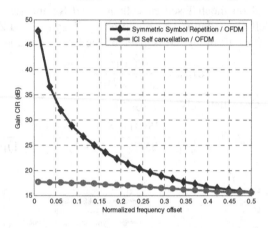

Fig. 3. Gain of the CIR ICI Cancellation and Symmetric Symbol Repetition compared to OFDM

Figure 3 plots the CIR gain of different algorithms studied. For a normalized carrier frequency offset ε which varies from 0 to 0.5, the ICI Self Cancellation gain compared to the OFDM varies from17.65 to 15.65dB. For the same normalized carrier frequency offset ε, the symmetric Symbol Repetition gain compared to the OFDM varies from 47.65 to 15.65dB. The algorithm of symmetric Symbol Repetition is therefore more efficient.

Two situations exist in a digital communication. The transmitter and receiver can be fixed or they can be moving. In the case of a fixed link, the CFO is constant and therefore the objective is to increase performance. The algorithm of SSR is most appropriate because he gives the best performance regardless of the value of CFO. In the case of a mobile link, the CFO is variable, we obtain stable performance. The ICI Self Cancellation algorithm is most appropriate because it gives more stable performance, because it is less sensitive to large variations of the CFO.

4   Conclusion

In this paper, we have studied the OFDM in a channel characterized by the carrier frequency offset. To reduce inter-carrier interference, we studied two different algorithms. If the objective is increased performance, then the algorithm of symmetric Symbol Repetition is required. If instead, the channelis variable, the algorithm of ICI Self Cancellation is required due to its stability.

References

1. Chang, R.W.: Synthesis of band-limited orthogonal signals for multichannel data transmission. Bell Syst. Tech. J. 46, 1775–1796 (1966)
2. Weinstein, S., Ebert, P.: Data transmission by frequency-division multiplexing using the discrete Fourier transform. IEEE Transactions on Communications 19, 628–634 (1971)
3. Armstrong, J.: OFDM for Optical communications. Journal of Lightwave Technology 27(3) (February 1, 2009)
4. Yang, Q., He, Z., Yang, Z., Yu, S., Yi, X., Shieh, W.: Coherent optical DFT-Spread OFDM transmission using orthogonal band multiplexing. Optics Express 20(3), 2379–2385 (2012)
5. Zhao, Y., Häggman, S.-G.: Intercarrier Interference Self-Cancellation Scheme for OFDM Mobile Communication Systems. IEEE Transactions on Communications 49(7), 1185–1191 (2001)
6. Sathananthan, K., Rajatheva, R.M.A.P., Ben Slimane, S.: Analysis of OFDM in the Presence of Frequency Offset and a Method to Reduce Performance Degradation. In: Proceeding of IEEE Globcom, vol. 1, pp. 72–76 (November 2000)
7. Yeh, H., Chang, Y., Hassibi, B.: A Scheme for Cancelling Intercarrier Interference using Conjugate Transmission in Multicarrier Communication Systems. IEEE Transactions on Wireless Communications 6(1) (January 2007)
8. Lee, J., Lou, H., Toumpakaris, D., Cioffi, J.: SNR Analysis of OFDM Systems in the Presence of Carrier Frequency Offset for Fading Channels. IEEE Transactions on Wireless Communications 5(12), 3360–3334 (2006)

Semi Supervised Learning Based Text Classification Model for Multi Label Paradigm

Shweta C. Dharmadhikari[1], Maya Ingle[2], and Parag Kulkarni[3]

[1] Pune Institute of Computer Technology,
Pune, Maharashtra, India
[2] Devi Ahilya Vishwa Vidyalaya, Indore, Madhya Pradesh, India
[3] EkLat Solutions
Pune, Maharashtra, India
{d.shweta18,paragindia}@gmail.com, maya_ingle@rediffmail.com

Abstract. Automatic text categorization (ATC) is a prominent research area within Information retrieval. Through this paper a classification model for ATC in multi-label domain is discussed. We are proposing a new multi label text classification model for assigning more relevant set of categories to every input text document. Our model is greatly influenced by graph based framework and Semi supervised learning. We demonstrate the effectiveness of our model using Enron, Slashdot, Bibtex and RCV1 datasets. We also compare performance of our model with few popular existing supervised techniques. Our experimental results indicate that the use of Semi Supervised Learning in multi label text classification greatly improves the decision making capability of classifier.

Keywords: Automatic text categorization, Multi-label text classification, graph based framework, semi supervised learning.

1   Introduction

Automatic text classification (ATC) is a prominent research area within Information retrieval. Multi label text classification problem refers to the scenario in which a text document can be assigned to more than one classes simultaneously during the process of text classification. The inherent ambiguity present in the content of textual data often makes the text document to be the member of more than one class simultaneously[3]. It has attracted significant attention from lot of researchers for playing crucial role in many applications such as web page classification, classification of news articles, information retrieval etc. Multi label text classifier can be realized by using supervised, unsupervised and semi supervised methods of machine learning. In supervised methods only labeled text data is needed for training. But availability of labeled data all the time is rare and processing of is expensive. Unsupervised methods relies only on unlabeled text documents; but it does not shows remarkable improvement in the performance. Semi supervised methods effectively uses unlabeled data in addition to the labeled data. Majority of existing approaches are supervised in nature[16]. Most of these lacking in considering relationship

V.V. Das and P.M. El-Kafrawy (Eds.): SPIT 2012, LNICST 117, pp. 178–184, 2014.

between class labels, input documents and also relying on labeled data all the time for classification. And also not capable of utilizing information conveyed by unlabeled data[17].

Hence through our paper we are proposing a multi label classification model using semi supervised learning so that classifier can handle labeled and unlabeled data. We are also aiming at handling input documents similarity along with correlation existing between class labels to improve decision making capability of our proposed classifier. We apply the proposed model on standard dataset such as Enron, Bibtex and RCV1 and Slashdot to test the performance. We also compare performance of our model with few popular existing supervised techniques.

The rest of the paper is organized as below. Section 2 describes relevant literature related to our proposed system; Section 3 describes our proposed classification model. Section 4 describes experiments and results, followed by a conclusion in the last section.

2   Related Work/Literature

Multi label learning problem is generally realized by problem transformation and algorithm adaptation methods. Few popular algorithms under these categories are binary relevance method, label power set method, pruned sets method, C4.5, Adaboost.MH & Adaboost.MR, ML-kNN, Classifier chains method etc[20]. These methods either decomposes classification task into multiple independent binary classification tasks[6], one for each category or the ranking function of category labels from the labeled instances and apply it to classify each unknown test instance by choosing all the categories with the scores above the given threshold[20]. Almost all of these methods are supervised in nature. These methods cannot utilize information conveyed by unlabeled data. The other common drawbacks include inability to handle relationship among class labels and can not scale to large data set.

Recently some new approaches for multi-label learning that consider the correlations among categories have been developed. Few eg. are generative model proposed by Ueda[26], Bayesian model proposed by Griffiths [27], Hierarchical structure considered by Rousu [28], Maximum entropy method proposed by Zhu[29], Latent variable based approach proposed by McCallum. But all these methods are also supervised in nature.

Few recent approaches effectively used semi supervised learning for multi label text classification. In 2006 Liu, Jin and Yan proposed Multi-label classification approach based on constrained non negative matrix factorization [8]. In this approach parameter selection affects the overall performance of the system. Zha and Mie proposed Graph-based SSL for multi-label classification in the year 2008[9]. But this approach was purely intended for classification of video files and not for documents. Chen,Song and Zhang proposed Semi supervised multi-label learning by solving a Sylvester Eq in the year 2010 [10]. In this approach they constructed graph for input representation and class representation as well but this approach is getting slower on convergence when applied in the situation where large number of classes and input data exists. In 2009 Lee, Yoo and Choi proposed Semi-Supervised Non negative Matrix Factorization based approach [11]. But this approach was not specifically meant for multi-label text classification.

Thus by identifying limitations of all these methods we feel that there is need to build intelligent text classifier for multi label scenario which can efficiently handle all these said issues.

3   Proposed Classifier Model

The objective behind designing the proposed classifier model is to improve accuracy of multi label text classification process by assigning more relevant set of classes to unclassified documents. Following Fig.1 shows architecture proposed by us to achieve the said objective. We are using both labeled and unlabeled documents for training as our classifier is based on semi supervised learning.

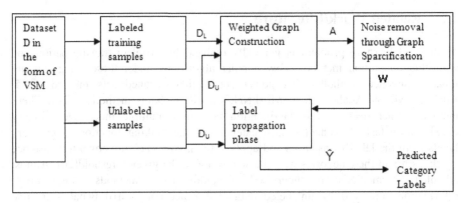

Fig. 1. Architecture of Classifier Model

We considered dataset D, which is in the VSM representation format. Out of which|D_L| documents are already labeled and |D_U| are unlabeled. We constructed Graph G(V,E) out of it. This graph is represented in the form of adjacency matrix A. Graph G consists of "n" no. of vertices such that n=|D_L| + |D_U| .The objective is to predict set of labels for D_U. Each vertex Vi represents document instance di . Relationship between pair of vertices is represented by edge E. The adjacency matrix A∈Rnxn is computed to represent the edge weight using cosine similarity measure. We have captured the correlation among different classes by computing matrix [B]kxk for representing relationship between classes.

In the next phase we attempted to remove noise by eliminating irrelevant documents prior to classification. We constructed graph W from Graph A through graph sparcification process; A⇒W∈Rnxn. In this, Matrix A is specified and reweighted using Knn approach and produce matrix W. This graph specification can lead to improve efficiency in the label inference stage. This stage is followed by classifier training phase which estimates a continuous classification function F on W i.e. F∈R|v|x|c| where |v| is number of vertices and |c| is number of class labels.F: W→Ŷ ...Where Ŷ is estimated label set.It estimates soft labels of unlabeled doc. By optimizing the energy function by generating confidence matrix [P]nxn. To this phase specified graph W acts as an input. Given this graph W and label information. This phase infers labels of unlabeled documents.

In the last Prediction phase we employed label propagation approach . It works on the smoothness assumption of SSL which states that "If two input points x1, x2 are in high density region are closer to each other then so should be the corresponding outputs y1, y2". Closeness between the two document instance can be identified by W. Relation between corresponding class labels can be computed by weighted dot product piBpj . If assignment of class labels pi and pj are relevant to doc. di and dj then we would expect Wi,j ≈ piBpj and uses following smoothness function to predict the labels of unlabeled doc.

$$\emptyset = \sum\nolimits_{i,j=1}^{n} \left(W_{i,j} - \sum_{i,k=1}^{m} p_i B p_j \right)$$

4   Experimentations and Result Discussion

We evaluated our approach under a WEKA-based [23] framework running under Java JDK 1.6 with the libraries of MEKA and Mulan [21][22]. Jblas library for performing matrix operations while computing weights on graph edges. Experiments ran on 64 bit machines with 2.6 GHz of clock speed, allowing up to 4 GB RAM per iteration. Ensemble iterations are set to 10 for EPS. Evaluation is done in the form of 5 × 2 fold cross validation on each dataset. We first measured the accuracy, precision, Recall after label propagation phase is over. We conducted experiments on four text based datasets namely Enron, Slashdot, Bibtex and Reuters. Table 1 summarizes the statistics of datasets that we used in our experiments.

Table 1. Statistics of Datasets

Dataset	No. of document instances	No. of Labels	Attributes
Slashdot	3782	22	500
Enron	1702	53	1001
Bibtex	7395	159	1836
RCV1	12,000	135	5000

Enron dataset contains email messages. It is a subset of about 1700 labeled email messages [21]. BibTeX data set contains metadata for the bibtex items like the title of the paper, the authors, etc. Slashdot dataset contains article titles and partial blurbs mined from Slashdot.org [22]. We measured accuracy, precision, recall and F-measure of overall classification process. Fig. 2 shows the result comparison for these different datasets.We used accuracy measure proposed by Godbole and Sarawagi in [13]. It symmetrically measures how close y_i is to Zi ie estimated labels and true labels. It is the ratio of the size of the union and intersection of the predicted and actual label sets, taken for each example and averaged over the number of examples. The formula used by them to compute accuracy is as follows:

$$Accuracy = \frac{1}{N}\sum_{i=1}^{N}\left[\frac{Y_i \cap Z_i}{Y_i \cup Z_i}\right]$$

In order to evaluate the performance of our classifier model using SSL approach, we compared the results of few popular supervised algorithm such as C4.5, Adaboost, ML-kNN, BP-MLL, SVM-HF (Algorithm adaptation method) and BR,RAkEL, MetaLabeler, CC,PS and EPS (problem transformation method).

Fig. 2 shows comparison of accuracy measured for each dataset; whereas Fig. 3 and Fig. 4 represents comparison of accuracy measured during experimentation between our classifier (referred as GB-MLTC) and supervised approaches on the same set of datasets.

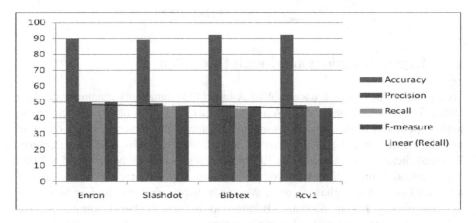

Fig. 2. Comparison of Results Measured Using GB-MLTC on Different Datasets

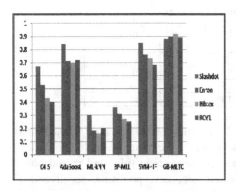

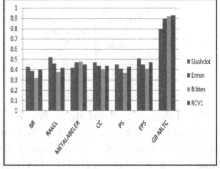

Fig. 3. GB-MLTC Vs Supervised Algorithm Adaptation Methods

Fig. 4. GB-MLTC Vs Supervised P.T. methods

5   Conclusion and Future Work

In our classification model we incorporated document similarity along with class label correlation in order to improve accuracy of multi label text classifier. We have used semi-supervised learning to utilize the unlabeled data for text classification. Experimental results show that our model offers reasonably good accuracy. Use of cosine similarity measure may ignore some aspects of semantic relationship between text documents which can affect accuracy. However In future, along with vector space model of text representation use of more robust feature extraction technique like LSI or NMF may be incorporated in order to reduce rate of misclassification.

References

1. Zhu, J.: Semi-supervised learning Literature Survey. Computer Science Technical Report TR 1530, University of Wisconsin – Madison (2005)
2. Chapelle, O., Schfolkopf, B., Zien, A.: Semi-Supervised Learning, 03-08. MIT Press (2006)
3. Tsoumakas, G., Katakis, I.: Multi-label classification: An overview. International Journal of Data Warehousing and Mining 3(3), 1–13 (2007)
4. Santos, A., Canuto, A., Neto, A.: A comparative analysis of classification methods to multi-label tasks in different application domains. International Journal of Computer Information Systems and Industrial Management Applications 3, 218–227 (2011) ISSN: 2150-7988
5. Cerri, R., da Silva, R.R.O., de Carvalho, A.C.P.L.F.: Comparing methods for multilabel classification of proteins using machine learning techniques. In: Guimarães, K.S., Panchenko, A., Przytycka, T.M. (eds.) BSB 2009. LNCS, vol. 5676, pp. 109–120. Springer, Heidelberg (2009)
6. Tsoumakas, G., Kalliris, G., Vlahavas, I.: Effective and efficient multilabel classification in domains with large number of labels. In: Proc. of the ECML/PKDD 2008 Workshop on Mining Multidimensional Data (MMD 2008), pp. 30–44 (2008)
7. Nigam, K., McCallum, A.K., Thrun, S., Mitchell, T.M.: Text classification from labeled and unlabeled documents using EM. Machine Learning 39, 103–134 (2000)
8. Liu, Y., Jin, R., Yang, L.: Semi-supervised Multi-label Learning by Constrained Non-Negative Matrix Factorization. In: AAAI (2006)
9. Zha, Z., Mie, T., Wang, Z., Hua, X.: Graph-Based Semi-Supervised Learning with Multi-label. In: ICME, pp. 1321–1324 (2008)
10. Chen, G., Song, Y., Zhang, C.: Semi-supervised Multi-label Learning by Solving a Sylvester Equation. In: SDM (2008)
11. Semi-supervised Nonnegative Matrix factorization. IEEE (January 2011)
12. Wei, Q., Yang, Z., Junping, Z., Wang, Y.: Semi-supervised Multi- label Learning Algorithm using dependency among labels. In: IPCSIT, vol. 3 (2011)
13. Godbole, S., Sarawagi, S.: Discriminative methods for multi-labeled classification. In: 8th Pacific-Asia Conference on Knowledge Discovery and Data Mining (2004)
14. Angelova, R., Weikum, G.: Graph based text classification: Learn from your neighbours. In: SIGIR 2006. ACM (2006) 1-59593-369-7/06/0008
15. Jebara, T., Wang, Chang: Graph construction and b-matching for semi supervised learning. In: Proceedings of ICML- 2009(2009)

16. Thomas, Ilias, Nello: Scalable corpus annotation by graph construction and label propogation. In: Proceedings of ICPRAM, pp. 25–34 (2012)
17. Talukdar, P., Pereira, F.: Experimentation in graph based semi supervised learning methods for class instance acquisition. In: The Proceedings of 48th Annual Meet of ACL, pp. 1473–1481 (2010)
18. Dai, X., Tian, B., Zhou, J., Chen, J.: Incorporating LSI into spectral graph transducer for text classification. In: The Proceedings of AAAI (2008)
19. Dharmadhikari, S.C., Ingle, M., Kulkarni, P.: Analysis of semi supervised methods towards multi-label text classification. IJCA 42, 15–20, ISBN: 973-93-80866-84-5
20. Dharmadhikari, S.C., Ingle, M., Kulkarni, P.: A comparative analysis of supervised multi-label text classification methods. IJERA 1(4), 1952–1961, ISSN: 2248-9622
21. http://mulan.sourceforge.net/datasets.html
22. http://MEKA.sourceforge.net
23. http://www.cs.waikato.ac.nz/ml/weka/
24. Read, J., Pfahringer, B., Holmes, G., Frank, E.: Classifier chains for multi-label classification. In: Buntine, W., Grobelnik, M., Mladenić, D., Shawe-Taylor, J. (eds.) ECML PKDD 2009, Part II. LNCS, vol. 5782, pp. 254–269. Springer, Heidelberg (2009)
25. Schapire, R.E., Singer, Y.: Boostexter: A boosting based system for text categorization. Machine learning 39(2-3) (2000)
26. Ueda, Saito, K.: Parametric mixture models for multi-labelled text. In: Proc. of NIPS (2002)
27. Griffiths, Ghahramani: Infinite latent feature models and the Indian buffet process. In: Proc. of NIPS (2005)
28. Rousu, Saunders: On maximum margin hierarchical multi-label classification. In: Proc. of NIPS Workshop on Learning with Structured Outputs (2004)
29. Zhu, S., Ji, X., Gong, Y.: Multi-labelled classification using maximum entropy method. In: Proc. of SIGIR (2005)
30. Ding, C., Jin, R., li, T., Simon, H.: A learning framework using Green's Function and Kernel Regularization with application to Recommender System. ACM, San Jose (2007) 978-1-59593-609-7/07/0008

An Insight into Task of Opinion Mining

Nidhi Mishra[1,*] and C.K. Jha[2]

[1] Buddha Institute of Technology Gorakhpur, UP, India
[2] Banasthali Vidyapith , Rajasthan, India
{mishra.nidhi7384,ckjha1}@gmail.com

Abstract. Recent years have brought the burst of popularity of community websites across the internet of opinionated text on web. Users express their views and opinions regarding products and services. These opinions are subjective information which represents user's sentiments, feelings or appraisal related to the same. People use such opinion rich sources to formalize knowledge and analyze it for further reuse. This leads to emergence of new field opinion mining which differs from traditional fact based information mining which are generally done by current search engines. With introduction of Blog track in TREC 2006, a considerable work has been done in this field which comprises of opinion mining at sentence level, passage or document level and feature level. This paper presents an insight into task of opinion mining. We find that task of opinion mining is directly related to degree of formalism of language used in data sources.

Keywords: Opinion Mining, Information retrieval, Sentiments, Blogs, Polarity.

1   Introduction

The Task of opinion mining [1] is involved with recognizing, classifying the opinionated text and determining the user's sentiments expressed in the text. The aim of information gathering is to find the demands and opinions of people. Users leave their comments and reviews through debate and personal notes on a variety of products and their services on various commercial websites such as online review sites and personal blogs. With increase in popularity of such opinion-dominated resources, there is growing need to mine the opinion linked contents to search out and identify the sentiments of others. There are two types of textual information in the entire world: facts and opinions. The facts are the objective expressions which describe about entities and their properties whereas the opinion are the subjective expression which describes people's opinions, feelings, emotions and attitudes towards entities and their properties. For e.g., fact: don-2 is the high budget movie in bollywood, and opinions: don-2 is the best action movie and in this shah rukh khan look was awesome. The opinion mining [1] [2] is generally associated with information retrieval (IR). In IR the algorithms function on factual data, whereas in opinion mining the algorithms function on subjective information. Hence opinion

---

* Corresponding author.

V.V. Das and P.M. El-Kafrawy (Eds.): SPIT 2012, LNICST 117, pp. 185–190, 2014.

mining is difficult task as compared to IR. The research in the field of opinion mining aims at classifying the opinion of a given text at the document level, sentence level, or feature level as positive, negative, or neutral [3] [4]. The applications of opinion mining are in (1) businesses and organizations: it includes product and service; market intelligence etc. and spends a group of money to track consumer sentiments. (2) Individuals: paying attention in other's sentiments when purchasing a product or use a service. (3) Ads placements: business and organization place ads in the user-generated content on web. Spam filtering refers to detection and removal of fake opinions that mislead the users by giving unworthy positive or negative opinions to some objects in order to sponsor or spoil the objects reputations. It is also a research issue in healthy opinion mining.

Rest of the paper is organized as follows Section 2 deals with brief review and discussion about task of opinion mining. Finally we conclude our discussion in Section 3.

2   Brief Review and Discussion about Task of Opinion Mining

In order to give more insight into the problem, in the subsequent subsections we describe various attempts to classify and formalize different opinion types. Hu and Liu [4] put most impact on their work and said that the components of an opinion are: **Opinion holder:** it is the person or organization that holds or gives a specific opinion on an object. **Object:** it is entity on which an opinion is expressed by user or company. **Opinion:** it is a view, attitude, or appraisal on an object done by an opinion holder. An **object** "O" is an entity which can be a product, person, event, organization, or topic, "O" is generally represented as a hierarchy consisting of components, its sub-components, and so on. Each node represents a component and has set of attributes of the component. O is the root node. An opinion can be determined on any node or its attribute. Hu and Liu, use the features in representing both components and their attributes. They present the review of a model as follows:

1. An object O is represented with a set of features, $F = \{f1, f2... fn\}$.
2. Each feature fi in F can be expressed with a finite set of words or phrases Wi, which are synonyms. That is to say: we have a set of corresponding synonym sets $W = \{W1, W2, ..., Wn\}$ for the features.
3. An opinion holder j comments on a subset of the features $Sj \subseteq F$ of object O.
4. For each feature $fk \in Sj$ that j comments on, he/she, chooses a word or phrase from Wk to describe the feature, and expresses a positive, negative or neutral opinion on fk. With regard to opinion there could be two types of opinions: Direct opinion and indirect opinion

- Direct Opinions: sentiment expressions on some identifiable objects, e.g. products, services etc.
    - o   E.g., "the picture quality of the mobile camera is good"
- Comparisons: relations establishing similarities or differences in between different objects.
    - o   E.g., "car x is cheaper than car y."

Table 1. Presents insight into opinion mining at different levels

Classification of Opinion mining at different levels	Assumptions made at different levels	Tasks associated with different levels
1. Opinion Mining at Sentence level.	1. A sentence contains only one opinion posted by single opinion holder; this could not be true in many cases e.g. there could be multiple opinions in compound and complex sentences. 2. Secondly the sentence boundary is defined in the given document	Task 1: identifying the given sentence as subjective or opinionated Classes: objective and subjective (opinionated) Task 2: opinion classification of the given sentence. Classes: positive, negative and neutral.
2. Opinion Mining at Document level.	1. Each document focuses on a single object and contains opinion posted by a single opinion holder. 2. Not applicable for blog and forum post as there could be multiple opinions on multiple objects in such sources.	Task 1: opinion classification of reviews Classes: positive, negative, and neutral
3. Opinion Mining at Feature level.	1. The data source focuses on features of a single object posted by single opinion holder. 2. Not applicable for blog and forum post as there could be multiple opinions on multiple objects in such sources.	Task 1: Identify and extract object features that have been commented on by an opinion holder (e.g., a reviewer). Task 2: Determine whether the opinions on the features are positive, negative or neutral. Task 3: Group feature synonyms. Produce a feature-based opinion summary of multiple reviews.

2.1 Document Level Opinion Mining

Document level opinion mining is about classifying the overall opinion presented by the authors in the entire document text as positive, negative or neutral about a certain object [5] [6].The work done by Turney [5] on review classification presents an approach based on distance measure of adjectives found in text from preselected words with known polarity i.e. excellent or poor. The author presents a three step algorithm which processes the documents without user care. First step, the adjectives are extracted along with a word that provides contextual information. Second step, the semantic orientation is captured. This is done by measuring the distance from words of known polarity. The mutual dependence between two words is found by analysis of hit count with AltaVista search engine for documents that contain two words in certain proximity of each other. Third step, the algorithm counts the average semantic orientation for all word pairs and classifies a review as recommended or not.

In contrast, Pang et al. [3] present a work based on classic topic classification techniques. The proposed approach aims to test whether a selected group of machine learning algorithms can produce good result when opinion mining is perceived as document level, with two topics: positive and negative. Authors present the results using nave bayes, maximum entropy and support vector machine algorithms and the performed tests shown the good results as comparable to other ranging from 71 to 85% depending on the method and test data sets.

Apart from the document-level opinion mining, the next sub-section discusses the classification at the sentence-level, which classify each sentence as a subjective or objective sentence and determine the positive or negative opinion.

2.2   Sentence Level Opinion Mining

The sentence level opinion mining is an action that is associated with two tasks [7] [8] [9]. First task is to identify whether the given sentence is subjective (opinionated) or objective. The second task is to find opinion of a subjective sentence as positive, negative or neutral. Riloff and Wiebe [10] do the task of identifying subjective sentences through a method called bootstrap approach which uses high precision classifiers to extract a number of subjective sentences. Authors achieve around 90% accuracy during their tests. Yu and Hatzivassiloglou [13] discuss both sentence classification (subjective/objective) and orientation (positive/negative/neutral). For the sentence classification, author's present three different algorithms: (1) sentence similarity detection, (2) naïve Bayens classification and (3) multiple naïve Bayens classification. In the second step for opinion orientation as positive, negative and neutral, authors use a technique similar to the one used by Turney [5] for document level opinion mining. The technique takes the average of log-likelihood ratio (LLR) scores of seed words in sentence and use thresholds to decide whether it is positive, negative and neutral. Wilson et al. [17] pointed out that not only a single sentence may contain multiple opinions, but they also have both subjective and factual clauses. It is useful to pinpoint such clauses. It is also important to identify the strength of opinions.

Like the document-level opinion mining, the sentence-level opinion mining does not consider about object features that have been commented in a sentence. For this the feature level opinion mining is discuss in the next sub-section.

2.3   Feature Level Opinion Mining

The feature level of opinion mining is to not only determine the subjectivity and opinion of an object but also what author liked or disliked about the object [12] [14]. The feature level opinion mining is associated with following tasks: the commented object features are extracting, determine the opinion (positive, negative and neutral) of the object and then group the feature synonyms and produce the result. Hu and Liu do customer review analysis [19] through opinion mining based on feature frequency, in which the most frequent features is accepted by processing many reviews that are taken during summary generation. In opposite to Hu and Liu, Popescu and Etzioni [11], improved the frequency based approach by introducing the part-of relationship and remove the frequent occurring of noun phrases that may not be features.

2.4   Tools and Techniques

- **Sentence Delimiter [18]:** The given document is segmented into individual sentences by the help of sentence delimiter like question mark (?), dot or full stop (.). Sometimes identification of full stop in the sentence does not mark the end of sentence such as date *12.1.2012,* hence the rule based pattern matching could be used to identify sentence boundary.
- **Part of Speech Tagger [16]:** The part-of-speech tagger tool is used to assigns parts of speech to each word of a sentence such as noun, verb, adjective, etc. for example – happy plays hockey, here happy is noun not adjective hence this sentence is not opinionated.
- **Named Entity Recognition [16]:** It is also known as entity identification that's seeks to locate and classify atomic elements in text into predefined categories such as the names of persons, organizations locations, expression of times, percentages, names of object, its parts etc. It is used for noun phrase only.
- **Sentiword Net [15]:** It is a lexical resource in which each Word Net synsets is associated to three numerical scores Obj(s), Pos(s) and Neg(s), describing how objective, positive, and negative the terms contained in the synset are.

3   Conclusions

This paper presents an insight into task of opinion mining. Opinion mining aims at recognizing, classifying and determining opinion polarity of the opinionated text. Most of the approaches presume that the given text is opinionated. There are cases where objective sentence could be opinionated e.g., opinion drawn about a person in news articles column. Hence just identifying subjective sentence to have opinionated content is not enough. Sentence boundaries are not clearly defined on such blog sites. We find that the language used whether it is formal or informal in the text have direct impact on opinion mining as informal text are difficult to be processed i.e., syntactical, semantically or higher level analysis is tough. The task of opinion mining becomes difficult if there are opinion spams in text. Detecting fake opinions is a research issue. Some of the opinions are time sensitive hence identifying latest opinions on the subject is another research issue. We observe that opinion mining at three level i.e., document level, sentence level and feature level have got positive and negatives associated with them which are already discussed in section 2. The performances of Natural language processing tools also contribute towards the effective opinion mining.

References

1. Liu, B.: Opinion Mining and Summarization. In: World Wide Web Conference, Beijing, China (2008)
2. Liu, B.: Web Data Mining, Exploring Hyperlinks. Contents and Usage data (2007)
3. Pang, B., Lee, L., Vaithyanathan, S.: Thumbs up? Sentiment Classification using Machine Learning Techniques. In: Proceedings of the Conference on Empirical Methods in Natural Language Processing, pp. 79–86 (2002)

4. Dave, K., Lawrence, S., Pennock, D.M.: Mining the peanut gallery: Opinion extraction and segment classification of product reviews. In: Proceedings of WWW, pp. 519–528 (2003)
5. Turney, P.: Thumbs Up or Thumbs Down? Semantic Orientation Applied to Unsupervised Classification of Reviews. In: Proceeding of Association for Computational Linguistics, pp. 417–424 (2002)
6. Das, St., Chen, M.: Yahoo! for Amazon: Extracting market sentiment from stock message boards. In: Proceedings of the Asia Pacific Finance Association Annual Conference (2001)
7. Hatzivassiloglou, V., Wiebe, J.: Effects of adjective orientation and gradability on sentence subjectivity. In: Proceedings of the International Conference on Computational Linguistics (2000)
8. Riloff, E., Patwardhan, S., Wiebe, J.: Feature subsumption for opinion analysis. In: Proceedings of the Conference on Empirical Methods in Natural Language Processing (2006)
9. Riloff, E., Wiebe, J.: Learning extraction patterns for subjective expressions. In: Proceedings of the Conference on Empirical Methods in Natural Language Processing (2003)
10. Wiebe, J., Bruce, R.F., O'Hara, T.P.: Development and use of a gold standard data set for subjectivity classifications. In: Proceedings of the Association for Computational Linguistics, pp. 246–253 (1999)
11. Popescu, Etzioni.: Extracting product features and opinions from reviews. In: Proceedings of the Conference on Empirical Methods in Natural Language Processing (2005)
12. Wilson, T., Wiebe, J., Hoffmann, P.: Recognizing contextual polarity in phrase-level sentiment analysis. In: Proceedings of the Human Language Technology Conference and the Conference on Empirical Methods in Natural Language Processing, pp. 347–354 (2005)
13. Yu, H., Hatzivassiloglou, V.: Towards answering opinion questions: Separating facts from opinions and identifying the polarity of opinion sentences. In: Proceedings of the Conference on Empirical Methods in Natural Language Processing (2003)
14. Bethard, S., Yu, H., Thornton, A., Hatzivassiloglou, V., Jurafsky, D.: Automatic extraction of opinion propositions and their holders. In: Proceedings of the Association for the Advancement of Artificial Intelligence Spring Symposium on Exploring Attitude and Affect in Text (2004)
15. Cardie, C., Wiebe, J., Wilson, T., Litman, D.: Combining low-level and summary representations of opinions for multi-perspective question answering. In: Proceedings of the Association for the Advancement of Artificial Intelligence Spring Symposium on New Directions in Question Answering, pp. 20–27 (2003)
16. Jin, W., Hay Ho, H., Srihari, R.: Opinion Miner: A Novel Machine Learning System for Web Opinion Mining and Extraction. In: Proceeding of International Conference on Knowledge Discovery and Data Mining, Paris, France (2009)
17. Wilson, T., Wiebe, J., Hwa, R.: Just how mad are you? Finding strong and weak opinion clauses. In: The Association for the Advancement of Artificial Intelligence, pp. 761–769 (2004)
18. Dey, L., Mirajul Haque, S.K.: Studying the effects of noisy text on text mining applications. In: Proceedings of the Third Workshop on Analytics for Noisy Unstructured Text Data, Barcelona, Spain (2009)
19. Hu, M., Liu, B.: Mining and Summarizing Customer Reviews. In: Proceedings of the Tenth International Conference on Knowledge Discovery and Data Mining, Seattle, WA, USA (2004)

DwCB - Architecture Specification of Deep Web Crawler Bot with Rules Based on FORM Values for Domain Specific Web Site

S.G. Shaila, A. Vadivel[*], R. Devi Mahalakshmi, and J. Karthika

Multimedia Information Retrieval Group,
Department of Computer Applications,
National Institute of Technology, TamilNadu, India
{shaila,vadi,devimaha,karthika}@nitt.edu

Abstract. It is well-known that obtaining deep web information is challenging task and it is required to choose suitable query values for crawling large data source. In this paper, we have proposed architecture specification of a deep web crawler with effective FORM filling strategy using rules. The rules are constructed by analyzing the FORM and combination of parameters. These FORM parameters are classified as most preferable, least preferable and mutually exclusive. For each successful FORM submission, the deep web data is extracted and indexed suitably for information retrieval applications. The performance of the crawler is encouraging when compared to a conventional surface crawler.

Keywords: Hidden web crawlers, Domain specific, Rule Set, Surface web, FORM values.

1 Introduction

Deep web sources can be dynamically retrieved based on the user's query using a well manageable crawler. The Deep web Crawler must interact with the FORM and have prior knowledge about the domain which improves in FORM filling capabilities and crawl more information. Since, the immense source of information buried into deep web, the first deep web crawlers is proposed with the complexity of interacting with web search interfaces [6]. Thus, crawlers are developed for extracting data from deep web databases [2] and to match deep web query interfaces [8]. A Source-Biased Approach [1] has used source-biased probing techniques, to allow interactions to decide whether a target database is relevant to the source database by probing the target with very precise probes. In [9], pages from Internet are generated dynamically and are structured to provide structured query interfaces and results. This approach works on single domain deep web resources. However, this process consumes longer time and sometimes valuable data may get ignored to find the probability of schema.

---

[*] Corresponding author.

V.V. Das and P.M. El-Kafrawy (Eds.): SPIT 2012, LNICST 117, pp. 191–196, 2014.

In [5], crawler autonomously discovers and downloads pages from the hidden web. The set covering problem is implemented for filling the FORM. However, working with such algorithm iteratively is a time consuming and downloading every page needs enormous amount of repository space. Deep web adaptive crawling based on Minimum Executable Pattern (MEP) [3] is proposed where minimal combination of elements in a query FORM is used for making successful query. Though, MEP is an efficient approach, it has a limitation on the size of result set. Hidden Web Exposer (HiWE) [6] has been developed, which interacts with FORM and a customized database to perform FORM filling. It is based on layout based information extraction technique. However, HiWE fails to recognize and respond to simple dependencies between FORM elements and lack of partial filling out the FORM. Vision based data-extraction (ViDE) [7] has focused on visual information of web pages and their implementation of web data extraction procedure. This approach involves both DOM tree analysis and visual analysis. When a website consists of web pages with visual dissimilarity, VIDE may not be automated. Fiva-Tech [4] is a page level web data extraction technique and applies tree matching, tree alignment and mining techniques. In a webpage, fixed pattern is identified and matched using a tree mining approach for extracting information. It has been observed that larger time is required to carry out all these tasks. Based on the above discussion, it is noticed that most of the work extracts information from deep web at the cost of huge processing time. Also, none of the approach has an efficient indexer, which can be effectively combined to use the crawler ideal time for indexing the already extracted information. Thus, it is imperative that a deep web crawler is required with architecture specification to crawl the surface web, deep web and with indexing capability. In addition, most of the approaches consume large time for processing FORM and it would be appropriate to analyze the FORM to acquire prior knowledge to reduce the FORM processing time. In this paper, these issues are handled and a suitable crawler architecture specification is proposed. This crawler has shown the ability in indexing, analyzing and mining web content from the hidden database.

The rest of the paper is organized as follows. The proposed work is presented in the next Section. In section 3, we present the experimental results and conclude the paper in the last section.

2   Proposed Work

In this paper, we propose an architecture specification of **Deep web Crawler Bot** (DwCB) and is shown in Fig. 1. From WWW, the URL pages are fetched and parsed with the help of URL fetcher and URL parser. The parsed web pages are verified for the FORM existence. The pages, which are not having FORM are crawled by Surface Web Crawler. The pages with the FORM are crawled by Deep web Crawler. Input elements of the FORM are analyzed and the Label-Value-Set (LVS) relationship of FORM is found out, using LVS manager.

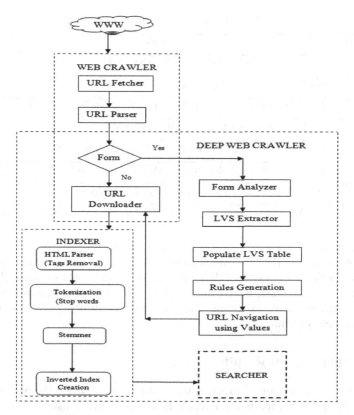

Fig. 1. Architecture Specification of DwCB

Using the LVS content of FORM, rules are generated and every FORM elements have their corresponding values. Based on the FORM analysis, prior knowledge is acquired and the values are populated to the FORM elements. Mathematically, we can represent L as label and $V=\{v1,v2,v3....vi\}$ is a fuzzy graded set of values. The values will be assigned to corresponding labels L using V. Intuitively, each vi represents a value that could potentially be assigned to an element e, if label: e "matches" L. Labels can be aliased i.e. two or more labels can share the same value set. Rules are generated depending on the LVS. The combinations of the values (Rules) that are populated should be navigated for crawling. The respective URLs are downloaded and the result is given to Indexer for indexing. We have considered real estate domain (http://www.99acres.com) and crawled the data from it. The rules for residential apartment and villa are shown in Table.1. Here, the rules depending on number of bedrooms in the apartment and villa are generated. The residential apartment (P_2) and villa (P_2) are considered in the property category, in bed room category eight levels $[B_1-B_8]$ are considered and in the budget category seven levels of cost prices $[R_1-R_7]$ are considered for generating the rules.

Table 1. Rules for real estate domain

`	Rules
1	If $(P_1 \&\& R_1)$then B_1-MP; $B_{2,3}$ -LP; others-ME
2	If (P_1 && R_2) then $B_{1,2,3}$ - MP; $B_{4,5}$ - LP; others - ME
3	If (P_1 && ($R_3 \parallel R_4 \parallel R_5 \parallel R_6 \parallel R_7$)) then $B_{1,2,3,4}$ -MP; B_5- LP; others - ME
4	If (P_2 && R_1) then $B_{1,2,3}$- MP; B_4 – LP; others - ME
5	If (P_2 &&($R_2 \parallel R_3 \parallel R_4$) then $B_{1,2}$- MP; B_3- LP; others - ME
6	If (P_2 && ($R_5 \parallel R_6$) then $B_{1,2,3,4}$ - MP; $B_{5,6}$ - LP; others - ME
7	If (P_2 && R_7) then $B_{3,4,5,6}$ - MP; $B_{1,2,7}$ -LP; others – ME
Where, MP - Most Preferable, LP - Least Preferable, ME - Mutually Exclusive.	

For instance, as per rule 1, the FORM is filled with values (P_1) as "residential apartment" with price (R_1) as "twenty lacks". Given these values, the *most preferable* value for this field is 1-bedroom (B_1) and *least preferable* for 2-bedroom (B_2) and 3-bedroom (B_3). In contrast, B_4, B_5, B_6, B_7 and B_8 are *Mutually Exclusive* values, i.e. this combination returns no result. Here, we have constructed this rule by giving different property locations.

3   Experimental Results

We carried out a number of experiments to study and measure the performance of DwCB. We present experimental result to compare performance of surface web crawler and DwCB. The number of web pages crawled by surface web crawler and deep web crawler for a deep website with respect to crawling time is considered. It is observed from the below graph that for any Deep Web resource, DwCB provides better result compared to a surface web crawler. Fig. 2, represents the number of documents crawled with respect to time. We have experimented for website http://www.99acres.com. As indicated in Fig. 2, DwCB crawled 2,100 web pages and surface web crawled around 250 web pages in 2 hours.

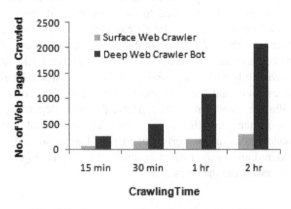

Fig. 2. Performance of DwCB compared to SWC

Another experiment is also carried out to find the number of relevant document retrieved in any particular context. A set of keywords is used as query and searched into both documents crawled by surface web crawler and DwCB. It is observed that the number of documents retrieved by DwCB is high compared to surface web crawler and is depicted in Fig. 3. However, as more FORMs are processed, the crawler encounters a number of different finite domain elements and is able to contribute new entries to the LVS table. In addition, the LVS manager uses these new entries to retrieve additional values from the data sources. As a result, at the end, the crawler successfully contributes crawling directly, almost a 2000 additional successful web pages.

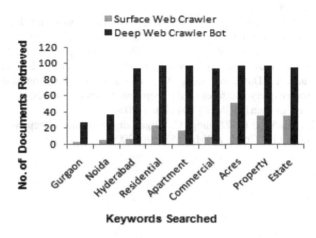

Fig. 3. Comparison ratio of response of DwCB Vs. Surface Web Crawler

4   Conclusion and Future Works

DwCB is provided with an enriched automated method to fill FORMs based rules for domain specific Web site. We have developed the system and extracted information from http://www.99acres.com. For this domain, the FORM is fetched, analyzed and a prior knowledge is acquired. During FORM filling procedure, rules are generated and the FORMs are filled with suitable value. The proposed architecture specification crawls more relevant documents in lesser time. The performance is superior compared to the conventional crawler. In future, we are trying to populate the LVS table dynamically depending on the domains chosen and thereby automating the rule generation.

Acknowledgement. The work done is supported by research grant from the Department of Science and Technology, India, under Grant DST/TSG/ICT/2009/27 dated 3rd September 2010.

References

1. James, C., Ling, L., Daniel, R.: Discovering Interesting Relationships among Deep web Databases: A Source-Biased Approach. World Wide Web 9(4), 585–622 (2006)
2. Craswell, N., Bailey, P., Hawking, D.: Server selection on the World Wide Web. In: Proc. of the Fifth ACM conference on Digital Libraries (ACM DL F00), San Antonio (2000)
3. Liu, J., Jiang, L., Wu, Z., Zheng, Q.: Deep Web adaptive crawling based on minimum executable pattern. Journal of Intelligent Information Systems 36, 197–215 (2011)
4. Mohammed, K., Chia-Hui, C.: FiVaTech: Page-Level Web Data Extraction from Template Pages. IEEE Trans. Knowl. Data Eng. 22(2), 249–263 (2010)
5. Alexandros, N., Petros, Z., Junghoo, C.: Downloading Hidden Web Content, Technical Report, UCLA (2004)
6. Raghavan, S., Garcia-Molina, H.: Crawling the hidden web. In: Proc. of the 27th International Conference on Very Large Databases (VLDB F01), Rome (2001)
7. Liu, W., Meng, X., Meng, W.: ViDE: A Vision-Based Approach for Deep web Data Extraction. IEEE Transactions on Knowledge and Data Engineering 22(3), 447–460 (2010)
8. Wu, W., Yu, C.T., Doan, A., Meng, W.: An interactive clustering-based approach to integrating source query interfaces on the deep web. In: Proc. of the 2004 ACM Conference on Management of Data (SIGMOD F04), Paris (2004)
9. Zhao, P., Li, H., Wei, F., Zhiming, C.: Organizing Structured Deep web by Clustering Query Interfaces Link Graph. ADMA, 683–690 (2008)

Efficient and Alternative Approach for Android Based Mobile Remote Control in a Bluetooth Environment

Husain Alhayki[1] and Jayavrinda Vrindavanam[2]

[1] Telecommunication Engineering, Caledonian College of Engineering, Muscat, Oman
alhayki1990@hotmail.com
[2] Department of Electronic and Computer Engineering, Caledonian College of Engineering, Muscat, Oman
jayavrindav@gmail.com

Abstract. The paper presents a novel method of design and implementation of a control system using Bluetooth technologies. The proposed system based on IOIO board, Bluetooth and android application endeavours to support user the ability to control the electrical devices from mobile devices, which must have android operating system. The proposed system design is simple, multifunctional, superior to previous approaches and can considerably economise the costs involved in developing such systems. The application has a variety of uses in offices, factories, laboratories and access controlled environments.

Keywords: Android, IOIO board, Bluetooth, SDK tools, ATD plugin.

1 Introduction

With the advent of mobile phones, a multitude of functions are added to such hand held instruments on a continuous basis, making such devices as 'versatile master control device'. The uses of such devices are extremely divergent. Such uses range from photography, video chats, daily planner, e-mail facility and so on. As an extension to such advancements, the main objective of this paper is to design and implement a new control system for devices using mobile phones which run with the support of android operating system through the support of Bluetooth technology as a medium of communication. There are many controlling boards that can be used in these applications such as Arduino, mbed, IOIO board etc, and each one has its own specifications and applications. Among the control boards, IOIO board specially designed to work with android phones with version above 1.5. In this paper, IOIO board is used to control the electrical devices with the help of a simple hardware circuit and also it will be used to interface with Bluetooth dongle that can send and receive control signal from android based mobile phone. The mobile device can be High Tech Computers (HTC) phones, Samsung phones, Samsung tablet etc, which must have android operating system. The paper shows that the proposed system is efficient, simple and more cost effective in comparison with the existing similar

V.V. Das and P.M. El-Kafrawy (Eds.): SPIT 2012, LNICST 117, pp. 197–203, 2014.
© Institute for Computer Sciences, Social Informatics and Telecommunications Engineering 2014

systems. This paper, after reviewing the prevailing literature, postulates how the proposed system is distinct. Further, the working of the proposed system, logic control circuit for controlling the electronic devices, flow chart of proposed system, results and conclusion are explained thereafter.

2   Literature Review

The proposed control system uses mobile devices with android operating system through the Bluetooth technology. Being one of the recent areas of research, papers dealing with similar systems are not considerable. There are studies which have looked into the android based control using different controller boards. In previous study [3], the authors presented various connection approaches to connect Android with the LEGO Mindstorms and NXT robotics system. The main approach can be classified into Microbridge, IOIO (which is pronounced as yo-yo board) and Google android open accessory development kit (Google ADK). Microbridge consists of some basic hardware which is an Arduino microcontroller board with USB host shield. The function of USB in this board is to connect with android phone using USB cable. It can interface the sensor and control actuators easily. The main advantage of this system is that it works with almost every android version but it requires the android debug bridge (ADB). The second approach is the IOIO board; it can be defined as a direct extension of the android devices. The main distinction is, it provides a PIC CPU with a fixed firmware. It provides a powerful application program interface (API) which benefits in including some specification, such as routines, data structure, object classes and variables. The API can be accessed to boards, for example, general input and output (I/O) pins or Serial Peripheral Interface Bus (SPI). It also provides an Inter Integrated Circuits bus (I2C), ADB protocol and a virtual Transmission Control Protocol (TCP) connection. Third approach is the Google ADK. This can be defined as a combination of the Microbridge and IOIO board. These boards consist of the hardware side of an Arduino microcontroller with USB host and an extension shield can be interfaced for buttons, joy stick, relays etc. It also provides a device API but it supports only newest devices like android version 2.3.4. The paper states that all three boards are under heavy development and it can be observed that applications based on such methodology are gradually entering the market.

In another study [2], the authors used the Bluetooth technology to turn a phone into controller for a toy–level car. The car has an operating lighting system, horn and motor system, which is controlled by using Arduino (similar to IOIO board). The Arduino board is connected to a Bluetooth modem which established a wireless serial communication to a remote device via Bluetooth.

Another study [4] has proposed a new system to control higher temperatures inside the car and the user is capable of controlling some of the car accessories by using his/her mobile phone. Once the car is fit with the Bluetooth and the control system, the car accessories can be connected with (PIC 16F877A) micro-controller which will work with 5 V and control can be done by mobile application. The benefit of the system is that the user has the ability to use the existing mobile devices for the controlling of the car accessories. The authors have used Java 2 micro edition (J2ME) in this system. Java [9] as a medium of communication uses technology of radio standard designed for less power consumption with a small range and supports low cost transceivers at each of the devices using the Bluetooth. In this type of radio technology, the physical layer used is frequency hopping spread spectrum (FHSS), which uses 79 channels of radio and continuously changes the frequencies in the rate of 1600 hops per second. In the basic mode, Bluetooth communication has a modulation of Gaussian frequency shift keying (GFSK). The Bluetooth transceivers operate in the license-free band which is used by the industrial, scientific and medical (ISM) radio band of frequencies of 2.45 GHz,; this is the band used in the wireless local area network (WLAN) devices and IEEE 802.11 compliant devices. The device that uses Bluetooth allows making communication each other through Bluetooth devices when they are setting in the range of the Bluetooth [5]. On the other hand, Android is a software stack for mobile devices that includes an operating system, middleware and key applications. It consists of kernel and low level tools, native libraries, Android Runtime and framework layer on top of all the applications. The first two applications and application frame work are written in Java and run in the Dalvik Virtual Machine and libraries. The Basic applications like contact, email, browser settings, Bluetooth etc., form part of the android package. Many of these applications can be multi-threaded depending upon their use and interaction. The Applications that can be added depends on the user requirements in Android Market, which is an online store for applications [1]. Further details on Android applications are available extensively in the standard literature. As evident from the previous studies, the latest advancement in this area uses a Bluetooth socket to interface WI-Fi with a system by using another mobile phone as server and such web servers are not economical. Hence, the proposed system is devised, which ensures direct communication without the involvement of server and superior to the systems explained in the previous studies.

3   Proposed System

In divergence of the system explained above, the proposed system uses two way switching, with reduced size without any complicated hardware parts. The proposed system also uses 3.0 Bluetooth version which provides data transfer speeds up to 24 Mbit/s. Further, the new system is multi-functional. The proposed system works with android version 1.5 and above. Further, the system design consists of four main parts, user interface, communication channel, controlling board and electronic circuits. The system structure is explained with the help of the following block diagram (Fig. 1 The proposed system).

Android Operating System. This is a type of operating system used for mobile handsets like smartphones, tablet computers like Samsung galaxy s2, HTC, Sony Ericson...etc. In the proposed system the authors have used Samsung galaxy S2 mobile with android operating system 4.0.3 (Ice Cream Sandwich) platform family with Bluetooth version 3.0 which is the latest version of Bluetooth. The authors also designed an application with eclipse software. The android system is used to send signals through the Bluetooth to another Bluetooth module to switch ON or OFF.

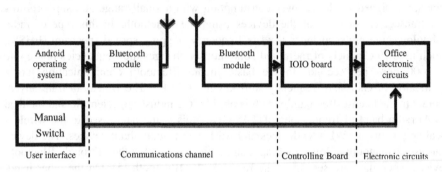

Fig. 1. The proposed system

Manual Switch. This block as shown in the figure identifies the alternative method to control office electrical appliance by using OR gate logic circuit. This will benefit the user incase the android system stops working for any reason. Thus, it is possible to switch on and off the electrical device by using two way switching.

Communication Channel. The communication channel used with Bluetooth operates under industrial, scientific and medical radio band (ISM) at frequency 2.4 GHz. The authors have used Samsung galaxy S2 mobile phone with 3.0 Bluetooth version at the transmission end and Bluetooth version 3.0 is interfaced with IOIO board on the receiving side. Bluetooth range can be covered up to 100 meters.

Logic Control Circuit. The controlling board used in the proposed system is the IOIO board which gives opportunity to connect electronic circuits to an Android operating system like android phone, tablet etc. Further, it can be controlled from Android application. As already stated, the android application can be written by using eclipse software. In the proposed system, the authors use 3 input & output (I/O) pins from 48 total pins.

Office Electronic Circuits. This block considers the electronic circuits forming part of the proposed system like light control, fan control, door alarm etc. As already stated, it can work for 'two way' switching, either from android operating system or manual logic control.

3.1   Android in Proposed System

The android operating system is responsible for sending and receiving control signal by using the Bluetooth technology. The functioning of the android application based programme structure depends on two programming conditions. The first condition is switch case; in this condition, each case will represent specified function like light control, door alarm, fan control. Second condition is 'if & else'; by using this function the researcher achieves the purpose of switching ON and OFF. For example, when the user activates any button that represents a particular electrical device like "switching on light", "on door alarm", "switching on fan" etc. it will send the signal through the Bluetooth to switch ON and display would show that it is switched ON. When the user wants to switch off any electrical device, the user can do so by activating the button and it will switch directly to OFF mode.

3.2   Logic Control Circuit for Manually Controlling the Electronic Devices

The authors have taken into consideration the criticality of using two way switching circuit in order to address any problem that might occur in android operating system. Accordingly, the authors have designed simple logic control circuit using an OR gate as it shown in the figure (Fig. 2 Logic control circuit for manually controlling the electronic devices). The truth table of the OR gate displays an output of 'high' only if the input is high. Otherwise, if both the inputs are low, the outcome will be zero which is equivalent to OFF. Generally this circuit is responsible for 'two way' switching, which gives opportunity to switch ON/ OFF the electrical devices either from the android phone using the Bluetooth or using the manual switch. The flow chart of the proposed system for door alarm, fan, and light is shown in the figure (Fig. 3 Flow chart of the proposed system).

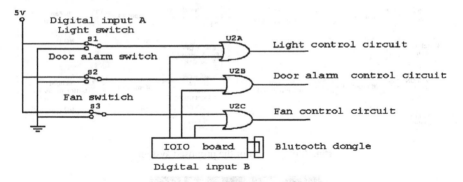

Fig. 2. Logic control circuit for manually controlling the electronic devices

4   Results and Discussions

The result of the designed system user interface is shown in the fig. 4. As evident from the figure, the system user interface acts like a switch. When the android user press any button that represents a particular electrical device, it will send a signal through the Bluetooth to switch 'ON' and display appears that it is 'switched on' and when the user wants to switch off any electrical device, the user can do it by activating another button on the handset. For controlling of fan, PWM controller is used. For example, when the user activates the first button, the display will change the status from 'ON' to 'OFF'. Similar process repeats for other applications as well.

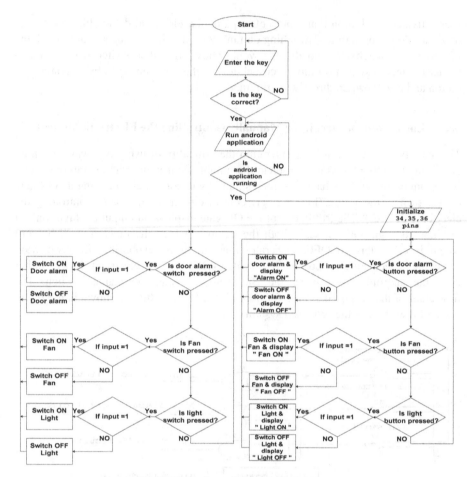

Fig. 3. Flow chart of the proposed system

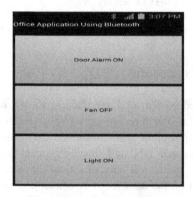

Fig. 4. The android application

5   Discussion and Conclusion

The paper has presented a novel design based implementation of a new control system for office or other electrical devices using mobile phone equipped with android operating system through Bluetooth technology as a medium of communication. The android program structure is built with the help of android software development kit (SDK) tools and android developer tools plugin (ADT). The system provides 'two way' switching either from android mobile phone or through simple switch. This has multiple applications at the office and other premises and the device can be used for appliances which can be remotely controlled. Hence, the design would lead to hardware reduction as well as cost savings, which would make such applications highly affordable to the users. Future work in this field that the authors would be pursing is to implement a system which integrates a wireless fidelity (Wi-Fi) technology with the mobile phone as a server, which would enable anywhere connectivity.

Acknowledgement. During the course of this work, the authors have discussions with several faculty members and other experts at the Caledonian College of Engineering. The authors would like thank each and every one of them for their guidance, encouragement and support.

References

1. Chandrian, P.: Efficient Java Native Interface for Android based Mobile Devices. Proquest LLC (2011)
2. Fitzgerald, J., Kim, B., Wolniewicz, J.: Bluetooth Ferrari Controller: Android Remote Controller App. (2011)
3. Göbel, S., Jubeh, R., Raesch, S.L., Zündorf, A.: Using the Android Platform to control Robots. Kassel University (2011)
4. Mamdouhi, H., Khatun, S., Zarrin, J.: Bluetooth Wireless Monitoring, Managing and Control for Inter Vehicle in Vehicular Ad-Hoc Networks. Journal of Computer Science 5(12), 925–932 (2009)
5. Mendoza, P.A.: An enhanced method for the existing Bluetooth pairing protocol to avoid impersonation attacks.a thesis. Proquest LLC, pp. 2–8 (2009)
6. Free software downloadable from:
   http://developer.android.com/sdk/eclipse-adt.html
7. Free software downloadable from:
   http://developer.android.com/sdk/index.html
8. Free software downloadable from: http://www.eclipse.org/downloads
9. Efficient Java Native Interface for Android based Mobile Devices, proquest (2011)
10. Bluetooth Wireless Monitoring, Managing and Control for Inter Vehicle in Vehicular Ad-Hoc Networks, proquest (2009)

A Resource-Independent Marker-Based Augmented Reality Application

Suhaifi Syazani[*], Abdullah Junaidi, and Ku Day Chyi

Multimedia University, Faculty of Information Technology,
Jalan Multimedia 63100 Cyberjaya Selangor Malaysia
{junaidi,dcku,syazani.suhaifi11}@mmu.edu.my

Abstract. Creating a marker based Augmented Reality (AR) usually requires a series of files such as marker files and 3d model files. The series of files that Marker Based Augmented Reality requires will limit its capability and reduces its reliability. These files and resources have to be loaded from storage such as a local machine or a web server. We propose a Resource Independent Marker Based Augmented Reality (RIMBAR) by encoding resources such as 3D model files as QR code and using the QR code itself as the marker. The AR system does not need any marker file or 3d model file. We processed, shortened and convert the content to make it fit into a QR code. Larger contents are then split to multiple markers and the data is joined together at the other end. Currently this system shows potential but further research needs to be done to remove the issues.

Keywords: QR Code, Augmented Reality, 3D Model Transmision.

1   Introduction

The dependence to the resources that Marker Based Augmented Reality requires will limit its distribution, capability and reliability. If the app needs to download its resource from the internet, the application performance will then be dependent on the speed of the user's internet connection. One solution is to install them on the machine running it. But, if the user wants to use many AR applications, it will be a cumbersome to install each one of them on their machine. Resource independent AR is not a concept useful to everybody in general. If the user has high speed broadband or are able to drive to the nearest shop to buy AR app CDs and DVDs this concept is totally irrelevant. If we want to deliver AR content for rural areas where it took 2 hours to go to town and the internet connection is using GPRS or worse 56k dial-up modems, resource independence is very important. The use case scenario for AR in these remote locations is mainly in education and medical purposes. Resource independence is also very useful for content that changes frequently. A magazine using a resource independent AR system only needs to generate the QR codes and print it on the magazine. No uploading or updating is necessary on their server. We

---

[*] Corresponding author.

V.V. Das and P.M. El-Kafrawy (Eds.): SPIT 2012, LNICST 117, pp. 204–210, 2014.
© Institute for Computer Sciences, Social Informatics and Telecommunications Engineering 2014

have developed a system that is able to distribute AR content via the medium of QR code. The system also has the capability to split the into multiple QR codes if necessary.

2   Previous Works

Previous attempts on resource independence have been done by [1] in a system called In-Place Augmented Reality. An AR marker is created with the image as the texture and model for the application. They also included a 2D elevation map to form the terrain model. The system created by [1] also allows embedding of behaviors. Icons representing transportation are included in the marker image and they used the red lines included in the marker as the path the marker will animate on. Their application however did not embed complicated models as they have to rely to height maps for 3D information. They also highlighted an issue of quality in its textures, that the qualities of the textures are dependant on the imaging devices used. Another attempt is done by [2] using a system that recognizes hand-drawn sketches, and converts them into 3D model for Augmented Reality. Notations written down on paper will also give the models physical properties. Both of the works are very close in achieving resource independance.

Delivery of content in multiple parts has been tried before by [4]. They came up with a system that uses XML data to provide the content location, provides the ability to do joint models with the minor models attached to a major model on another QR code. However, the application did not embed the content directly inside the QR codes itself and it has to be downloaded.

Using QR code as an Augmented Reality marker has been executed several times in the past. A system that uses a QR code to carry the URLs of the model that their system fetches from a server was created by [5] and [3]. The first proof of concept FLARToolkit with QR codes was created by [6] in 2009. However, he did not embed the resources in his proof of concept. These past work have hinted on a possibility that content can be embedded inside QR codes. Recently, [7] has created a system that can dynamically generate QR code using an ink senstitive to variations of temperature. The ability to change QR code on-the-fly will give our system greater practicality as no QR code needs to be printed.

3   Resource Independent Marker Based Augmented Reality (RIMBAR)

The system is divided into two parts which is the deployment/developer system and the user system.The developer system processes the models and textures. It will process, inspect, and perform necessary conversions. The developer system also determines how many part should the data be split into and to how many QR Codes. The user system contains the FLARToolkit engine, the QR Code decoder and Papervision3D as the 3D engine. The user system will read the QR code, parse it, recreate the 3D scene and augment it to the live feed. The processes involved in Developer Module and Client Module are listed in Table 1.

Table 1. The processes involved in the RIMBAR module

Developer Module	Client Module
1. Loading the VRML file	1. Read the QR code
2. Parsing the VRML file	2. Parse the QR code data
3. Compress the VRML text	3. Recreate the 3D scene
4. Split the content to multiple QR codes if necessary.	4. Track the QR code as an AR marker
5. Generate the final QR code containing the model	5. Overlay 3D model on top of the QR code

3.1 Compressing the VRML File

The file on its own is quite long and beyond the encoding capacity of one QR code. Therefore the 3d formats undergo a process of shortening. Firstly, the whitespaces inside the strings are removed. The empty-spaces are counted as one character by the QR code encoder. Unnecessary empty-spaces will decrease considerably the amount of data encodable. Then, the words inside the strings are replaced with shortened codes. The system will check series of words inside an XML file, and if the words are found inside the string, it will then be replaced with a shortened code. Figure 1 below shows a sample of VRML string after shortening.

b301 t6 { t8 0.1722 0 -5.974 c10 [t6 { t8 0 16.09 0 c10 [s3 { a4 a2 { m3 m1 { d2c2 0.7686 0.3451 0.8824 } } g2 b3 { size 32.93 32.18 33.3 } }] }] }

Fig. 1. Sample of VRML string after shortening

Table 2. Result of the shortening process of Box.wrl model

	Character Count	QR code required to fit the data
Raw unedited VRML	466	3
Whitespace removal	229	1
Dictionary replacement	135	1
Final Outcome	135	1
Reduction of Character Count	71.03%	
Reduction of QR	67%	

However, the shortening process as we found out later does not totally solve the problem. Although the results are promising as shown in Table 1, it is not enough for our goal to fit in complex models. If one box is 135 characters long, one QR code will be full if we put two boxes. That is not practical. Both formats contain a plethora of information. However, not all of them are needed for Papervision3D to recreate the scene. Therefore, we created our own proprietary format. This particular format carries the exact information that the Papervision3D needs to reconstruct the scene. We called this format the QRF format. Figure 2 shows a sample of the QRF format.

MDL,g3 b3,m1 d2c2 0.7686 0.3451 0.8824| ,t16 0.1722 0 -5.974| ,s11 32.93 32.18 33.3|

Fig. 2. The same VRML as used in Figure 1 after conversion to QRF

The use of QRF allows for a significant decrease in the size of the VRML string as it only contains the information needed to reconstruct the scene. Using the QRF format allows more complex scenes to be embedded into QR code.

3.2   Multiple QR Codes

There is a need to split contents as we have set the limit of 250 characters per QR code. Indeed the capacity of QR can take much more than 250. But, as the numbers increase, we found that it becomes harder for the QR code reader to read.

We are able to embed larger 3d scene by splitting such information into multiple QR codes. Part information metadata is attached to the split string. Whenever the program decodes the QR codes, the metadata will inform the system the number of parts does the system need to decode and recombine before processing the final output. Once all the parts are present, a parser will parse the codes and recreate the 3d scene. The process is shown in Figure 3.

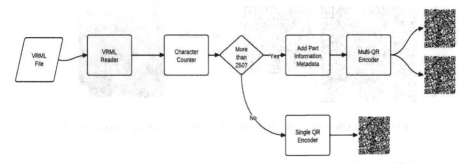

Fig. 3. Process of QR splitting

By splitting the information, large amounts of data can be encoded into multiple QR codes. It is possible, with the help of this system and metadata to encode data into any number of QR codes. However, too many QR codes part will be very cumbersome to scan.

3.3   Recovery of 3D Models

To recover the data, we have to piece together the jigsaw puzzle that we created using the developer system. Firstly, the QR code is scanned using a QR code reader. We used Logosware' QR Code Reader as the QR code reader. The code reader then passes the decoded information back to the system. The system will then look for metadata that is embedded together with the QR code. By using the metadata the system will determine the part that the current data belong to in the whole total set of data. If all the parts of the data are present, a parser will then parse the document. Parsed information values needed for recreating the scene is then passed on to the 3dcreator() function to recreate the 3d scenes in Papervision 3D. Finally, Papervision3D augmented the model on top of the live video.

3.4   Embedding and Recovery of Image Textures into QR Code

We are able to encode textures into QR codes by transmitting the pixel color values instead of the whole image. The system iterates through the pixels and builds a table or list of the color of each pixel. This information is then passed to the QR code encoder to encode as QR code. During recovery, the system takes the data and recreates the pixels according to its original color. However we found out that in context of transmitting large images, this method is not at all practical if compared to the methods used by [1] because 2 QR Codes is required to transmit a very small image as shown in Figure 4.

Fig. 4. Two QR codes that carries the pixel values of a 6 by 6 pixel image

3.5   3D Pose Estimation

To estimate the position of the 3D graphics, we employed a normal marker tracking approach with a twist to make it robust. Firstly, we generated a marker using the position detection pattern on the QR code. In order to place the 3D object at the center of the QR we used the transformation matrix from all 3 position detection pattern. Similar to the works by [6], we assume that the markers are on a flat paper and the position of the pattern faces the same direction, then the center of the QR code can roughly be obtained by calculating the average of the 3 transformation matrix of the 3 position detection patterns. Instead of selective averaging we averaged all the components of the transformation matrix. Overall, the method works with one QR code, and continues to work with multiple QR codes. If there is 4 QR codes, averaging the transformation matrix will result in the marker being in the middle of the QR code formation. Our approach provides a new level of robustness to occlusion as shown in Figure 5 below.

Fig. 5. RIMBAR still works with almost all the QR code covered

By using our method, almost the whole QR code can be covered. If there is at least one position detection pattern remain uncovered, the model will still appear. In order to smooth out temporary loss of detection that happens especially when the marker is moving, a timer is used to prevent the 3D object from disappearing upon loss detection of all the position detection pattern. Such temporary disturbance rarely happens for a long time. Usually within the range of less than 1 or 2 seconds before the application can detect the position detection pattern again.

4   Future Research

Coping with temporary occlusion with Kalman filter as demonstrated by [3] will be a useful feature for this system and we intend to implement it in our second version of the system. Usage of High Capacity Color Barcodes such as Microsoft Tag will largely improve the ability of this system to carry more information without the need to split the data (into multiple barcodes). At the time of writing, there is no Microsoft Tag reader for PC. Microsoft Tag reader is however available for smartphones with Android iOS, and Symbian. In our attempt to build mobile solution, using Microsoft Tag instead of QR code is very much possible.

This system if it can be used as mobile apps will prove to be very useful as mobile phones and tablets are easier to carry around especially when the user goes to a remote area. The application is already built using Flash to ease the transition to mobile apps by using AIR for Android and AIR for iOS.

5   Conclusion

We proposed a Resource Independent Marker Based Augmented Reality (RIMBAR) by encoding resources such as 3D model files to QR code and using the QR code itself as the marker. We found that this method can transmit models in an acceptable manner. But in order to transmit textures and images, it is not feasible.

References

1. Hagbi, N., Bergig, O., El-Sana, J., Kedem, K., Billinghurst, M.: In-Place Augmented Reality. In: IEEE International Symposium on Mixed and Augmented Reality (2008)
2. Bergig, O., Hagbi, N., El-Sana, J., Billinghurst, M.: In-Place 3D Sketching for Authoring and Augmenting Mechanical Systems. In: EEE International Symposium on Mixed and Augmented Reality 2009 Science and Technology Proceedings, ISMAR (2009)
3. Jian-tung, W.C.-N., Shyi Hou, T.W., Fong, C.P.: Design and implementation of augmented reality system collaborating with QR code. In: 2010 International Computer Symposium (ICS), pp. 414–418 (2010)
4. Kan, T.-W., Teng, C.-H.: A framework for multifunctional Augmented Reality based on 2D barcodes. In: ACM SIGGRAPH 2010 Posters, p. 1 (2010)
5. Kan, T.-W., Teng, C.-H., Chou, W.-S.: Applying QR code in augmented reality applications. In: Proceedings of the 8th International Conference on Virtual Reality Continuum and its Applications in Industry, pp. 253–257. ACM
6. MakC:Augmented reality and QR codes, http://makc3d.wordpress.com/2009/10/30/augmented-reality-and-qr-codes/7
7. Peiris, R.L., Fernando, O.N.N., Bee, C.S., Cheok, A.D., Ganesan, A.G., Kumarasinghe, P.: dMarkers: ubiquitous dynamic makers for augmented reality. In: Proceedings of the 10th International Conference on Virtual Reality Continuum and Its Applications in Industry, pp. 217–224. ACM

Personalized Web Search Ranking Based on Different Information Resources

Naglaa Fathy[1], Nagwa Badr[1], and Tarek Gharib[2]

[1] Ain shams University, Faculty of Computer and Information Sciences,
Cairo, Egypt
[2] Faculty of Computing and Information Technology King Abdulaziz University Jeddah,
Saudi Arabia

Abstract. The goal of personalized search is to provide user with results that accurately satisfy their specific goal of the search. In this paper, a hybrid personalized search re-ranking approach is proposed to provide users with results reordered according to their interests. User preferences are automatically learned into a concept-based user profile. This profile is then employed in the re-ranking process with other information resources to personalize results. Our experiments have shown interesting results in enhancing the quality of web search.

Keywords: Search Personalization, User Profile, ODP, Re-rank, Concept Hierarchy.

1 Introduction

In web search, users usually submit a short query consisting of a few keywords. However, given different interests of users and ambiguities in natural language, it is likely that query words of two users may appear exactly same even though information needs are different. In this paper, a hybrid personalized search re-ranking model is proposed based on learning conceptual user profiles implicitly. The user profile represents user's potential interests from his search history. More specifically, the user profile consists of user's interesting concepts obtained from a concept hierarchy of topics. This user profile is then exploited in the re-ranking process along with other information collected from the reference hierarchy and original search engine's ranking in order to personalize search results for each user.

2 Related Work

Personalized re-ranking considers user's interests to bring more relevant search results on the top few [1], [2], [3]. In [4], a vector of weighted terms from visited URLs is defined to represent each user. However, this approach cannot distinguish words having multiple meanings. The user models in [5], [6] are presented by semantic networks of user's past queries. However, these approaches may become deficient when query words do not exist in the dictionary used by the system.

V.V. Das and P.M. El-Kafrawy (Eds.): SPIT 2012, LNICST 117, pp. 211–214, 2014.

3   Proposed Personalized Re-ranking Architecture

This paper proposes a hybrid personalized search model that involves learning concept-based user profiles implicitly from user's search history as shown in Figure 1.

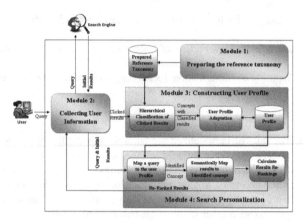

Fig. 1. Proposed Personalized Web Search Architecture

We used the Open Directory Project (ODP) [7], [8] as reference concept hierarchy of topics. Each concept is represented by vector of terms from the first 30 URLs using vector space (TF-IDF) mechanism [9]:

$$\text{Normalized term weight, } ntc_{ij} = (tf_{ij} * idf_i / \Sigma\, tc_{ij}.)\,. \tag{1}$$

Where tf_{ij} is the frequency of term i in document j and idf_i is the inverse document frequency of documents containing term i. Additionally, we implemented Google Wrapper [10] in order to implicitly collect information from users. The wrapper logs the queries, search results, and clicks per user. As subsequent step, data obtained by observing user search history are used to learn and construct concept-based user profile. The vector space classifier [9] is used in order to hierarchically classify clicked search results into ODP concepts [11]:

$$\cos(\vec{c},\vec{d}) = \frac{\vec{c} \bullet \vec{d}}{\|\vec{c}\|\|\vec{d}\|} = \frac{\vec{c}}{\|\vec{c}\|} \bullet \frac{\vec{d}}{\|\vec{d}\|} = \frac{\sum_{i=1}^{n} c_i d_i}{\sqrt{\sum_{i=1}^{n} c_i^2}\,\sqrt{\sum_{i=1}^{n} d_i^2}}\,. \tag{2}$$

Where c_i, d_i denote the weight of term i associated to concept c and weight of term i in the document d respectively. Eventually, each concept in the user profile contains two documents. The first document is called the **taxonomy document** which contains the same information as in the reference taxonomy. The second document is the **Personal document** and it holds all the information that was extracted from a user's classified clicked search results.

When user submits a query, it is mapped to the taxonomy documents in the user profile to identify the concept that most represents the query by equation 2. Next, the semantic similarity method in [12] is employed to map search result R_i to each document associated with the query's concept. The importance of concept's taxonomy document C_T and personal document C_P that represent query q is measured as follows:

$$\text{Score } (R_i) = CosSim \ (q, C_T) * SemanticSim \ (R_i, C_T) + CosSim \ (q, C_P) * \qquad (3)$$
$$SemanticSim(R_i, C_P) \ .$$

Finally, Google original ranking is combined with the previous information resources; taxonomy and personal rankings as follows (with $0 \leq \alpha \leq 1$):

$$\text{Final Rank} = (1 - \alpha) * OriginalRank + \alpha * Score \ (R_i) \ . \qquad (4)$$

4   Experimental Evaluation

In order to evaluate the effectiveness of the proposed method, 6 users with different interests were invited to search through our personalized search interface for 10 days. Average Rank [13] and Precision [14] were used as the evaluation metrics. We set α to 0.2 since it produces lower average error and provides the best improvement in personalized search.

4.1   Experimental Results

Figure 2 reports the average improvement of the proposed re-ranking model over original ranking day by day for all users with two different methods for mapping documents to the user profile; semantic similarity and cosine similarity. It is observed that the average improvement of using the semantic similarity for re-ranking over search engine's original ranking is 35.23 %. Figure 3 shows the average precision for the proposed hybrid re-ranking model, concept-only re-ranking model and non personalized Google search results. Results show that the proposed personalized re-ranking method provided better precision at all top-n documents.

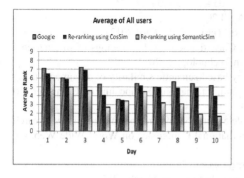

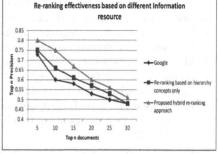

Fig. 2. Quality of Personalized Search day by day (lower is better)

Fig. 3. Average Precision for the top-n documents

5   Conclusion and Future Work

In this paper, a hybrid re-ranking method is employed with concept-based user profile enriched with user's clicked search results to improve web search. We plan in the future to conduct a large scale experiment for longer period with more participants.

References

1. Li, L., Yang, Z., Wang, B., Kitsuregawa, M.: Dynamic Adaptation Strategies for Long-Term and Short-Term User Profile to Personalize Search. In: Proceedings of Joint Asia-Pacific Web Conference / Web-Age Information Management Conference, pp. 228–240 (2007)
2. Mohammed, N.U., Duong, T.H., Jo, G.S.: Contextual information search based on ontological user profile. In: Pan, J.-S., Chen, S.-M., Nguyen, N.T. (eds.) ICCCI 2010, Part II. LNCS, vol. 6422, pp. 490–500. Springer, Heidelberg (2010)
3. Chirita, P., Nejdl, W., Paiu, R., Kohlschutter, C.: Using ODP Metadata to Personalize Search. In: Proceedings of the 28th Annual International ACM SIGIR Conference on Research and Development in Information Retrieval, pp. 178–185 (2005)
4. Matthijs, N., Radlinski, F.: Personalizing Web Search using Long Term Browsing History. In: Proceedings of the 4th ACM International Conference on Web Search and Data Mining, pp. 25–34 (2011)
5. Mianowska, B., Nguyen, N.T.: A Method for User Profile Adaptation in Document Retrieval. In: Proceedings of 3rd Asian Conference on Intelligent Information and Database Systems, pp. 181–192 (2011)
6. Sheng, Yan, et al.: A Personalized Search Results Ranking Method Based on WordNet. In: Proceedings of 6th International Conference on Fuzzy Systems and Knowledge Discovery, pp. 500–504 (2009)
7. Open Directory Project, http://www.dmoz.org/ (last visit on April 2012)
8. Gabrilovich, E., Markovitch, S.: Harnessing the Expertise of 70,000 Human Editors: Knowledge-Based Feature Generation for Text Categorization. Journal of Machine Learning Research 8, 2297–2345 (2007)
9. Vector Space Model, http://en.wikipedia.org/wiki/Vector_space_model (Last visit on April 2012)
10. Google, http://www.google.com.eg/ (last visit on April 2012)
11. Pulijala, A., Gauch, S.: Hierarchical Text Classification. In: Proceedings of International Conference on Cybernetics and Information Technologies (2004)
12. Madylova, A., Öğüdücü, Ş.G.: A taxonomy based semantic similarity of documents using the cosine measure. In: Proceedings of the 24th International Symposium on Computer and Information Sciences, pp. 129–134 (2009)
13. Dou, Z., Song, R., Wen, J.-R.: A large-scale evaluation and analysis of personalized search strategies. In: Proceedings of the 16th International Conference on World Wide Web, pp. 581–590 (2007)
14. Precision, http://en.wikipedia.org/wiki/Precision_information_retrieval (last visit on March 2012)

Security Metrics: Relevance in Securing Educational Institutions

Pooja Tripathi[1] and Saurabh Gupta[2]

[1] Scholar, Mewar University Rajasthan
[2] POS, Minister of Home Affairs,
Sr.Technical Director of NIC
{Tripathipoojamail,Nic.Saurabhgupta}@gmail.com

Abstract. Security is easy; simply stop all communication with the external world: be recluse or isolated and you are secured. Every enterprise whether it is in education or defense or IT sector, everyone wants to keep its data, information and knowledge secured from intruders and competitors and even wants to expose the right kind of data, information and knowledge to its enterprise partner, employees, customers, government and stakeholders. Educational Institutions tend to deal in abstract concepts and knowledge that may not deliver tangible outcomes for years, decades and even for centuries. Educational Institutions faces unique information security threats as well as increasingly frequent and severe incidents such as information theft, data tempering, viruses, worms, and terrorist activity constitute significant threats to security of various universities. In this paper we strive to present the problem which the educational institutions are facing and endeavor to find the solution for it through security metrics.

Keywords: Security metrics, Vulnerabilities, IDS, Vulnerabilities estimation, Security posture, Denial-of –Service.

1   Introduction

Security has always been prime concern for any institution, with increase in interaction and exposure with other world this has become contextually more important. In the current scenario various enterprise are investing significant amount of resources for developing the tangled solutions that are caviling to daily operations and long-drawn out success with recent economic downturn. With shrinking IT budgets in an enterprise, IT departments are seeking more efficient, effective and innovative ways to solve problems. Empowerment of users and experimentation in the learning process are one of them. However, it often causes enterprise to struggle with their security issues. It has been discovered that empowering non-technical users results in the security exposure of network, applications, workstation, or servers. All such exposures threaten the stability of the IT environment if not handled properly, hence can result in compromised servers and possibly lost data [2]. According to the Ward and Peppard [2002] "Most organizations in all sectors of industry, commerce, government and education are fundamentally dependent on their information system"[1].

V.V. Das and P.M. El-Kafrawy (Eds.): SPIT 2012, LNICST 117, pp. 215–221, 2014.
© Institute for Computer Sciences, Social Informatics and Telecommunications Engineering 2014

Certain obvious questions strike to our mind when we talk about the security from an enterprise perspective:

✓   What are the specific threats to an enterprise?
✓   What are the security controls are in place?
✓   How sensitively information are being disposed?
✓   What backup/recovery policy is in place?

Despite advancement in IT security many Educational Institutions remains vulnerable to exploitation especially the human attitude threats. Educational Institutions generally collect large amount of data is about their operations and because there are common elements to the data which is collected, these have often emerged as metrics by which educational institutions are assessed at both national and international level [3]. There exist a large number of suggestions for how to measure security, with different goals and objectives. In many cases the goal is to find a single overall metric of security. However, given that security is a complex and multi-faceted property, we believe that there are fundamental problems in finding such overall metrics. Thus, we are currently developing a framework for security metrics that is based on a number of system attributes taken from the security and the dependent ability disciplines [18]. Having metrics related to different types of attributes facilities making quantitative estimation of the concept of combined security and dependability and improves our understanding of the underlying system properties [19].The educational sector has been mark as being heterogeneous, comprise of insulated information system that keeps stakeholders information [4]. Any universities X is said to have certain security postures, and university Y is said to possess a certain security posture different from X, connecting X and Y will result into more vulnerable system than the individual system (Fig-1).

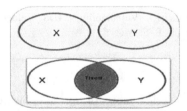

Fig. 1.

To ensure the interconnected system results into a moderate secure environment it is important to estimate the security of each enterprise systematically to reveal the overall security posture [5].

2   Study Design

We pursue the answers of the following questions in the study while when we are discussing about the Security metrics in context with the Universities:

➢   How information security can be improved at the educational institutions?
➢   What kind of security matrix to be determined to safeguard institution?

> ➢ What is the role of "User awareness" in security matrix?
> ➢ What kind of security matrix prevailing?
> ➢ How information security risks at the various educational institutional are determined?
> ➢ How various educational institutions are reducing information security risks?
> ➢ What is the impact of using security matrix in various universities?

3   Need and Benefits of Security Matrix

The metrics "gathering" process often leads to identification of security inconsistencies or holes. The motivation for seeking security metrics comes from different fact from an economic perspective , organization wants to know the return-on –investment(ROI), how much protection is gained per each additional investment[10][11]. Security metrics initiative can set the foundation for enabling organizations to identity risk levels, priorities corrective actions, raise awareness and helps to get answers for unclear questions such as: "Am I more secure today than before?", "How do I compare to others?" & "Are we secure enough?" This increases the confidence of the users towards institution. *Metrics is a quantities measures of degree to which a system, component, or process possess a given attribute, a calculated or composite quality based upon two or more years.* Measures or metrics in particular promote visibility, informed decision making, predictability, proactive planning and help avert surprises. [14]

It is impossible to get accurate figures for the number & cost of security breaches mainly because organizations are either not aware that the breeches has occurred, or reluctant to publicize it, for fear of ruining their reputations or destroying the trust of their stakeholders. However, in one instance the impact of malicious software in the form of worm/viruses attacks on the Internet was estimated to have caused $32.8 billion in economic damage for august 2003(Berghal 2003). In the recent years it has become widely acknowledge that human factors play a part in many security failures (Werich and Sasse 2002, Whiteman 2004). Technical threats are usually more high profile and grab much media and financial attention; however non-technical human and physical threats are sometimes more effective and damaging to information security. Non technical threats include Act of God (i.e. Fire, Flood, and Explosion). Threat analysis is necessary for specifying a concrete and comprehensive set of requirements so as to build all needs of security mechanisms for efficiently protecting the system. Moreover when conducted on an existing system, a correct evaluation and assessment of the threats and vulnerabilities allows us to priorities them. This analysis of prevailing security of the system would facilitate to propose an optimal enhancement plan. [17].

4   Plan for Building the Security Metrics in an Enterprise

Effective planning for security metrics implementation will serve as strong foundation for secured institution; below mentioned figure will enable us to plan for secured future institution (Fig-2).

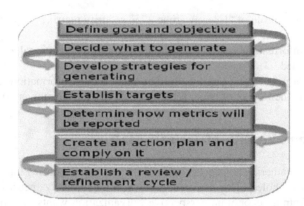

Fig. 2.

✓ Starts with statement of objective that must be collectively executed to accomplish the goal.

✓ Step 2 would focus on identifying the Security posture for which defects could be detected and managed. It would identify those standards for which compliance should be tracked.

✓ Step 3 defines strategies for collecting needed data and deriving the metrics those must be developed.

✓ In step 4 appropriate benchmarks would be identified and improvements target sets. This process provides fresh ideas for managing an activity, but also can provide comparative data needed to make metrics more meaningful.

✓ Step 5 emphasizes on Graphic representations (Dashboards), as they are particularly effective so that the end product can be visualized early on by those who will be involved in producing the metrics.

✓ Time to get the real work done. Step 6 defines action plan, the action plan should contain all tasks that need to be accomplished to launch the security metrics program, with expected completion dates.

✓ Final step emphasizes on formal, regular re-examination of the entire security metrics program which should be built into overall process. Certain Queries Should answered on priority during the review process.

• How much effort is it taking to generate the metrics?

• Are the metrics useful in determining new courses of action for the overall security programs?

• Is there reason to doubt the accuracy of any of the metrics?

5   How Security Metrics Works

The above figure (Fig-3) is just an approach to explain how security metrics works. Firewall is the primary component and provides protection at the perimeter level to ensure access policy control and it does not provide extensive threat detection capabilities due to the large amount of traffic handled. Security Metrics integrates vulnerability estimation with its IDS (Intrusion Detection System) which monitors all network traffic and analyze the traffic in real-time. On the basis of IDS an IT administrator is notified in real time when an attack occurs. When an attack is launched, the system automatically looks at the last vulnerability estimation database for the attack target. An analysis is initiated to discover if the target is vulnerable to attack. If the target is not vulnerable then no alert is sent to the administrator. Attack Prevention require insertion into flow of traffic(two network interface connections) where an IDS simply sniffs exiting traffic and does not need to block the dataflow (one network interface connection).If the alert is real then an alert is sent to the administrator.

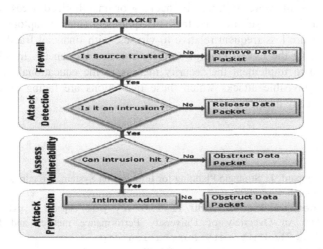

Fig. 3.

6   Vulnerability Estimation by Security Metrics

Vulnerability is defined as "a flaw or weakness in the security procedures, design, implementation, or internal controls that could be accidentally triggered or intentionally exploited and a result in security breech or a violation of the systems 'security policy" [20]. An attacker probes the System for weaknesses using vulnerability detection tools. Each vulnerability is ranked by risk on a scale of 0 to 9 with 9 being highly critical. The computer will fail if any vulnerability has a risk of 4 or above.

A good vulnerability estimation system will point out holes which we could never have found our self and tell about password problems, programming errors and basic architecture issues without the high price tag of a security consultant. All security components are launched at each target when a test is initiated. Security Metrics reports contain instructions, security patch links, and helpful information needed to immediately repair identified issues. With the help of Security Metrics a Pass/Fail scoring system can be developed for Vulnerability Estimation. Each security issue is rated according to its risk to our security. If our computer or server passes our tests, we can be assured that we are protected from thousands of potential hacking attacks.

7   Conclusion

Over the last few years, information security has changed and matured, moving out of the shadow of government, the military and academia into fully fledged commercial field of its own. Although there can be no agreement on the actual figure and percentages, empirical evidence from a number of security Surveys over the past years (Comp TIA, 2010: Comp TIA 2011: PricewaterhouseCoopers, 2008; Richardson, 2004) shows similar trends and patterns of security breaches. Information security breaches are increasing year on year. The most common type of attack is from viruses and malware, followed by hacking or unauthorized access to networks resulting vandalism of websites and theft of equipment (mainly laptops). Denial-of-service attacks are less frequent relative to viruses, with financial fraud and theft of information being the lowest kind of security breach experienced. In this paper we have just tried to implement the security metrics in the educational institutions to overcome the invisible attacks which these institutions are facing along with the working of security metrics.

References

1. Ward, J., Peppard, J.: Strategic Planning for Information System, 3rd edn. John Wiley and Sans Ltd., Chichestor (2002)
2. http://net.edu0cause .edu/ir/library/pdf/eqmo337.pdf
3. Tonich, D.: An Overview of University Performance metrics and Rankings,12, http://www.My Universty.Australlia.org
4. Payne, S.C.: A guide to security metrics. SANS Institue (2006)
5. Jafari, S., Metenzi, F., Fitzpatrick, R., Shea, B.O.: Security metrics for e-health care Information Systems.A Domain soecific Metrics Approach. IJDS 1(4) (December 2010)
6. Cuilhong, W.: 2010 2nd International Conference on The problems in Campus network information security and its solutions in industrial and information system (IIS) (2010)
7. AI-Akhras, M.A.: Wireless Network Security Implementation in Universities. In: 2nd Information and Communication Technologies, ICTTA 2006 (2006)
8. Zhu, J., Liu, L.: University network security risk assesment based on fuzzy analytic hierarchy process. In: 2010 International Conference on Computer Application and System Modelling, ICCASM (2010)
9. Kvavik, R.B.: Information Techonology Security: Goverance, Strategy, and Practice in higher education. Educause Centre for Applied Research (October 2004)
10. Rathbun, D., Homsher, L.: Gathering Security Metrics and Repairing the Rewards. SANs Institute (2009)
11. Beres, Y., Mont, M.C., Griffin, J., Shin, S.: Using Security metrics Coupled with Predictive Modeling and Simulation to assess Security Process. Hewlett-Packard Development Company (2009)
12. Kyobe, M.: Towards a frame work to guide compliance with IS Security policies and Regulations in a university. IEEE (2010) 978-1-4244-5494-5
13. McCoy, J.: Are we ready for a chief Information Security Officers (2005), http://www.docstoc.com/docs/18364711/Are-we-ready-for-a-chief

14. Sckimkowitch, S.E.: Key components of information Security Metric Program plan (2009), http://webcache.googleusercontent.com/search?q=cache%3AJolzW7iux3

15. Lane, T.: Information Security management in Australian Universities: An Exploratory analysis (2007), http://eprints.qut.edu.au/16486//

16. Jones, H., Soltern, J.: Facebook:Threats to privacy (2005), http://swiss.ai.mit.edu/6095/student-papers/fall05-papers/facebook.pdf

17. Stango, A., Prasad, N.R., Kyriazanos, D.M.: A Threat Analysis Methodlogy for Security Evalution and Enhacement Planning.

18. Jonsson, E.: Towards an integrated conceptual model of security and dependability. In: The First International Conference on Availability, Reliability and Security, ARES 2006, p. 8 (April 2006)

19. Almgren, M., Fu, Z., Jonsson, E., Kleberger, P., Larsson, A., Moradi, F., Oovsson, T., Papatriantafilou, M., Pirzadeh, L., Tsigas, P.: Mapping Systems SecurityReasearch at Chalmers.

20. Cole, E.: Network Security Bible, p. 61

Author Index